BUDDHISTS IN INDIA TODAY

Buddhists in India Today

Descriptions, Pictures and Documents

DETLEF KANTOWSKY

Translaed from the German by Hans-Georg Tuerstig
Foreword and Comments by Eleanor Zelliot

MANOHAR
2025

First published 2003
Reprinted 2021, 2022, 2023, 2024, 2025

ISBN 978-81-7304-511-0

Published by
Ajay Kumar Jain *for*
Manohar Publishers & Distributors
4753/23 Ansari Road, Daryaganj
New Delhi 110 002

Printed at
Replika Press Pvt. Ltd.

Contents

Foreword

I WELCOME THIS English edition of Detlef Kantowsky's *Buddhisten in Indien heute* because it is both innovative and imaginative. Buddhism in India today is in a complex situation, bursting with life and not always understood. Dr Kantowsky has tackled six facets of the Indian Buddhist world, leaving aside the Tibetans, who are covered in much other literature; small groups of Buddhists left over from the ancient Buddhist period; the foreign Buddhist institutions clustered around the Bodh Gaya temple; and the recent conversion movements in Delhi, Kerala, and elsewhere in India. He brings great personal interest and much personal opinion to his narrative, and also offers much in the way of written documents and photographs. For instance, the way that Bodh Gaya is represented in various maps and the tedious but fascinating inner workings of the Bhikkhu Sangha are unusual and valuable sources for the student of the Buddhists in India today.

Dr Kantowsky's personal, even at times opinionated, commentary is of special value to me because it allows me to doff my strictly historical hat and write anecdotally of what I know of Ambedkar Buddhism, the TBMSG, and the Vipassana movement also in a personal way. As he notes, I have been bound by my historical approach and have not contributed as much as I know to the body of knowledge about Buddhists today. I also disagree with some of Dr Kantowsky's facts and judgements, and he has most graciously allowed me to place my comments at the end of his narrative, after which he will comment again. I hope that the result will be a book that engages the reader in a fruitful journey along the many paths of contemporary Indian Buddhism. And even if the journey is beset with questioning and wondering, that can also lead to knowledge.

A third value of this volume is that Dr Kantowsky as a European has made much use of German sources as well as most of the Asian and American material. His bibliography is of great worth. Initially there were two bibliographies, the first for the article (Chapter One) reproduced from an earlier publication. We have combined these and placed one bibliography at the end of the volume, adding an occasional English source. I have added some English sources when those were available and I have also given a few more references in a bibliography at the end of my Comments.

One more note: translations from Hindi to German to English and the varied sources for material have resulted in some differences in spellings, and we seek the reader's indulgence for a non-standardized use of names and terms. For instance, the Pali *dhamma* and the Sanskrit *dharma* have been used as the original source indicated, even when this seemed incorrect for the Theravada *v.* Mahayana tradition. We have also not tried to standardize the *o v. a* ending for such names as Mahathero/Mahathera, again following the source as best we could.

I am grateful to Hans-Georg Tuerstig for the initial translation from the German, to the University of Konstanz for allowing the publication of the English edition, and to a fine editor at Manohar Publishers & Distributors who took infinite pains with the manuscript.

Northfield, Minnesota
USA

ELEANOR ZELLIOT

Preface

My descriptions of Buddhists in present-day India begin with a report about the literature on the social situation and the ritual practices of the New Buddhists. This analysis will be complemented by the following chapters and deepened through observations about and documents concerning the following:

- The Maha Bodhi Society, founded in Ceylon in 1891 as the bearer of a movement for the revival of Buddhism in the country of its origin.
- Bodh Gaya as the central place of Buddhism, where, in 1891, the Buddhist renewal movement began with the goal of recovering and reclaiming the main temple from Hindu domination and use, and to transform the place of enlightenment into a place of worship and devotion for all Buddhists from around the world.
- Nagpur as the central place of a New Buddhist movement, supported by former Untouchables. Here, on 14 October 1956, following the example of their caste-comrade Dr Ambedkar, whom some honoured as a Bodhisattva, several hundreds of thousands of Mahars and a few others publicly took refuge in the Three Jewels: the Buddha, the *dhamma*, and the *sangha*. Prior to this, they renounced Hindu traditions and deities.
- The Buddhist organization, the Trailokya Bauddha Mahasangha Sahayak Gana (TBMSG), founded in 1976 in Pune and sponsored by the Friends of the Western Buddhist Order (FWBO) based in England in order to help develop a form of socially committed and spiritually motivated lay Buddhism suited to the conditions of the country.
- The All India Bhikkhu Sangha, in which at present 574 monks who mainly come from a New Buddhist background in Maharashtra are registered. The leaders of the Sangha claim to represent the interests of all Buddhists in India and recently demanded that they be entrusted with the guardianship and administration of the Maha Bodhi Mahavihara in Bodh Gaya.

- The Vipassana International Academy, founded in 1976, now in Igatpuri in Maharashtra. The Buddhist method of meditative self-purification, taught by S.N. Goenka, has spread all over the world. I have added to this an autobiographical statement by S.N. Goenka.

With the help of pictures and documents, I have tried to describe vividly this colourful mixture of organized and/or practised Buddhism in today's India, where each form finds its particular expression. I wanted to give those who are interested the opportunity to carefully study the materials and form their own opinion about what Buddhism represents in present-day India. However, the following limitations should be considered:

1. I did not enter into a discussion of the Dalits and the special significance they could have for the New Buddhist movement. The title of Eleanor Zelliot's collection of essays, *From Untouchable to Dalit: Essays on the Ambedkar Movement*, rightly points to the existing interdependencies. However, it does not deal with the different levels of activity among the various protagonists: those of the Untouchables, those of the Dalits, and those of the Ambedkar Buddhists. It is not the case that all Untouchables in India see themselves as Dalits even if this is often maintained by concerned observers from abroad. (See the *Evangelischer Pressedienst* 14, 1994 and 1995 for this usage, which predicts a breakdown of traditional structures.) Speakers of various groups within the Dalits do not accept the New Buddhists as brothers, but accuse them of achieving a mobility advantage through their own educational institutes through which they remove themselves from their common background (Jogdand, 1997).

   The Dalit movement is not a large reservoir in which the anti-Hindu resentments of all Untouchables come together in order to fight in the name of Ambedkar for the imposition of that equality which he laid down in the Constitution of India. The election to the Indian Parliament (Lok Sabha) in February 1998 clearly showed that the protest of the lower classes in India is still largely determined by regional characteristics and specific influential factors. True, the term Dalit, i.e. *the broken ones, the crushed ones*, is also widely used today by the Untouchables themselves in order to emancipate themselves from the supposedly loving embrace of God as his children (Harijans) through the change of heart of caste Hindus and to clearly characterize their actual situation. At the same time, however, the shared usage of a word alone cannot bring about shared features in regard to political action among all the Dalits of India.

Meanwhile, even the New Buddhists in Maharashtra no longer form a homogenous group exercising uniform political influence because some people who successfully climbed out of the Dalit milieu do not like to be reminded that they came from an Untouchable background. They have dropped out as potential advocates of specific forms of political agitation and legal protest.

These notes may be sufficient to enable an understanding of why I did not enter into a discussion of the complex socio-political context which lies hidden behind the term 'Dalit'. I simply attempted to lay the foundation for an appropriate comprehension of the main characteristics of Buddhism in today's India. It is self-evident that Buddhists do not operate in empty space. This becomes evident from the example of the controversy around the occupation of the Temple Management Committee in Bodh Gaya, which is certainly a worthwhile subject for a detailed exposition elsewhere!

2. I did not comment on all Buddhists in India who, with their own temples and hostels, are nowadays present in Bodh Gaya, a place that forty years ago was almost empty. For instance, the Chinese from Kolkata, who have their own large temple in Sarnath and recently in Bodh Gaya as well, are not included. The Tamang, who emigrated from Nepal to eastern India and became quite successful, also do not get a chance to speak here. I also did not pursue the happy pilgrims from Bhutan and Sikkim, even though their facilities in Bodh Gaya are truly inviting. These as well as various other Tibeto-Buddhist schools are nowadays represented by their own buildings and thus underline Bodh Gaya's special importance for international Buddhism. However, they are only indirectly important for the renewal movement in India.

This is true for the Tibetans in exile in India as well. Even though they rule the Buddhist scene in Bodh Gaya on Tibetan New Year, they are not important for the renewal of classical Buddhism within the meaning enunciated by Anagarika Dharmapala, or of a socially committed Buddhism in the style of Dr Ambedkar. Moreover, certain Indian Buddhists have lately asked themselves whether the international attention focused on Tibet and the worldwide radiating charisma of the Dalai Lama do not in fact draw attention away from the actual problems of the Buddhist renewal in India.

This topic too would be worthy of a detailed description which should pay special attention to the Central Institute of Higher Tibetan Studies, founded in 1967 in Sarnath at the suggestion of Jawaharlal Nehru. This has grown into a very beautiful and internationally renowned teaching and research institute (see the publications of the Central Institute of Higher Tibetan Studies listed in the Bibliography at the end of this volume).

3. I also did not want to go into the current situation of the Buddhist renewal movement in south India, especially in Andhra Pradesh and Karnataka (see Ahir, 1991: 105f. and 121f.) because in this respect I lack an unmediated opinion. The south Indian Buddhism which is newly forming could eventually become very important since it represents the attitudes of the anti-Brahminical protest of the Dravidian south. However, it does not see itself as New Buddhism in the sense of Ambedkar's teachings but goes back to the rich Buddhist heritage of south India from where Bodhidharma once set out to carry the message of 'Great Emptiness' further to the East.

4. I did not load my descriptions with broader questions such as:

   - the special relationship between Buddhist orthodoxy and New Buddhist heterodoxy (see Buss, 1998: 71–80);
   - the typical Indian tendency to integrate a social protest movement through the granting of political recognitiion, but nevertheless simultaneously maintaining the system of social discrimination;
   - the special opportunities and limited possibilities of a historically unique lay Buddhism emerging from below.

The last subject is especially very important for committed Buddhists and their Christian dialogue partners. Nevertheless, the international discourse among English-speaking members of the educated elite has little in common with the actual facts of the everyday practices of the New Buddhists in India today. Often it is not really recognized that

Buddhism as a way of life follows its own unique cultural patterns of persistence and worldly interpretations, especially in India.

To show the present situation of Buddhism in India today with the help of a few examples and thus to help us better understand it is the point of the following narrative.

Bodman, Germany
December 1998/2541

DETLEF KANTOWSKY

Acknowledgements

19-58 An article published in *Bauddhavidyasudhakaran, Studies in Honour of Heinz Bechert. On the Occasion of His 65th Birthday*. Edited by Petra Kieffer-Pülz and Jens-Uwe Hartmann, Swisttal-Odendorf: India et Tibetica Publisher, 1997: 361–96. Reprint used with the kind permission of the editors and publishers.

61 Photograph, D. Kantowsky, February 1998.

63 Photograph, D. Kantowsky, February 1998.

65 Activities of the Maha Bodhi Society, Sarnath Centre. Reprint page 1 used with kind permission of Ven. D. Wimala Thero.

67 *Dharmadoot: Kartika Purnima Special*. Sarnath/Varanasi: Maha Bodhi Society, India, 1997, inside back cover.

69-72 100 Years of the Maha Bodhi Society of India. Bodh Gaya: *Sambodhi*, Vol. 2, No. 2, 7 and 8 December 1991: 104–7.

73 Ibid., no page number.

74 *The Maha Bodhi, Centenary Volume 1992*, The Maha Bodhi Society of India, 4 A Bankim Chatterjee Street, Calcutta 700 073, p. 3.

75 Ibid.: 7.

76 Ibid.: 308.

77 Ibid.: 311.

78 Ibid.: 312.

79 *The Maha Bodhi*, Vol. 104, 2539 BE (CE 1996), No. 1, inside front cover.

80 Ibid.: inside back cover.

82 Back cover of *The Buddha Message*, Vol. I, No. 1, Bombay: Buddha Society, May 1928.

84 Back page of a six-page leaflet introducing *Sangiti*, Newsletter, Vol. I, Bodh Gaya, January-February 1998. Published by the Buddhagaya Buddhist Cultural Centre, c/o Daijokyo Buddhist Temple, Bodh Gaya, Gaya, Bihar, 824 231, India.

86 *An Appeal of the Chakma Buddhist Temple Construction Committee* (Bodh Gaya). Given to me by Priya Pal Bhikkhu in Bodh Gaya, March 1998.

88 Two photographs, D. Kantowsky, Bodh Gaya, February 1998: The sign under the Donation Chart stands on the Main Road. The Donation Chart is on a board at the entrance to the office of the Buddhagaya Temple Management Committee.

91 Copy from: S. Dhammika, *Middle Land, Middle Way. A Pilgrim's Guide to the The Buddha's India.* Kandy: Buddhist Publication Society, 1992: 80.

92 Map of Bodh Gaya circulated by the leading travel agency in Bodh Gaya: Middle Way Travels, (Mr Shubhabuddin), House No. 11, Gautam Buddha Road, Bodh Gaya, Bihar 824 231.

93 Bodhi leaves, one printed with an image of the Buddha, original size.

94-5 Map distributed to the participants of the Monlam 1997. Monlam is celebrated from the third to the twenty-fourth day of the first month of a new year (i.e. February–March) in order to accelerate the arrival of The Buddha Maitreya.

96-7 '100 Years of the Maha Bodhi Society of India', op. cit.: 54–5, 102–3.

98-9 Appeal, sent to me by Priya Pal Bhikkhu, with a letter dated 10 August 1998.

100 From: *Buddhayana Zeitung*, July 1998/2542: 6, 7.

101-3 English text of a twelve-page leaflet, back page in Chinese letters.

104-5 Photographs (D. Kantowsky) of the wall poster on the fence of the Chinese Temple in Bodh Gaya, February 1998. All text blocks ran continuously on a banner approximately 4.5 metres long.

106-7 *Times of India*, New Delhi, 24 October 1998.

108-10 Multicoloured leaflet, distributed in Bodh Gaya by the Root Institue for Wisdom Culture.

113 Photo of the inner cover of *Revival of Buddhism in India.* Dr Ambedkar Centenary Year, 1990. Pamphlet of the Trailokya Bauddha Mahasangha Sahayak Gana, Pune, 1991.

116 Title page of a pamphlet of the People's Education Society, Anand Bhavan, Dr Dadabhai Naoroji Road, Fort, Bombay 400 023.

118 Inside title of the *College Annual Magazine*, 1996-7, Milind College of Science, Nagsena Vana, Aurangabad 431 002. The heading above the picture reads: People's Education Society (Mumbai)'s founder. Below the picture is: Bharatratna Bodhisatva Dr Babasaheb Ambedkar, the dates of his birth and his entering into Parinirvana.

120 Reduction of a coloured poster. Published and produced for sale by The Buddhist Society of India (Regd.), Delhi State, Buddha Vihar, Ambedkar Bhavan, New Delhi 110 055. Also in the picture, apart from Dr Ambedkar and President Rajendra Prasad, are (from left): Jawaharlal Nehru, Sardar Vallabhbhai Patel, Chakravarti Rajagopalachari, Maulana Abdul Kalam Azad.

121-2 From the *College Annual* 1991 and 1992, Milind College of Science, Nagsena Vana, Aurangabad: 6-7.

123 Birth Centenary of Dr Babaṣaheb Ambedkar. Mumbai: People's Education Society, 1991: 3.

124 Postcard, Samyak Cards, Ambedkar Bhawan, New Delhi 110 055.

125-34 Pamphlet, designed and produced by the Directorate of Advertising and Visual Publicity, Ministry of Information and Broadcasting, Government of India, November 1993.

136 Brochure of the Karuna Trust with a description of their work in India. The Karuna Trust, St. Marks Studio, Chillingworth Road, London N7 8QJ, Great Britain. No date, *ca.* 1996.

141 Ibid., same brochure.

143 Front and back pages of a coloured *vade mecum*. 6 × 9 cm, welded together in plastic, TBMSG, Dapodi, Pune.
The Threefold Refuge repeated three times and the Five Shilas.

147-8 The *Karuna Report*. Annual Report 14 and Supporters' Newsletter 1995. The Karuna Trust and Aid for India, 186 Cowley Road, Oxford OX4 1UE, Great Britain.

149 The Karuna Trust and Aid for India. *Annual Report* 12, 1993: 9.

160-88 From the Archives of the All India Bhikkhu Sangha, Camp Office Wat Thai, Sarnath. Reprint of all documents with kind permission of Ven. Sasanarashmi Mahathero, General Secretary, AIBS.

193 *Vipassana Meditation: An Introduction*, Vipassana Research Institute, Dhammagiri, Igatpuri 422 403. Back page of an eight-page pamphlet.

197 *Buddhayana Zeitung*: Vol. 9, No. 3, January 1998/2541: 1 and 6. Bauddhayana Centre, Stephensonstraat 13, 2561 XP Den Haag, The Netherlands.

200 *Sayagyi U Ba Khin Journal*, a Collection Commemorating the Teaching of Sayagyi U Ba Khin. Published to mark the Twentieth Anniversary of his demise. Igatpuri: Vipassana Research Institute, 1994 (1st edn. 1991).

207-12 Eight-page pamphlet from the Vipassana International Academy, Dhammagiri, Igatpuri 422 403. Two pages containing the application form and the questionnaire concerning personal data have been omitted.

213 *Vipassana Pagoda Souvenir*, 26 October 1997, Mumbai: Global Vipassana Foundation, no address given, 1997.

214 Ibid.: XXXIII.

215 *India 1965*. Publication Division, Ministry of Information and Broadcasting, Government of India, Delhi, 1965, between pp. 26-7.

216 Ibid.: 26.

CHAPTER ONE

Buddhists in India Today: A Report on the Literature, especially about the New Buddhists

WHEN ANTON GUETH (1878–1957) arrived in Bombay in the spring of 1903 on his search for a Buddhist way of life and purification practice, he soon had to realize 'that Buddhism had died out in India 700 years ago' (Hecker, 1996: 59). So he travelled via Colombo to Burma, where, in September 1903, he was ordained a novice in the Ngda Khi pagoda. 'After about four or five months, i.e. in January or February 1904', he later recalled in an autobiographical sketch, 'I received the full ordination into the order under the name Nyânatiloka from my superior U. Kumara Mahathera. Thus, I became the first European from the continent in the history of European Buddhism who was accepted into the Buddhist order' (Hecker, 1995: 19-20).

Nowadays, seekers of Eastern spirituality do not have to travel beyond India if they want to meet Buddhists. In the home country of the Buddha, more than 6.5 million Buddhists were counted in the census of 1991. However, in 1890 only 50,000 Buddhists were supposedly left in India (Ahir, 1991: 189), and even in the census of 1931 only 157,000 Buddhists were counted in the area that constitutes India today (excluding what is now Pakistan and Bangladesh). Most of them lived in the North-East Frontier Agency (101,000); 38,500 were in the mountainous areas of the North-Western Provinces; and the remaining 17,500 were scattered throughout India (Ling, 1980: 137, fn. 4).

The table on page 20 shows the increase in the numbers of Buddhists since 1951 in the various states and Union Territories of India. It documents the special significance of the New Buddhist movement which was founded by Dr B.R. Ambedkar (1891–1956) in Maharashtra and which had its major influence mainly in this state. Diwan Chand Ahir (born in 1928 in the Punjab), himself a practising Buddhist and the author of many books about Buddhism in India, described the situation as follows.

Buddhists in India 1951, 1971 and 1991

States	1951	1971	1991
Andhra Pradesh	230	10,035	22,153
Arunachal Pradesh	unknown	61,400	111,372
Assam	22,628	45,212	64,008
Bihar	1,092	4,806	3,518
Gujarat	198	5,469	11,315
Haryana	in Punjab	845	2,058
Himachal Pradesh	unknown	35,937	64,081
Jammu & Kashmir	unknown	57,956	69,706
Karnataka	1,707	14,139	73,012
Kerala	90	605	223
Madhya Pradesh	2,251	81,823	216,667
Maharashtra	2,487	3,264,223	5,040,735
Manirpur	33	495	711
Meghalaya	in Assam	1,878	2,934
Mizoram	in Assam	22,647	54,024
Nagaland	47	179	581
Orissa	969	8,462	9,153
Punjab	1,660	1,374	24,930
Rajasthan	4,361	3,642	4,467
Sikkim	39,397	62,617	110,371
Tamil Nadu	1,179	1,148	2,128
Tripura	15,403	42,285	128,260
Uttar Pradesh	3,221	39,639	221,433
West Bengal	81,665	121,504	203,578
All States	189,018	3,847,920	6,441,448

Union Territories	1951	1971	1991
Andaman & Nicobar Island	unknown	1,707	322
Chandigarh	in Punjab	92	699
Dadra & Nagar Haveli	–	73	200
Delhi	503	8,720	13,900
Goa, Daman & Diu	56	260	271
Lakshadweep	–	–	1
Pondicherry	unknown	21	39
Total Union Territories	559	10,873	15,432

India Total	189,577	3,858,793	6,456,880
Population (in million)	361,9	548.2	846.3
Buddhists (as per cent of total pop.)	0,052	0,703	0,763

SOURCES: Figures for 1951 from 'India 1965' (1965: 19); for 1971 and 1991 from 'Landerbericht Indien' (1995:30).

Figures for Buddhists in 1951 and 1971 from D.C. Ahir (1991: 201/2), in 1991 from informations) by the Office of Dhammaviriyo Mahathero, Member of the 'National Commission for Minorities' (Government of India, Lok Nayak Bhavan, New Delhi 110 003), in February 1996.

INDIA: State Boundaries, 1991

In modern India, both the Theravada and the Mahayana traditions of Buddhism are prevalent. 92% of the Indian Buddhists follow the Theravada tradition, and the remaining 8%, who live in the High Himalayas, are Mahayanists. The Indian Buddhists can be further divided into four distinct groups:

Firstly, there are survivals from the Buddhist period. Mainly this type is represented by the Barua Buddhists of Bengal, the Chakma tribe of Tripura and Mizoram, and the Buddhists of Ladakh, Himachal Pradesh (Lahul, Spiti, Kinnaur and Pangi valleys) and Arunachal Pradesh (NEFA).

Secondly, there are the ethnic overlaps from Nepal, Thailand and Burma such as the Tamangs and Sherpas who are mainly settled in the Darjeeling and Jalpaiguri Districts of West Bengal, and the Tais of Assam.

The third category of Buddhists is represented by those who were attracted towards Buddhism as a result of the missionary movement spearheaded by the Maha Bodhi Society.

The followers of Dr. Ambedkar, who adopted the Buddhist way of life in October 1956 and after, form the fourth group.

The Tibetans, who followed in the footsteps of His Holiness the Dalai Lama in 1959 and after, form yet another group.

Of all the groups, the followers of Dr. Ambedkar or the neo-Buddhists as they are sometimes called, form the most dominant group. They are over 90% of the total population of Buddhists in India. Majority of the neo-Buddhists are in Maharashtra (40 lakhs). The rest are scattered throughout India. As the mass movement launched by Dr. Ambedkar is still making steady progress, the position of this group is likely to improve further. (Ahir, 1991: 189; subdivisions mine)

Though it would be quite difficult to account exactly for the percentage figures given by D.C. Ahir above, it is true that the vast majority of Buddhists in India today do not follow the Mahayana tradition. There are several works discussing the Barua Buddhists noted by Ahir in the first group. There is also the question of how clearly we have a tradition here which can be traced back to the beginning of Buddhism in India.[1] I will not pursue this question here because the answer can only contribute to

[1] Heinz Bechert was the first to specifically treat this subject in his early works on Buddhists in Bengal and Bangladesh (1967/8, 1968, 1973a, 1973b). These studies were consolidated into an essay that appeared in 1977 under the title *Zur Geschichte des Theravâda-Buddhismus in Ostbengalen* (On the History of Theravâda Buddhism in East Bengal). Then he published a short article in 1982 specifically on the Châkmâs and their history as an ancient Buddhist people (or community). Anjana R. Das (1993) discussed specifically the special form of Theravâda Buddhism among the Baruas.

A less detailed overview is an essay by Trevor Ling (1990) which also analyses the 'ethnic overlap', as D.C. Ahir (1991: 189) calls it, of Buddhists in and around

the understanding of the situation of Buddhists in India insofar as it might help to explain the very limited contacts between these Old Buddhists and the New Buddhists.

An interdisciplinary research team recently presented comprehensive and, in its accuracy, exemplary documentation about Buddhists and Buddhism in Ladakh (Crook and Osmaston, 1994). It familiarizes one with the hard realities and special conditions as well as the lamaistic spirituality found in the villages located in the Himalayas. In his portrayal of Himalayan Buddhism, which is arranged according to the main regions, Ahir (1993) gives us a good overview of Buddhists in the mountainous areas of northern India.

I will also not discuss the specific minority problems of the ethnic overlaps in West Bengal and Assam, mentioned by Ahir in the second group. Instead, I will concern myself mainly with the New Buddhists, the followers of Dr Ambedkar in the fourth group.[2] It is important to know what special problems they have in their association with the third category

---

Darjeeling. Based on the census data and his own observations, Ling shows that these are settled workers who migrated from the neighbouring regions of Nepal, Sikkim, and Thailand which were populated by Buddhists.

Though less detached and analytical, the views of locally based individuals of the region are important additions to the accounts of outsiders, i.e. Western academics. In this context, I would like to point to the contributions of the Asian Buddhists Conference for Peace (*Bodhi-Enlightenment*, Dhaka: Fine Art Press, 1990) with contributions by Enamul Haque, Shamsul Hosain, Karuna Barua, Dr Annisuzzaman, Latifa Akanda, and Prajnavangsha Thero.

A. Somananda Bhikkhu, who was supported by the government of Thailand and trained there as a monk, wrote a history of Theravâda Buddhism in his homeland, Bangladesh (1975). Also written by an insider is the short description of Buddhism in Bangladesh, comprised of biographies of the Sangharajas since 1864 (S.B. Barua, 1990).

[2] Here, however, we will not discuss Dr Ambedkar himself. Bernd S. Jurgens published his dissertation (University of Munich) in 1994 in which he describes in detail the religious philosophy of Ambedkar. However, he does not discuss the current Buddhism of Ambedkar's successors.

Martin Baumann (1991) wrote a short and precise essay on the connections between the committed Buddhists in the West, i.e. the Friends of the Western Buddhist Order (FWBO), in England, recently also in Germany, and the Ambedkar movement in India. The first part of this essay also describes the characteristics of the special form of Buddhism as developed by Ambedkar.

Sangharakshita (Dennis P. Lingwood, born 1925, founder of the FWBO)

of Buddhists, the Maha Bodhi Society, in order to justify Ahir's positive evaluation of the further development of Buddhism in India. However, no information regarding this sensitive question is available. Therefore, I will not pursue it any further here but will take it up later basing my comments on my own observations.

Finally, we are also not concerned here with the Tibetans in exile in India. It should only be noted that it is certainly no accident that the enthusiastic reception of Tibeto-Buddhist spirituality in Germany does not match the corresponding descriptions of the actual practice of Tibetans in India. The Myth Tibet in its desired purity can indeed only survive if it is detached from the actual way of life of Tibetans. This has recently

---

wrote a book *Ambedkar and Buddhism* (1986), which is mentioned again and again by those interested in Dr Ambedkar as especially successful. Similarly useful is *Dr. Ambedkar: The Liberator* by Bhadant Anand Kausalyayan (1991), which comes from the New Buddhist movement in India itself and which was originally written in Hindi. Bhadant Anand Kausalyayan (1905–88) came from the Punjab. In 1928 he was ordained in the Vidyalankara Pirivena (Sri Lanka). Since his return to India in the mid-1930s, he belonged to the group of the most prominent supporters of the Buddhist renewal movement. His biography of Dr Ambedkar in Hindi (*Yade Babana hotey*) came out in 1968 (see in detail Ahir, 1989: 81–8).

Since the mid-1960s, Eleanor Zelliot (Professor Emerita at Carleton College in Northfield, Minnesota, USA) has undertaken very comprehensive and continuous research on Ambedkar himself, as well as on the way of life practised by the New Buddhists. A portion of her essays, not always easily accessible, is now fortunately available as in omnibus volume, *From Untouchable to Dalit*. Its bibliography also includes the latest subjects on the subject in general (Zelliot, 1992, 3rd edn. 2001). Complementing this is a historically and materialistically oriented study by Gail Omvedt, *Dalits and the Democratic Revolution* (1994), which includes material on Hyderabad and Andhra.

The contributions to the Ambedkar Centenary Commemoration Volume (Kadam, 1993) provided by the Buddhist Forum and Research Institute in Pune have—and this is especially common on such occasions in India—a strong hagiographic tinge and do not even try to pretend to maintain an analytical distance from their subject. The brief study of L. Kenadi (1995), published in anticipation of his dissertation (Jawaharlal Nehru University, New Delhi), is unfortunately very superficial and does not go beyond the commonly known secondary material.

The brief comparison of the positions of Gandhi and Ambedkar by D.C. Ahir (1995b) summarizes once again the reasons for Ambedkar's resistance against the Mahatma's embrace of the 'Harijans'.

been shown quite succinctly by Mathiassen (1996). Apart from periodic self-portrayals in exile publications such as the *Tibetan Review* (New Delhi), the works of T.C. Palakshappa (1978) and Girija Saklanie (1984) remain valid studies of the attempts to preserve a specific socio-cultural configuration in the Indian Diaspora.[3]

Material and Method

One can properly understand the New Buddhist way of life and practice only against the background of the values of Hinduism; these values determine all levels of daily and especially ritual activities through precise rules governing the relations between superior and subordinate, and of precepts and prohibitions in all economic, commensal, and connubial matters. Politicians and social reformers repeatedly declare their interest in bringing about change, but in spite of this it is still not an individual's choice to decide who produces or exchanges what with whom, who can share a meal with whom, and, most of all, who can marry whom. These choices follow social norms, and accordingly the same castes are always rewarded, whereas for others access to even the simplest means of existence (which may be deemed worthy of a human being) is forbidden. The Untouchable Dr Ambedkar who was born a Mahar, a caste at the bottom of the social hierarchy, wanted to shake off this centuries-old institutionalized discrimination and unfair treatment. Thus, in Nagpur, on 14 October 1956, at a large public ceremony, he together with more than five lakh like-minded people renounced the commitments of Hinduism and converted to Buddhism. The end of a talk that Ambedkar had given twenty years earlier during a Mahar conference (text on pp. 54–5) is an impressive testimony to his feelings, and the vows that are binding for the members of the Bharatiya Bauddha Maha Sabha (Buddhist Society of India),[4] which Ambedkar founded in 1955, clearly show his understanding

[3] An interdisciplinary study on young Tibetans in Switzerland (*Junge Tibeter in der Schweiz*, see Brauen, Kantowsky) was presented in 1982. Prominent Tibetans collaborated in this study such as Gyaltsen Gyaltag (representative of the exile government for the safeguarding of Tibetan interests in Europe, who is based in Zurich) and Kelsang Galtsen (now in Dharmshala, India, who is responsible for the contacts of the exile government in India with Europe and the European Union).

[4] The Bharatiya Bauddha Maha Sabha was founded in 1955 by Dr Ambedkar. After his death, it was continued by his son Yashwant Ambedkar and after the

that his turning towards Buddhism had to be preceded by a fundamental turning away from the rituals of Hinduism. Otherwise, liberation from the teachings and practice of Hinduism did not seem possible:

Buddhist's Oaths

1. I will not regard Brahma, Vishnu and Mahesh as Gods nor will I worship them.
2. I will not regard Rama and Krishna as Gods nor will I worship them.
3. I will not accept Hindu deities like Gauri, Ganapati, etc. nor will I worship them.
4. I do not believe that God has taken birth or incarnation in any form.
5. I do not believe that Lord Buddha was the incarnation of Vishnu. I believe this propaganda is mischievous and false.
6. I will never perform any *Shraadha* nor will I offer any *Pinda*.
7. I will never act against the tenets of Buddhism.
8. I will never get any *Samskaar* performed by Brahmins.
9. I believe in the principle that all are equal.
10. I will try to establish equality.
11. I will follow the Eight-Fold Path of Lord Buddha.
12. I will follow all the ten *Paramitas* of the Dhamma.
13. I will have compassion for all living beings and will try to look after them.
14. I will not lie.
15. I will not commit theft.
16. I will not indulge in lust or sexual transgression.
17. I will not take any liquor or drink that causes intoxication.
18. I will try to mould my life in accordance with the Buddhist preachings, based on Enlightenment, Precept, and Compassion.
19. I embrace today the Bauddha Dhamma discarding the Hindu religion which is detrimental to the emancipation of human beings and which believes in inequality and regards human beings other than the Brahmins as low born.
20. This is my firm belief that the Bauddha Dhamma is the best religion.
21. I believe that today I am taking a New-Birth.
22. I solemnly take an oath that from today onwards I will act according to the Bauddha Dhamma.

Sabbe Satta Suknee Hontu
(Zelliot, 1978: 103-4)

---

latter's death (1977) by Ambedkar's wife Savita Ambedkar. This society has branches in all major cities in Maharashtra, with a head office in the Ambedkar Bhavan, Gokuldas Rasta, Mumbai (Ahir, 1991: 136).

I will try to investigate and analyse the available studies dealing with the other ways of life which the 'new birth' of Buddhists has brought about (see the twenty-first of the vows). The question is: what can one observe among the New Buddhists in the way of introducing new patterns of behaviour concerning the central economic, connubial, and commensal areas of their lives. Writings which go beyond this will not be analysed here; these include the special hermeneutics of a New Buddhist fresh attempt at liberation (Queen, 1994), specific developments in the area of New Buddhist iconography (Tartakov, 1994) and, concerning the history of ideas, the question of the relationship between the fresh attempt of Ambedkar's social reform movement and the classical social ethics of Buddhism (Redmond, 1994). Such a discussion in Western academic communities may be quite interesting for an academic dialogue; however, in the present context we will simply deal at the micro-level with the actual day-to-day activities of the New Buddhists. What do the few available studies on the subject tell the person who wants to know in greater detail the characteristics of New Buddhism in India today?

Early Studies

Some studies are less useful than others for this rather specific question. Though they look at New Buddhism in India as a phenomenon dependant on social conditions, the studies mostly depict the movement only in a historically descriptive way, as, for example, Harold C. Coward in his contribution to the omnibus volume *Religion in Modern India*, first published in 1981 and again in 1995. His essay gives us a clear idea of the various developmental phases of the revival of Buddhism in modern India. However, concerning today's forms of expression and appearance, he can only conclude very generally the following:

> Reverence has evolved over the years into a kind of hero-worship of the sort that Ambedkar himself hated. In the rural villages statues of him are seen garlanded with flowers, and the utterance of his name is a prayer for many. But though devoted to him as their hero, these poor and generally uneducated peasants typically have little knowledge of the Buddhist teaching he championed. In fact, many who became Buddhists through the conversion ceremonies have received little further instruction in the teaching and practice of Buddhism. While Buddhists in name they carry on many of the very Hindu customs and rituals that Ambedkar was attempting to overcome. Although it has liberated some untouchables into an alternative life, for many little has changed as a result of their conversion. (Coward, 1995: 282)

The study by Deodas Liluji Ramteke, *Revival of Buddhism in Modern India*, unfortunately does not include an analysis which reaches to urban localities or the village level of behaviour at all. In the final chapter, 'The Ideal Social Order' (Ramteke, 1983: 231ff.), he only derives from texts by Ambedkar a description of what a brave new world of Buddhism should look like in the social, political, ethical, and monastic areas so that one can overcome the discrimination of the *varna* system.

Important references to the changed conditions in the area of economic relations and commensality, however, are found in the work of Arjunrao Bhujangrao Hiramani on social change in two villages in the Marathwada area of Maharashtra. His field research dates back to 1971 and shows that New Buddhists succeeded in discarding the degrading duties of the Mahars within the framework of the division of labour in these villages:

> The conversion from the Hindu fold is one of the most important factors that brought about social change among the Buddhists. The data show that most of the Buddhist families have taken to agricultural labour after abandoning their traditional services. When such change took place in them, their relationships with the villagers based on *baluta* came to an end. The relationships between the Buddhists and the villagers formerly were shaped not only on an economic basis but also on a social basis. Almost all menial and degrading jobs were to be performed by the Buddhists under obligation to the higher castes. Their present occupation as agricultural labourers has not brought any appreciable economic dividends either. But they do not now work under compulsion. The compulsion, if any, is economic and indirect and not social. (Hiramani, 1977: 202)

> The villagers now get their work done by employing a servant or by themselves. The dead animals are in many cases dragged by the respective owners themselves who bury them in their fields, or allot the work to a person belonging to the Mang caste who is paid Rs. 2 to 5 for this work. The sweeping of a courtyard of the higher caste is done by themselves, and the sweeping of the village streets is assigned to the servants appointed by the village. Grampanchayat. The breaking away of the Buddhists from the *baluta* system, therefore, has led to some concomitant changes in inducing others to step in. (Hiramani, 1977: 243)

Even though it was possible in these two villages to avoid traditional degrading duties without significant sanctions, the former Mahars did not at all become pure and touchable as New Buddhists. Furthermore, even they themselves continued to act in a discriminatory way towards the other low castes and did not accept food from them:

> The Buddhists even after their conversion are still treated as the former Mahars in commensal relations. Their touch is still treated as polluting. And hence if and

when food is served to them the higher castes take the usual precautions. The Buddhists do not accept food from the Nhavi, Dhobi, Kaikadi, Dhor, Chambhar and Mang. (Hiramani, 1977: 264)

These findings/conclusions from the studies undertaken in 1971 largely agree with the data that T.S. Wilkinson had collected ten years earlier in two villages near Nagpur. He too found that the Mahars were able to discard their polluting activities in the framework of traditional caste duties without significant sanctions from other castes of the village because the Chamars were ready to remove the carcasses of dead animals (Wilkinson, 1972: 86). Unfortunately, the study does not further explore the questions of commensalism. However, it does contain an exact and useful description of a Buddhist marriage ceremony.

Generally, those interviewed thought that they could observe improvement in their economic situation mainly because they did not have to celebrate any longer the extravagant Hindu festivals and ceremonies which often involved lifelong debts. Below is a description of a simple New Buddhist marriage ceremony:

For the wedding ceremony the bride and bridegroom sit in front of a table or stool on which are placed the pictures of the Buddha and Dr. Ambedkar. An earthen pot full of water, with a few mango leaves dipped in it, is kept in front of the bride and the groom. A white thread is tied around the neck of the pot. The bride and groom fold their hands in reverence and the two ends of the thread are passed between the palms of the folded hands of each of them and held in that position until the oath-taking is over. It is preferred to have a Bhikku (Buddhist monk) preside over the ceremony, but since there are so few of them, a leading person of the community is generally asked to preside; he recites the *Tri Saran* and the *Panchsheel* in Pali, and during this recitation the assembled gathering showers white flowers on the couple at short intervals. Then the two are administered the following oaths:

Bridegroom:

1. I shall give due respect to my wife.
2. I shall not insult her.
3. I shall prove myself worthy of my wife by refraining from intoxicating and alcoholic drink, and shall abstain from adultery.
4. I shall make my wife happy by giving her wealth and fulfilling her necessities.
5. I shall satisfy my wife by giving her ornaments and clothes.

Bride:

1. I shall keep my house neat and clean.
2. I shall win the heart of my husband, members of my family and relatives,

elderly persons and servants of my house, by my good and decent behaviour.
3. I shall prove worthy of my husband by abstaining from adultery, deceit and prostitution.
4. I shall protect the wealth of my husband earned by good means.
5. I shall be vigilant over every work of my house and shall not show any kind of negligence.

After taking these oaths, the bride first garlands the groom and vice versa, by which act they publicly accept each other as husband and wife. Having done this, they garland the portraits of the Buddha and Dr. Ambedkar, while the assembled gathering shouts 'Bhagwan Buddha ki jai; Aur Babasahib Ambedkar ke jai' (Praise be to thee Lord Buddha, and Praise be to thee father Ambedkar). The ceremony is concluded with the Bhikku or any other person presiding by reciting the Jaimangal and the Ashta Mangalgatha in Pali.

The marriage dinner is also a simple affair, and no non-vegetarian dishes or alcoholic drinks are served. Many respondents said that in the past no wedding was considered complete without these two items, which not only added to the expenses but was one of the main reasons for quarrels and disorderliness. (Wilkinson, 1972: 97–8)

The ceremony was simplified and shaped by the elements of the Buddhist lifestyle. However, as far as the selection of marriage partners (by the parents!) is concerned, the same strict rules of endogamy still applied among the New Buddhists in the villages under investigation. The marriage partners came from the *jati* (lit. birth group) of the Mahars, who are the only ones considered eligible for marriage. True, Babasaheb Ambedkar again and again called on his followers to break the central kernel of the caste system through inter-caste marriages. But how could one follow his request and emulate his example (Dr Ambedkar's second wife was a doctor, born a Brahmin) in a village setting? (Wilkinson, 1972: 94).

The other contributions in this volume, *Ambedkar and the Neo-Buddhist Movement*, published in 1972 by the Christian Literature Society in Madras (now Chennai), do not examine in detail the question chosen for the present volume, except for a study by Richard W. Taylor (1972). There, in a footnote, one reads that the rejection of the traditional forms of labour can be sustained only if alternative opportunities are available in the vicinity:

In one village the Buddhists refused to perform their traditional tasks and when harvest time came in 1957 the ruling landlord and farmer class took revenge for it. The landlords refused to employ the Buddhists. This large and remote village in the Wardha District had a population of around 6,000 in the late 1950s of whom about 1,400 were Mahars—all of whom became Buddhists. Many of them later returned to their traditional roles out of economic necessity. (Taylor, 1972: 134)

Taylor also comments on the attitude of caste Hindus about their new status. At least one student expressed his frustration about Hinduism: 'Now we are the bloody Buddhists instead of the bloody Harijans.' (Taylor, 1972: 135).

To what extent people turned away from Buddhism after they returned to their traditional roles is unknown. However, the study by Adele Fiske on the understanding of religion by New Buddhists contains indirect references to this question. She shows that the rejection of Hinduism was formulated more clearly and distinctly than the positive turn towards Buddhism. In conclusion, she interprets the results of her research (survey, by questionnaire: out of 200 written in Marathi or English, 114 came back) to the effect 'that the Neo-Buddhist concept of Buddhism is primarily that of a religion of liberation of the oppressed in society' (Fiske, 1972a: 107 and 119). To what extent, however, the New Buddhists continue to believe in the teaching of self-deliverance through Buddhism even when the social conditions improve rather than deteriorate remains a question.

Early on Owen W. Lynch (1969) referred to the special problems which result from a conversion to Buddhism in view of a policy of protective discrimination especially for Untouchables:

> One who openly professes to be a Buddhist is not eligible for the special help given by the government to the Scheduled Castes under its 'protective discrimination' policy. A Buddhist in Uttar Pradesh cannot stand for reserved seats in an election, nor can he apply for government jobs reserved for Scheduled Castes. His children cannot claim eligibility for remission of fees, grants, and scholarships given to the Scheduled Castes for educational purposes.
>
> In such circumstances, then, the Jatav will engage in 'bridge actions'. Vis-a-vis the state or nation he will activate his Scheduled Caste status, which requires that he be a Hindu, since this carries with it the benefits of 'protective discrimination'. However, in situations in which he is not facing a government official, he will activate his Buddhist status. (Lynch, 1969: 147)

Lynch's study of the caste of the Jatavs in Agra, Uttar Pradesh, is frequently mentioned as an example which shows what we are still missing in terms of detailed knowledge of the concrete living conditions in a New Buddhist neighbourhood. Ravindra S. Khare (1984) does include in his study of the Chamars in Lucknow 17 New Buddhist households (in a spot check of 69 households)—one of the quarters he also called Baudhabagh. However, his detailed observations concern the overriding question of the various kinds of protests by the lower castes in India in general. According to his account, the Ambedkar movement is only one of four typically Indian expressions of this lower caste protest. In summary, he describes how they become an everyday affair:

The democratic inspiration of Ambedkar translates into the routine rhetoric and politics of the regional and local leaders. The changing group dynamics of local leaders and their immediate interests further parochialize the original inspiration. A national leader-hero like Ambedkar is best recalled as a past thaumaturge, remembered more and more only by erecting his statues and icons (with appropriate ceremonial panegyric). The national dimensions of his plan are continuously disembled under parochial practical pressure. (Khare, 1984: 144)

Fiske (1972b) arrived at quite similar conclusions in her study of the organizational forms and patterns of cooperation among the many Buddhist organizations in India. She found that they partly existed only as letterheads and that their representatives were not well informed about Buddhist movements in general.

Although an editorial published in the first issue of *Buddhist India* in 1927 called for the formation of an all-India Buddhist organization, and at least fifteen Buddhist organizations existed prior to Dr. Ambedkar's conversion in 1956, little evidence was found of inter-organizational communication and cooperation during the course of this survey in 1966-67. Even among the component units of the largest of the Buddhist organizations, the Buddhist Society of India, there was little coordination of programs, publications, and related activities. An assessment of the situation in 1964 was provided by D.C. Ahir in a form letter distributed in 1966 to Buddhist leaders and organizations throughout India.

'Though there are more than 3 million registered Buddhists and over 20 million potential Buddhists in India – Buddhism has not so far attained national status in this country. This was reflected to a great extent at the time of the 7th Conference of the World Fellowship of Buddhists held at Sarnath in November, 1964. From India as many as ten delegations participated in this conference but most of them had no or little knowledge about each other before reaching Sarnath. The reason being that there does not exist an active All India Body of Buddhists and information about numerous Buddhist Societies and Organisations in the country is not available from any one place.'

This statement was accompanied by a request for information concerning the existence in each locality of 'Buddhist Societies and Organizations, Schools, Colleges, Viharas, Customs and Festivals and Buddhist Literature etc.' Responses to this query were to be published in the *Bhartiya Buddhist Directory* established by Mr. Ahir, the managing editor, in collaboration with Ven. Anand Kausalyayan. In spite of the obvious usefulness of such information for the furthering of communication and integration within the movement, as of June, 1967, Mr. Ahir had received very few replies, and as of 1970, this work had not been published. (Fiske, 1972: 140)

The four studies of Adele Fiske (1972a and b), Ravindra S. Khare, and Owen W. Lynch go beyond the limited question chosen here, but I quoted them to at least hint at the larger picture.

Eleanor Zelliot has produced the most comprehensive, the most continuous, and certainly the most committed research on this subject. In the introduction to her selected essays, she writes: 'My life has continued to be dominated by Babasaheb Ambedkar and his movement. No other Western scholar has studied the movement as a whole' (Zelliot, 1992: v). At the same time, however, she points out that all her articles were written for conferences, journals, omnibus volumes, and encyclopedias. She still has not published her Ph.D. thesis, 'B.R. Ambedkar and the Mahar Movement' (University of Pennsylvania, 1969).

The essay which Zelliot co-wrote with Joanna Rogers Macy for a conference on the History of Buddhism, organized by A.K. Narain in 1976 at the University of Wisconsin (Macy/Zelliot, 1980), is most important for our question here. Eleanor Zelliot has written the second part of this jointly authored work. This part was incorporated into the volume of her collected essays under the title 'Tradition and Innovation in Contemporary Indian Buddhism: Activities and Observances'. It contains important information about the New Buddhist arrangement of festivals. First, she notes an expansion of Buddhist rituals. The Three-fold Refuge has been expanded, and Dr Ambedkar is a central iconographical element of each New Buddhist arrangement:

> The presence of the picture of Ambedkar in all Buddhist *vihāras* and at all Buddhist functions seems to set Indian Buddhists today apart from the main Buddhist tradition. The inclusion of 'Babasaheb' Ambedkar as an object of reverence is the most visible innovation in the practice of contemporary Buddhists in India. The Buddha and Babasaheb in plaster, stone, poster-art and painting, in song and drama and story, the two seemingly of near-equal importance, rarely one without the other, are continual evidence that contemporary Indian Buddhism proudly combines its own tradition with that of the main Buddhist tradition. Ambedkar is neither worshipped nor prayed to, nor of course is the Buddha. No *pūjā* is performed, no *navas* (vows) are made to either figure, so their functions are not those of a Hindu god. But at every occasion, both figures are garlanded, the Buddha first; incense is lit; and Bhagwant Gautam Buddha and Parampujaya Babaseheb Ambedkar are addressed before the speaker acknowledges the Chairman of the function and the 'Brothers and Sisters'. (Zelliot, 1992: 224)

Another broadly-accepted way of honoring Ambedkar is to add the diminutive of his first name, Bhimrao, to the list of refuges, i.e. Bhiman saranam gacchami, so that the 'Three Jewels' become four:

I go for refuge to the Buddha;
I go for refuge to the Dhamma (doctrine);
I go for refuge to the Sangha (order of monks);
I go for refuge to Ambedkar.

The place of such rituals is no longer a *mandir* (temple) but, following Buddhist terminology, is now called a *vihara*. However, this is now also a place where lay men and women meet for conversations and for mutual instruction. It is no longer only a permanent residence of monks or nuns as in other Buddhist countries.

The new buildings dedicated to the Buddhist religion in Maharashtra, as well as the old buildings converted to Buddhists' use, are called *vihāras*, the technical term for the residence of the Buddhist monks. The words for temple in Marathi, *deul* and *mandir*, are studiously avoided, and the only term for a gathering place in the old Buddhist tradition seemed to be *vihāra*. The need of today's Buddhists, however, is not so much living quarters for bhikkhus as a meeting place for the laity, a place where the image of the Buddha can be kept, the community can gather for lectures on Buddhism or for *wandana* and children can be instructed. As in the case of other lay elements in Buddhist structure, there was in India no living model for the place of gathering of the Buddhist community, so the multi-purpose *vihāra* came into being.

The *vihāra* most often is a plain rectangular structure, embellished, where possible, with architectural detail from the most accessible models of Buddhist structures: the caves of Ajanta and the stupa of Sanchi. These buildings are newly built whenever the Buddhists of some locality have the money and the cooperative spirit to create a symbol of their newly accepted faith. In many villages, the *cāudi* (communal hall) of the old *Mahārwādā* (the quarters of the Mahar, somewhat removed from the village proper), does double service as community meeting room and center for Buddhist activities. I have seen few Hindu temples converted to Buddhist use, probably because few were completely in the hands of those Mahars who converted.

The *vihāra* of Buddhists today is not an imitation of a Hindu temple. There is no *pujāri* or ritual priest, there is no stream of individual worshippers paying homage to the image. The *vihāra* serves chiefly as a symbol of the community's faith and as a center for the community to gather as Buddhists. And since knowledge is seen as a Buddhist virtue both Buddhist and secular education can easily be combined with its religious functions. (Zelliot, 1992: 226–7)

In spite of this strong position enjoyed by the laity, one can recognize the first signs of the formation of religious specialists. Moreover, the knowledge of foreign monks is being used, even if they cannot express themselves in the local language and even though they do not want to stay a long time because the unfamiliar frugality of the New Buddhist communities does not quite agree with them:

Now, after twenty years, it seems clear that Buddhism in India will continue its strong emphasis on the laity and lay leadership. It is still the lay leadership that does most of the teaching and preaching, writes most of the religious material that continues to flow from the movement, collects the money and plans the *vihāra*. But there are increasing numbers of Marathi-speaking bhikkhus appearing, it seems not so much from the need of the community as from their own individual commitments to Buddhism. . . .

The function of the bhikkhus in Buddhist society in Maharashtra seems primarily to be teaching, although it seems also true that the very presence of a bhikku is an important symbol of the identity of a Buddhist group. I have met many sorts of bhikkhus during my visits to India. In the 1960s the Ven. Sangarakshita of England and Kalimpong devoted half of each year to teaching in Maharashtra and Gujarat. He preached many sermons, his English being translated into Marathi by one of the young Buddhist students, and he also conducted *samnera*, a period of ten days or so in which Buddhist laity lived as monks. . . .

Singhalese, Burmese and Japanese bhikkhus have been of service to the community at various times, their effectiveness dependent upon their ability to communicate and their attitude toward the still generally economically and socially depressed community. (Zelliot, 1992: 229–30)

How do the New Buddhist communities portray themselves to outsiders? On what special occasions does the new religious identity become visible? As is well known, processions in India are often a cause for the outbreak of brutal excesses because they are aimed at provoking the emotions of people of a different faith. Serious clashes such as those which erupt on the occasion of Hindu or Muslim festive processions are not mentioned by Zelliot (1992: 231) in connection with the four holidays of the New Buddhists:

The anniversary of the day of the conversion, October 14, is celebrated as Dhamma Diksha Day by those who can return for a great ceremony to the field in Nagpur where the 1956 conversion was held; others hold local observances of varying sorts. Buddha Jayanti, the day of observance of the Buddha's birth, has been observed since 1950, when Ambedkar arranged for the celebration as a public occasion in Delhi. The Jayanti is a time for speeches, music, drama on Buddhist themes and occasionally a solemn procession. Ambedkar's death day, December 6, is a time for quiet and sorrowful gatherings, and talks or music by one of the many singers or singing groups in the community predominate.

Ambedkar's birth date, April 14, on the other hand, is a noisy and joyful occasion. Here the borrowings from the processions found in Hinduism, Islam and Jainism are clear. As in the Muslim Moharram or the Hindu Ganapati festival, local groups form committees, which plan their contribution to the city-wide procession. In Poona, the central point is the statue of Ambedkar near the railway station, and groups of dancing, shouting youngsters and older men march from their scattered localities to Ambedkar Square. The Maharashtrian dance game *legim* often is played by the marchers, as in the Ganapati festival, although the Buddhists have at least one girls' group, which the Hindus do not. One group rented the city zoo's elephant in 1976 to carry Ambedkar's photograph in the procession.

Unfortunately, the New Buddhist variant of the Mahar movement has only partially been of interest for Zelliot's historically oriented research question (she calls her collection of essays *From Untouchable to Dalit*), and she has not pursued this problem in any detail. This may have something to do with the fact that New Buddhism in Maharashtra is a new subject for investigation by the social sciences, and is very difficult to deal with. In addition, the observation of the actual world, life, and practices of the local groups could easily lead to a devaluation of their efforts if they are measured against the normative standards of Buddhist precepts. For Ambedkar has, with good reason, modified these by way of social reform, and it is well known that this earned him the hostility of the Maha Bodhi Society in Kolkata and of many old Buddhists as well!

However, this leads us beyond our chosen subject of investigation. Thus, we may only conclude here that, based on earlier studies, it is impossible to outline an exact picture of New Buddhist behaviour at the economic, connubial, and commensal levels as has been attempted above. And the few more recent studies are not of much help either.

More recent investigations

Recently, Timothy Fitzgerald, who himself has worked on Buddhists in Maharashtra, summarized the position of current research in this way:

> A great deal has been written in English about Dr. B.R. Ambedkar and the movement he started from biographical, historical and political points of view. Some of this literature is scholarly, sympathetic, and critical (Zelliot); but much of it fails to penetrate through the 'official' position to the minds and lives of actual Buddhists. Also, there appears to be little or no research of a specifically anthropological or sociological kind providing a detailed account of the structure of social relations in specific communities, rural and urban. There is nothing that

I have found which one might compare to Owen Lynch's study of Jatavs in Agra City (1969). (1994: 17)

This assessment agrees with the sources which Zelliot (1992: 262–3) notes in a new appendix to her earlier collection of articles. They do not go beyond the few publications which we can only note briefly below. Due to the long-standing and persistent efforts of Diwan Chand Ahir, we have quite a complete list of *bhikkhus* and *viharas*, as well as of the Buddhist societies and institutions in India (Ahir, 1991: 97–133 and 134–40). Nevertheless, we know virtually nothing about their members, their activities, and their influence, because the Buddhist journals of the country (Ahir, 1991: 173–4), especially the ones in English, continue to publish only interpretations of Buddhist texts and give instructions for a right livelihood and ethic (see Ahir, 1995); they do not report on the actual practices of today's Buddhists.

Unfortunately, the autobiographical accounts written by members of the Friends of the Western Buddhist Order (FWBO) concerning their energetic mission in the Indian branch of the order, called the Trailokya Bauddha Mahasangha Sahayak Gana (TBMSG), also do not serve as a source for the study of the New Buddhists in general. The founder of the order, Sangharakshita (Dennis Lingwood, born in 1925 in England), once described the special missionary enthusiasm of this movement quite vividly:

Even though they had not had anyone to teach them, the vast majority of those who had embraced Buddhism in response to Ambedkar's call had lost neither their faith in their great leader's vision nor their desire to learn more about the religion to which he had directed them. The evidences of that faith and that desire were to be found all over Maharashtra, and even beyond. Wherever I went, in the course of that preaching tour in the winter of 1981–82, I saw not only scores of newly constructed Buddhist temples but hundreds of lifesize—and more than lifesize—busts and statues of Ambedkar. Cast in bronze, or merely moulded in plaster, the familiar figure was to be seen in every town and village, in death as in life, dominating the lives of his people and reminding the whole nation of the principles for which he had stood.

Wherever I went I moreover saw, as I had seen time and time again all those years ago, how overwhelmingly grateful Ambedkar's followers were for whatever Buddhist teaching they received. This time, however, they would not have to wait for years before they heard another lecture on Buddhism. This time they were in contact with a new Buddhist movement, a movement that was the direct continuation of Ambedkar's own work for the Dharma, so that even after I had gone there would be plenty of opportunities for them to hear lectures, to learn how to meditate, and to go on retreat. There would, in short, be plenty of opportunities for them to practise Buddhism. (Sangharakshita, 1986: 172)

Meanwhile, many possibilities for such practices exist outside the daily routine, and this can be attributed mainly to the special efforts of Dhammachari Lokamitra. He is a Western member of the order which controls from Pune the activities as well as the appropriate use of the donations with which the work of the TBMSG is financed by the West through the FWBO. In his contribution to a seminar in March 1991, which was organized by the Bhikkhu Jagdish Kashyap Institute of Buddhist and Asian Studies in Sarnath, he summarized his work until then as follows:

> The Mahāsangha has been functioning for 12 years in India. There are about 20 centres of activity, mostly in Maharashtra, but regular or occasional activities take place in Gujarat, U.P., A.P., M.P., Goa and Karnataka. These are at present run by the 82 Indian Dhammacharis.
>
> The Mahāsangha runs many Dhamma retreats lasting from a couple of days to a week or more. Thousands of people have attended these, during which they are introduced to meditation, Dhamma study, friendship in the Dhamma, and puja, in fairly ideal conditions. Despite their short duration, most people experience higher, more positive mental states, and a joy they have not experienced before.
>
> Besides its numerous direct beneficiaries the social work shows that Buddhists can themselves bring about effective social change, especially through the practice of the Dhamma. The common commitment to common ideals helps to transcend personal, social and political differences which otherwise have fragmented the community. While many sincerely start social projects, very few succeed simply because their positive mental states are not strong enough. Before long greed for money and power, confusion and infighting cripple most such attempts. Through Dhamma practice these negative states can be worked upon and the positive one strengthened making the actual work much more effective.
>
> The Mahāsangha helps give others a vision of the new society that Ambedkar was convinced Buddhism could bring about. An essential aspect of that new society was the absence of caste. Through the development of *maitrā* barriers between people (usually very deep-rooted) are weakened. The Mahāsangha has members from a wide range of backgrounds, but within it no hierarchy based on birth, social position, profession, or education exists. Within India, while most members of the Mahāsangha come from the previously so-called Mahar community, there are members from different communities outside Maharashtra. Within Maharashtra itself, work has been started with people from the so-called Matang community. In such communication the old caste conditioning of the Indian members is not reinforced and they experience themselves only as fellow human beings and brothers and sisters in the Dhamma. In these ways and more the Mahāsangha is able to begin to set an example of a truly casteless society. (Lokamitra, 1994: 62–4, abbreviated)

This portrayal shows that in the work of the TBMSG we encounter a special case of Buddhism in India today which should be judged according to the criteria of educational and developmental aid. This excerpt also explicitly shows what is possible in the area of social work in India, if corresponding resources with the accompanying personal commitment flow from outside. This is neither intended to degrade the engagement of the FWBO nor to assume that a genuine Indian Buddhist movement with similar socio-political goals and comparable influence could not exist. However, it remains a fact that so far one searches for them in vain. Moreover, the history of the Sarvodaya movement in India (Kantowsky, 1980) does not make one feel optimistic about the outcome.

In spite of these restricting remarks, I would nevertheless like to quote four observations by Terry Pilchick. As a member of the FWBO, he was asked by Sangharakshita to write a report in order to give outsiders in the West an insight into the special character of the work which Lokamitra and the Dhammacharis of the TBMSG perform. We thus have the description of an insider, intended to mobilize good will for the movement. However, it contains some remarks which are interesting for our question. On the occasion of a mission tour by Sangharakshita, Pilchick repeatedly met with representatives of Buddhist groups, about which one Buddhist said (Pilchick, 1988: 55):

> Mr. Kamblay sat beside him (i.e. Sangharakshita) and lamented the decline of the local Buddhist community: men were taking to drink, families going into debt because of dowry weddings, people were worshipping the old gods; there was even a rumour that some of them had been participating in animal sacrifices. He feared that in time the entire community would forget Ambedkar's message and revert to Hinduism.

In the report quoted earlier, Lokamitra drew attention to the retreats which were organized by the TBMSG, and to the transformative influence they see within the New Buddhist groups. Pilchick (1988: 98–9) also points to the special atmosphere of such meditation exercises which, in his opinion, is unusual under typical Indian conditions:

> Generally speaking, I had found that nobody in India ever seemed to go for a walk simply for the sake of it, and certainly never went alone. But now people were strolling around the pathways, idling time away, even stopping in fields to peer into the hearts of wild-flowers, or to watch the insects that flitted about among the leaves. It was almost bizarre to be among Indians, for whom the group seemed such a natural, fundamental part of life, and yet to feel the group dynamic dissolving. In its place there emerged, over the hours and days, a genuine spirit of sangha, of 'spiritual community', as we looked at each other and spoke with the growing awareness that we were each unique beings with a

unique potential, no longer just group-members. The chanting became gentler and more harmonious as we started listening to our own voices in relation to the others'. During the 'communication exercises' we could look at each other directly, for minutes on end, without dissolving into hoots and squawks of embarrassed laughter. Group-based familiarity gave way to appreciation, to real sensitivity, real friendship. The silent periods became relaxed and satisfying; there was a thrill in the air, a quiet excitement.

The observations regarding the orthodox *bhikkhus* and their competence are somewhat pejorative, but they agree with the accounts of Dhammaviriyo Mahathero. In his capacity as a representative of Buddhist interests in the National Commission for Minorities, he informed me during an interview in February 1996 that the question of educating *bhikkhus* was a generational problem which would solve itself in the natural order of dying off. According to his information, ex-Sannyasins would soon cease to exist. Pilchick (1988: 126–7) still met them and found them to be a disturbance to the dedicated educational work of the TBMSG:

At any Dhamma event in Maharashtra, the monks enjoy a kind of traditional right to be at the centre of the action—and the limelight. They are usually, though not always, friendly folk, and seem content with their lot in a worldly sort of way. For all that, even the chummiest of them give the impression that they are searching for a role—that of Dhamma teaching being denied them by their lack of knowledge and experience. Few have received any training, and most have little idea, if any, of what the spiritual life is about. Some of the older ones, I heard, were Hindu sannyasis before the conversions; afterwards they simply got themselves ordained as monks so that they could continue their undemanding lives undisturbed.

The trouble with having them up on stage is that they will distract people from the fact that this talk is a gateway to TBMSG—which has something practical to offer in the way of instruction, facilities, and follow-up. If they are moved by the talk a few people will probably invite an Order member to come and lead a meditation course in their locality, or even try out a retreat. The long-term effects could be profound. But if they fail to realize that there is a distinction between TBMSG and other elements in the local Buddhist world, then their response to the talk might go no further than feeding a few monks for a day.

Finally, we have similarly critical descriptions of the direct meeting with *bhikkhus* in Pune (Pilchick, 1988: 172–3), which supposedly should explain to British readers that without the TBMSG once again everything would go its usual Indian way:

Going over to the community house for lunch one day, I found an old monk seated in the dining area. He was as thin as the proverbial rake and, when the food was served, ate hungrily and copiously, oblivious of anything else.

Nobody seemed to know quite who he was, but when Lokamitra joined us, he explained that our guest was the incumbent at a vihara just a few miles outside Poona. A group of Buddhist politicians and businessmen had donated money, raised some more, and built a fine vihara. But now that it was finished, with a monk installed, nobody knew what to do with it. The monk had therefore come along, with the trustees' blessing, he said, to ask whether TBMSG could take it over, since he believed it was the only movement capable of putting the facility to good use.

A few days later I found another monk at our lunch-time gathering. In bold contrast to the first, this gentleman was huge of bulk, highly jovial, but remarkably sparing in his appetites. Once upon a time he had been a famous singer-bard figure in Maharashtra. Even as a monk he still liked to work through the medium of 'music programmes'. A few years ago, after one such programme, a millionaire had dropped a small fortune into his lap as a gesture of devotion. He had used the money to buy some land, but since then nothing more had been done. Now he wanted TBMSG to take the land over, perhaps to build a vihara, or a hostel for students from poor families.

Similar offers had been made in Ahmedabad, Aurangabad, and Hyderabad.

As illustrative as these quotations from the works of members of the order are, it should have become clear by now that they are generally not an unbiased source of information about New Buddhists in India. They try to meet a determined programmatic claim, and besides this, they include only a selective minority of New Buddhists—those who are connected to the TBMSG.

The B.A. thesis of Shaun Linsley also does not add to our knowledge in the present context. It is based solely on an eight-week stay in Pune in the summer of 1988, deals exclusively with the work of the TBMSG, and tells us little about the New Buddhist surroundings in general. Only indirectly (and in a negative way) do we learn something about other New Buddhists:

One main difference that was perceived between the TBMSG and other organisations was that Meditation was seen as an essential part of Buddhist practice. Replying to the question, 'What difference is there between the Bharatiya Bauddha Mahasabha (the Buddhist organisation founded by Dr Ambedkar and the main Buddhist organisation in Maharashtra) and the TBMSG?' one senior Dharma Chari replied:

'They are concentrating on, for example, how to work the marriage. There should be, how do you say, on marriages, on births, on name-giving ceremonies—that these should be performed the same way everywhere. So there is a lot of stress on these things, rather than on the practice of the Dharma, on how to practice the Dharma. I mean there is no meditation. I mean I don't know how many people meditate, but very rarely. Meditation is the backbone of our movement, the other organisations are not teaching meditation. (Linsley, 1989: 46–7)

We read complete agreement with this assessment of an informant in the conclusion of this study:

The Neo-Buddhist movement in India has developed rather disjointedly because of political involvements and a lack of religious guidance. The FWBO is beginning to strongly influence the ways in which Buddhism is perceived. The influence is most clearly recognizable in the changing attitudes by the Neo-Buddhists with regard to meditation and the moral code of the Precepts. A redefinition by many Neo-Buddhists, of the role of Buddhism in the social context would also appear to be taking place, particularly with regard to the active involvement of Buddhists in social work. (Linsley, 1989: 62)

As stated above, there are several studies dealing with the work of the TBMSG intentionally written from an insider's viewpoint. The field in and around Pune is indeed comparatively easily accessible, and it is not difficult to find informants. As is common for similar help organizations, people have become used to the arrival of interested Westerners who want to gather information about the influence and the effect of measures which are financially supported from abroad.

Timothy Fitzgerald, lecturer in the Department of International Culture at the Aichigakuin University in Japan, also mainly worked on the TBMSG. At the same time, however, he gathered comparative data in several villages in Marathwada and in the university milieu of Nagpur. Accordingly, he distinguishes three types of Buddhism in Maharashtra:

1. Village Buddhism as a variant of Hindusim.
2. Intellectual Buddhism as secular rationalism and social democracy.
3. Modernist soteriological Buddhism as represented by TBMSG.

Fitzgerald's accounts concerning the first type (1994: 20–1) agree largely with the information which we could extract earlier from the descriptions of the forms of expressions of New Buddhism at the village level:

Type 1 Buddhism, put most negatively, is the kind of Buddhism which has not really changed anybody or anything very radically. The new identity is of a purely communal kind, and concerns the identity of a caste group in relation to other castes. Buddhists may have changed some practices (for instance, they may have refused to do *balutedari* duties such as scavenging, or given up eating beef), but they still recognise caste and sub-caste hierarchy, and practise endogamy, commensality, and even untouchability. Alongside the ostensibly "Buddhist" practices such as the chanting of the Three Refuges and the Five Precepts on Purnima and Jayanti days, they may still continue to worship the old Hindu gods; and Buddha and Ambedkar themselves may have been defied and added to the pantheon.

Frequently, I have been told that while pictures of Buddha and Babasaheb Ambedkar are kept in the front room, in the back-room you find pictures of Hindu gods and goddesses. In my experience many Buddhists do not have a back-room, since they often only have one room. Therefore this expression, which has been repeated so frequently, may have been intended figuratively. It has also been frequently stated that Buddha and Dr. Ambedkar have been deified. Dharmachari Lokamitra writes as follows (Buddhism in the Modern World: An Appreciation of Dr. Ambedkar's Contribution to Buddhism, Pune: TBMSG, 1991):

Both Dr. Ambedkar and the Buddha have been effectively deified by many. They have become the objects of prayer for a son, a promotion, to pass an examination and so forth. Palkis have been seen with the bust of Dr. Ambedkar on festival days around Pune. . . . In the same way many other confusions have crept into the practice of the Dhamma. Bhikshus take the place of the purohit. Paritran chanting takes the place of the Satya Narayan Puja. Buddha Vasi takes the place of Kailas Vasi and so on. (Fitzgerald, 1994: 19)

The expression of the second type of Buddhist intellectualism is quite different. Fitzgerald (1994: 22 and 23) thinks that there he could detect not only a rejection of the popular Buddhism of the villages, but also a rejection of the central basic assumptions of classical Buddhism:

Buddhism means equality, human dignity, self-help, rejection of caste inequality, rejection of reliance on supernatural agencies, acceptance of scientific rationality, modern education, democracy, the rights of the individual. Typically, the traditional concepts of Buddhist soteriology are interpreted in materialistic and secular ways. For instance, I was frequently told that 'karma' either has no meaning, or, alternatively, means 'action which has social consequences'. Though this is not incompatible with the traditional Buddhist concept, it has lost all meaning of 'moral causation', and thus has been severed from the soteriological nexus. Also, rebirth is unambiguously rejected, except in the diluted and materialistic sense given to it by Dr. Ambedkar, the natural process whereby the physical elements which make up the body, and which at death rejoin the mass of similar elements floating in space, recombine in the production of another body. The traditional concept of moral causation over several lives is consistently absent from this account, as is the idea that meditation progressively releases the mind from attachment and thus from the cycle of rebirth. Whereas Nirvana has always had a transcendental meaning (admittedly difficult to state and disputed by the schools), for Type 2 Buddhism it is typically explained as a correct analysis of the causes of suffering in society. The meaning of 'soteriology' (What must I do to be saved?) has become almost completely secularised.

The emphasis is consistently on suffering as being caused by the social institutions of caste and untouchability, and salvation or liberation (Nirvana) as being achieved through concerted social and political action. This is a fundamentally secularised version of Buddhism; and at its strongest and starkest it seems to have virtually no connection with the traditional Buddha Dharma, but to be an Indian name for a thoroughly modern western concept of the world.

In the summary of this attempt at a typology of Buddhism as it is practiced in Maharashtra, Fitzgerald claims (1994: 26) that, in spite of the social commitment, the soteriological variant of the TBMSG represents a regionally specific expression which unites modern conceptions with traditional elements:

Type 2 Buddhism is concerned with universal values; but it tends to state the secularist and materialist values of the Rights of Man so strongly that it is difficult to see anything distinctively Buddhist about it. However, Type 3 Buddhism, which is equally concerned with universal values, re-interprets traditional South Asian Buddhism in such a way that it retains its identity as a genuinely Buddhist soteriology while at the same time embracing the social, democratic and anti-supernaturalist principles of Type 2 Buddhism.

More important than the attempt at describing a typology of Buddhists in Maharashtra, however, is, in our context here, the information, however brief, which Fitzgerald (1994: 27) gives us regarding the actual circumstances in the villages. There, just as before, New Buddhists are discriminated against in accordance with their Mahar origin. Also as before, they themselves continue to behave in accordance with caste practices by avoiding contact with those castes that are traditionally regarded as lower than their own. Moreover, old precepts and prohibitions of commerce and commensalism among them are not revoked simply by publicly declaring their faith in Ambedkar's Buddhism:

In all the villages I visited Buddhists told me they were superior to the Mang; and in one village with an exceptionally high standard of Buddhist morals they told me they made the Mang beg for water from their well. It seems that Buddhists here are reluctant to give Mang water because they still do polluting traditional duties such as clearing and skinning carcasses – duties which Buddhists also used to perform, but which they have refused to do since 1956.

Those who are familiar with the conditions in India will not be surprised that this typical caste orientation in economic and commensal matters corresponds to strict endogamic rules:

In Marathwada, not only will Buddhists not marry into other castes, but they still practise sub-caste endogamy. Most of the Buddhists whom I met in Parbhani district belong to the Somash sub-caste. In three different villages I was told the same ranking order of subcastes. I don't know how reliable these notions of sub-caste ranking are; but there does seem to be a ranking concept. And sub-caste endogamy seems to be universal among rural Buddhists. (Fitzgerald, 1994: 27–8)

The authors of studies based on theories of modernization which follow the idea of an urban-rural continuum (*Stadt-Land-Gefälle*) will always object to such findings. They maintain that the villages simply lag behind since under conditions of widespread illiteracy, the messages of change are not as easily conveyed as they are in cities, especially among the well educated. However, the case studies of Fitzgerald (1994: 28) point in quite a different direction and show (once again!) that, beneath the veneer of modern enlightenment, patterns of behaviour continue to exist which are (still!) characteristic of the Hindu caste system in general—and not just in the villages:

All the eight lecturers I interviewed in Nagpur city told me that they didn't believe in sub-caste marriage restrictions. It was an old tradition and no longer relevant now that they were Buddhist. Six out of eight were married. All married women of Buddhist families; and four out of six married women of the same sub-caste. Five out of six marriages were arranged by the man's father or relative. Only one claimed to have had a so-called 'love marriage', and he refused to tell me his wife's sub-caste. One of the two unmarried men told me that his father would probably arrange for him to marry a woman from the same sub-caste (Lardwan). Three of the six weddings took place in the man's natal village, one in the local block-level town and one in Nagpur.

It seems difficult to avoid the supposition that, even for these highly educated urban-dwelling Buddhists, not only caste endogamy but sub-caste endogamy is still prevalent. It can also be noted that, economically-speaking, these are middle class Buddhists. All eight of the lecturers I interviewed have relatively high incomes; most own a small plot of land in the city to build a house on; most have helped their families buy agricultural land in the natal village; all employ a daily home help. However, though they live in typically middle class nuclear families in the city, they are structurally linked into the joint family household of the husband's village.

With typical British understatement, Fitzgerald summarizes these observations and their meaning for a proper understanding of the New Buddhist forms of living in Maharashtra in this way:

To return to the villages of Marathwada, the following tentative generalisation can be made, if for no other purpose than to provide a hypothesis for further research. The Buddhists here practice sub-caste endogamy; recognise a sub-caste hierarchy; are in 'dispute' with Matangs and other scheduled castes over relative status. Given the evidence of the urban lecturers it may be that this hypothesis has wider validity. (1994: 29)

A dissertation presented by Dipak Kumar Samanta and published in 1991 by the Anthropological Survey of India on the occasion of the centenary celebration of the birth of Dr Ambedkar unfortunately does not go beyond the findings of Fitzgerald. Samanta spent time during 1973 and 1974 in two villages in Maharashtra, each time for five months. Barbadi, district Wardha, lies within the trading area of Nagpur. At that time, 19.4 per cent of the total population (1,312 inhabitants) were New Buddhists (all former members of the Mahar caste). In Tasgaon, district Kolhapur, 25 per cent of the total population (1,170 inhabitants) were Mahars, but none of them had converted to Buddhism. This interesting comparative material is unfortunately not analysed further. The author remains on a purely descriptive plane and at the end comes to a very general conclusion:

The Nava Bouddha of Barbadi have accepted the new faith in their day-to-day life. A Nava Bouddha greets another saying 'Jai Bhim', Bhim being the first name of Ambedkar. During a marriage ceremony the bride and the bridegroom take their oaths before the photographs of Lord Buddha and Ambedkar. They bless the newly married couple with flowers instead of traditional *jowar* (millet) and powdered charcoal instead of vermillion is used for the *tika* mark on the forehead of the guests assembled. (Samanta, 1991: 109)

In contrast to this general assessment, Samanta does include a quite detailed account describing how the New Buddhists of Barbodi oriented themselves on the known model ,of Hinduism. They obviously only exchanged certain movable pieces of the Hindu ritual for Buddhist elements:

In their search for a new identity the Nava Bouddha, instead of finding alternatives fall back upon establishing close parallels to Hinduism. According to Buddhist practice, it is not necessary that a monk should be present at the solemnization of a marriage. There are sacred books prescribing the process and anybody can chant the relevant couplets. In actual practice, however, the engagement of a Buddhist monk (a parallel of a Hindu priest) as a sacred specialist is preferred. Marriage is generally solemnized before the image of Lord Buddha and a photograph of Dr Ambedkar. The couple takes an oath before them. There is also a practice of exchanging garlands as the Hindus do. The couple takes their oath while standing. The man who chants the couplets wishing the marriage success does it in a manner reminiscent of a Hindu marriage. The contents of the couplets are different but the tune is the same. The customary offering of betel leaf and areca nut to the assembled guests is still an important item in the marriage. The Nava Bouddha, instead of putting red ochre on the forehead of the guests, now put charcoal powder. Among the Hindus the guests bless the couple by throwing turmeric-coloured rice. The Nava Bouddha do it with flowers. After taking the oath the couple is taken to the Buddha temple to gain the blessings of the divine power. Marriage is held during the daytime and the marriage season corresponds to that of the Hindus. (Samanta, 1991: 48)

Finally, I reproduce two observations from Samanta concerning Barbadi because they remind us once again of the hard core of precepts and prohibitions governing commensalism in the daily routine of Indian villages. At the same time, they clarify why, given a corresponding influence, New Buddhists retreat from and boycott the institutions of the village's own administration if their claim to equal treatment is not recognized and acceded to:

Prior to the construction of the present panchayat building the panchayat meetings used to be held at the house of the Sarpanch (Chairman of the panchayat). In those days the Sarpanch was usually elected from higher caste Hindu groups. During such meetings the host used to offer a cup of tea to the participants. The Nava Bouddha members had to bring their own cups for the tea. As they felt offended at this discrimination, they all refused to carry a cup for the tea and thereby forfeited the offer. They demanded that the host provide the cup or tumbler. The then Sarpanch had agreed to this, provided the Nava Bouddha washed them after drinking tea. For sometime it carried on like this, till the Nava Bouddha (Mahar) revised their demand and asked for equal treatment in this respect, which the higher caste Hindus found impossible to grant. The issue has remained unsettled since then.

A few of the higher caste Hindu sometimes invite the Nava Bouddha on certain ritual occasions. Glasses and leaf plates are supplied and used plates are lifted by the Mang. The Nava Bouddha also reciprocate. Persons holding public offices like the Sarpanch and members of the panchayat enjoy a different status and have some political obligations. The higher caste Hindus maintain no distance under such circumstances. They accept the betel leaf and areca nut. However, they do not participate in the marriage feast. The Nava Bouddha also do not insist on it. The high caste Hindus do not accept cooked food from the Nava Bouddha, who are not allowed to fetch drinking water from wells belonging to them. The Nava Bouddha and Chambhar labourers are not considered for the job of cleaning and sinking wells located in the hamlets of the higher caste Hindus. (Samanta, 1991: 52 and 53)

Fitzgerald has shown us how New Buddhists behave towards castes that are traditionally considered lower than their own. The above-mentioned examples of public conflicts on the issue of commensalism, regulated by rules inherent in the caste system, have equivalents on an individual level. We find formal behaviour at public occasions among ritual unequals who do usually disregard caste precepts. They can only attempt to find more or less private solutions (Samanta, 1991: 52). (Note: 'lift the plate' means to pick it up and throw it away.)

One Mali boy of this village had a Nava Bouddha classmate. They were very close friends, too. They both hold white collar jobs now. At the time of his marriage the Mali youth wanted to invite his friend. He was aware of the implications of inviting his friend, he was in a dilemma. How he would ask him to lift his used leaf plate, if he himself considered this unjust? On the other hand, he did not have the courage himself to lift the leaf plate [*sic*] used by a Nava Bouddha as this would lead to criticism and social boycott. To compromise between his conscience and the possibility of social conflict he invited his friend separately to a meal, and himself lifted the used leaf plate.

Once again, it must be emphasized that these examples are not intended to supply new information but are meant only to remind us of the well-known realities of Indian society. However, based on reports about the Westernization of India and trusting the declarations of official representatives, these realities are being suppressed again and again—not only by the Indian elites themselves but also by their dialogue partners in the West. Therefore, it is useful to apply well-known patterns of action to the example of the New Buddhists, and this once again brings to our awareness what is still the case in India (Kantowsky, 1995: 25–65 and 110–32). If one is ready to look closely, as Jayashree B. Gokhale did, then it becomes evident that the New Buddhist movement has not reached its goals on the collective level of the actions of society in general (Gokhale, 1986: 272) and that it has not succeeded in escaping Hinduism and its characteristic social discrimination:

In the years since 1956 the expectations entertained for Buddhism on the collective level have not been fulfilled. Although social relationships among Untouchable and lower-caste communities have been altered as a result of the conversion, the direction of these changes has been to vitiate and erode unity: the opposite of what was intended. Buddhist identity has become another distinction that separates Mahar-Buddhists both from other Untouchables and from caste Hindus.

Based on the evaluation of many documents and texts in regional languages, Gokhale concludes that the findings on the level of individual behaviour do not fully correspond to the already well established failure of the New Buddhist movement on a more general social level. Just as

Zelliot (1992: 267–331) found many years before in her work on Dalit literature, Gokhale also found that many New Buddhists were successful in developing a new identity and could express this very effectively through literature:

> On the individual level and in terms of the Mahar-Buddhist community alone, the adoption of Buddhism has been a major success. Testimony by the new converts, in the form of interviews, personal accounts, and essays reveals the emphatic nature of the change in mental habit and self-conception that has occurred as a result of the Buddhist conversion. It has produced a new foundation for individual self-respect and community pride, and it has had a significant effect on the cultural renascence (with the Dalit Sahitya or 'Literature of the Poor and Downtrodden') of the Mahar-Buddhist community in recent years. There has been great cohesion and self-awareness on the part of the new converts and their parent community, but new cleavages among all Untouchables and lower castes have also appeared. (Gokhale, 1986: 273)

Summary

This overview of the sociological literature regarding the patterns of behaviour among the New Buddhists in Maharashtra is on economic, connubial, and commensal matters, the three central areas of daily life in India. The New Buddhists follow a social reformist variant of Theravada Buddhism developed by Dr B.R. Ambedkar.

In the area of economic life one could make the following observations:

1. Almost all New Buddhists, i.e. approximately 90 per cent of all Indian Buddhists, come from the caste of the traditionally Untouchable Mahars.
2. Whenever possible, New Buddhists refuse to do the polluting and ritually discriminatory duties traditionally associated with their caste. This rejection is mostly successful if it is possible to find alternative employment outside the village. Otherwise, one observes that in times of hardship, New Buddhists may be forced to resume the polluting work of the Mahars.
3. New Buddhists avoid contact with castes which have taken over their polluting work or which continue to hold on to the performance of work traditionally considered polluting.
4. Even if New Buddhists are successful in joining ritually more or less neutral professions, they are looked down upon as former Mahars and are discriminated against.

In the area of commensal behaviour one could make the following observations:

5. New Buddhists change their eating and drinking habits. Meat, especially that of cows that have died and which was their former prerogative, is no longer eaten. They publicly renounce alcohol and other intoxicating drinks, following Buddhist prescriptions of virtuous conduct.
6. New Buddhists avoid commensality with castes regarded as impure; in one case they refused to grant members of an impure caste access to a well.
7. New Buddhists do not publicly participate in the Hindu holiday calendar but celebrate among themselves four holidays that are inspired by Buddhism. They commemorate the Buddha's birth, Ambedkar's birth and death, and the large mass conversion which took place in Nagpur in 1956.
8. Though they attempt, following the New Buddhist vows, to strip the holidays of Hindu ritual significance, it nevertheless seems that through the deification of the Buddha and Ambedkar they have revived and continue to practice a naïve popular piety and devotionalism.
9. In spite of all efforts to Sanskritize their behaviour, New Buddhists are not accepted as equals in matters concerning food and drink. They continue to face discrimination in the matter of seating arrangements, eating and drinking utensils, as well as kinds of food.
10. In the context of public life in modern times, as at formally egalitarian village assemblies, New Buddhists can occasionally reinforce their ritual equality; however, on other occasions there is usually discrimination which accentuates once again the supposed impure origin of the Mahar Buddhists.

In the area of connubial behaviour one could make the following observations:

11. The connubial connections of New Buddhists are arranged by the parents, follow classic rules of endogamy, and are patrilocally oriented.
12. Even among university lecturers who were articulate and active in matters of social reform, inter-caste marriages were not observed, and the marriages were arranged by the parents according to the rules of endogamy. The households of such modern urban nuclear families were, through a large number of duties, patrilocally connected with the village of origin of the bridegroom's parents, who were financially supported by their son.

13. Marriage ceremonies do not take place in the house of the bride's parents but in a *vihara*, the place of worship and for social gatherings of New Buddhist communities. They are comparatively short and simple. Only vegetarian dishes, without alcohol, are served, and people try to keep the expenses within manageable limits. In this way, they try to escape the lifelong debts incurred by the bride's parents which are customary among Hindus and which result from the expenses of dowry and the cost of feeding and entertaining of hundreds of guests for several days.
14. If a *bhikkhu* resides nearby, he will perform the simple ritual of marriage. However, in the majority of the reported cases, trustworthy laymen led the ceremony and recited the marriage formulas in Pali.
15. Overall, one could observe that full-time *bhikkhus* were of lesser importance for the New Buddhist communities than lay leadership. According to the understanding of Buddhism as taught by Ambedkar, their function can generally be taken over by enlightened members of the community. Moreover, it seems that most New Buddhist communities are not in a position to provide permanently for religious specialists.

A special form of New Buddhism in India in the shape of the TBMSG was sponsored by foreign financial and educational aid. Their work focused at first mainly in and around Pune. The Western initiators maintain that the measures of social work initiated there and supported by meditation training will one day have a multiplying effect beyond the narrow circle of those who have been directly affected. To what degree this hope will come true remains to be seen. The obvious success of the TBMSG and the well-aimed public relations work of the FWBO for the activities of the subsidiary organization should not distract us from the overall findings.

Considering their founder's goals of social reform, the New Buddhist movement has had only limited success. The Buddhists neither succeeded in escaping from the discrimination of Hinduism nor in renouncing discrimination towards the other lower castes. Though their 'new birth' as Buddhists resulted in the rejection of traditional polluting occupational roles, they did not at the same time arrive at commensal and connubial practices that transcended the social barriers between the different castes. Thus, it seems that New Buddhism today has become the name of a new, although still ritually underprivileged caste which is not defined by the occupation of its members. The fact that New Buddhists succeeded in being included in the List of the Scheduled Castes in order to regain the advantages of protective discrimination confirms this interpretation.[5]

New Buddhist authors project the idea in their writings that this development, which concerns the entire society, can, on the individual level of interpretation, be compensated by a new feeling of self-worth and by corresponding emancipated strategies of action. However, it cannot

[5] Those Scheduled Castes who converted to Buddhism in 1956 lost the advantages of protective discrimination as Untouchables. However, in the early 1960s in Maharashtra, protective discrimination was reintroduced—at least in the area of education. Since 1971 and by order of the central government, protective discrimination is again valid for New Buddhists all over India:

'3. The Government have carefully considered the matter and are of the view that the Scheduled Castes converts to Buddhism still suffer from social and educational backwardness and are in need of assistances.

4. It has accordingly been decided that any person who professes the Buddhist religion and who either himself or any of whose ancestor were at any time member of a caste specified in the Schedule to the Constitution (Scheduled Castes Orders) in relation to the State/Union Territory in which he resides will be eligible for the grant of Government of India Post-Matric Scholarship.

Provided that the Income of the student's parents or guardians does not exceed Rs. 500/- per month.'

From: No. 14/1/169-SCT (1), Government of India, Ministry of Education and Social Welfare, New Delhi, 30.10.1971.

Through 'The Constitution (Scheduled Castes) Orders (Amendment) Act, 1990', Buddhists can—just like the Sikhs before them—be recognized as Scheduled Castes and, given the proof of corresponding requirements, they are entitled to claim special privileges for their education and for government service. Cf. *The Gazette of India*, Extraordinary, Part II, Section 1, New Delhi, 4.6.1990, p. 2:

'3. In paragraph 3 of the Constitution (Scheduled Castes) (Union Territories) Order, 1951, for the words "or the Sikh", the words "the Sikh or the Buddhists" shall be substituted.'

The passage referred to reads:

'No person who professes a religion different from the Hindu or the Sikh religion shall be deemed to be a member of a Scheduled Caste.'

In the new version it thus now reads:

'No person who professes a religion different from the Hindu or the Sikh or the Buddhist religion shall be deemed to be a member of a Scheduled Caste.'

Regarding the range of problems presented by such a re-integration (which had the consequence that even New Christians demand the same provision or classification) see the essay of Dieter Conrad (1995: 314ff.).

be ascertained whether or not this is true. Though such written autobiographical statements of intellectuals are easily or at least more easily accessible to us, we should be careful about consulting them as a source for the study of the actual patterns of communication in the villages of Maharashtra and elsewhere!

Appendix
Ambedkar's 1936 Conversion Speech*

Religion is for man; man is not for religion.
*If you want to gain self-respect** change your religion.*
If you want to create a cooperating society, change your religion.
If you want power, change your religion.
If you want equality, change your religion.
If you want independence, change your religion.
If you want to make the world in which you live happy, change your religion.
*Why should you remain in a religion that does not value your manhood?***
Why should you remain in a religion that does not let you enter its temples?
Why should you remain in a religion that does not give you water to drink?
Why should you remain in a religion that does not let you become educated?
Why should you remain in a religion that bars you from good jobs?
Why should you remain in a religion that dishonours you at every step?
*That religion which forbids humanitarian behaviour***
between man and man is not religion
but a reckless penalty.
*That religion which regards the recognition of man's self-respect***
as sin is not a religion
but a sickness.
That religion which allows one to touch a foul animal
but not a man
is not a religion
but a madness.
That religion which says that one class may not gain knowledge,
may not acquire wealth,
may not take up arms,
is not a religion
but a mockery of man's life.

---

* Final sequence of a speech by Ambedkar in 1936: 'Mukti kon Pathe?' (What Path Freedom?), Bombay: Bharat Bhushan Printing Press, 1936, as translated by Eleanor Zelliot (1978: 102–3).

** The Marathi word *manuski*, a key word in the Mahar movement literature, is used four times in this segment of Ambedkar's address. It may be variously translated as humanitarian attitude, self-respect, manhood, and humanity. Its literal meaning is 'of man'.

The excerpt is the end of the speech, arranged as free verse to stress its rhythmic qualities.

That religion which teaches that the unlearned should remain unlearned, that
the poor should remain poor,
is not a religion
but a punishment.
Do not say: men who treat animals with more respect that humans
and who respect all Brahmans as Gods
are religious.
Do not say: men who feed ants with sugar
and let men go without water
are religious
Do not say: men who embrace another religion
and push their own far from them
hate society.

Supplement

The new publications which were consulted after the completion of the report on literature do not disprove the conlusions of my analysis:

Timothy Fitzgerald has looked at his data, as I have already reported, with a slightly different theoretical question in mind, and he once again emphasizes (1997: 240–1) that Buddhists in rural areas behave according to caste considerations, and discriminate against people who are, according to their judgement, *impure*:

> The Buddhists in the villages of this region are not only placed by others into a system of hierarchical relations; they implicitly endorse such a system by ranking themselves as superior to other scheduled castes such as Mangs, Dhors and Holars. I have evidence in a neighbouring taluka (Kalumnori) of Buddhists forcing Mangs to beg for water from a Buddhist well. Buddhists told me they were reluctant to give Mangs water because they still performed polluting occupations such as skinning dead animals.

Similar are also the findings of Ramesh H. Kamble, who interviewed ten New Buddhists from a rather traditional background who had no great hopes of achieving upward social mobility, and ten from a more modern background, who did rise socially. His interviews substantiate the theme (Kamble, 1996: 89) that the turning to Buddhism for most people today is determined first of all by the need to leave Hinduism and not so much by their belief in Buddhist practice and teachings:

We have seen that the emphatic assertion of all Buddhists studied was that by being Buddhist they meant they were not Hindus. However, the cultural identity of one segment of common Buddhists exhibits that despite being Buddhist, their cultural-religious life is also characterised by adherences to superstitious beliefs and practices. And in case of the other segment of common Buddhists, we witnessed a mere ritualistic embracing of Buddhism.

According to their own conception of themselves, New Buddhists found a new identity outside of Hinduism. However, the Hindu majority does not accept this new awareness and still treats the *Nav Bouddhas* (already this term indicates devaluation) still as Mahars, openly or more discretly, depending on the social situation:

> From the case studies I have made it may be concluded that all Nav-Bouddhas observed assert that they are not Hindus, and that as Buddhists they have arrived at a self-identity of their own. However, despite their rejection of Hinduism, and separate existence as Buddhist, the caste-Hindus continue to treat them as Mahars. For, in the minds of caste-Hindus, Buddhist has become a synonym for Mahar. In case of the common Nav-Bouddhas this equation is explicit, whereas, in case of conscious educated Nav-Bouddhas it assumes an implicit form. (Kamble, 1995: 30)

More important than the generalizations of Kamble, which are based on only 20 interviews, are the results of Uttara Shashtree. She interviewed 212 'Lower Class Neo-Buddhists' and 20 'Educated, Well-placed Neo-Buddhists' in different residential areas of Pune and summarizes her findings as follows:

> There is a large gap between the ideal and the real for the Neo-Buddhists. They themselves have realized this gap. By embracing Buddhism the neo-Buddhists sought and claimed higher status, but as yet they did not feel that they have reached their goal.
>
> In fact, after India's Constitutional declaration of egalitarian ideology, no caste considers itself inferior to any other castes (though the feeling of superiority to some others continues). But in the case of new-Buddhists the situation became complicated as the conversion to Buddhism intensified the aspirations for status of this up-started group to a maximum level. Their frustration is more because the conversion brought about a change in their conception of themselves, and in reality they found that in the eyes of the outer world their conversion meant only a change of label, from Mahar to 'Nav-Boudha', or to 'Mahar-Boudha'. (1996: 144)

According to my own assessment, the descriptions offered by Neera Burra of living conditions of New Buddhists in rural Maharashtra are the most differentiated ones. The following example from her work shows (Burra, 1996: 164–5) how multi-layered the overlapping of New Buddhist and Hindu practices on the concrete level of action is:

Birth, marriage and death are three important occasions that I studied. With respect to birth, ceremonies are not frequently performed except when there is a son born after many daughters or when there is a birth after a long childless marriage. Out of the 10 births between 1980 and 1983, there were ceremonies only on two occasions. On both occasions, the ceremonies performed were according to Hindu rites and, importantly, the pictures of Ambedkar and the Buddha were removed at the time of birth. The explanation given to me was that Ambedkar, a man of learning to whom respect was due, should not be present at the time of the pollution which accompanies birth. Out of 102 Mahars interviewed about birth ceremonies, the answers were as follows: 25 persons said they performed Buddhist ceremonies; 67 said they performed Hindu ceremonies, six people said that there was no Buddhist equivalent to a Hindu rite and four were not sure.

It seems to me that the final suggestion of Burra (168–9) is especially important: we misunderstand the New Buddhist movement if we see it mainly as an aspect of religious conversion, whereas most of all it has been an attempt to overcome social discrimination:

My experience of rural Mahars suggests that it would be perhaps misleading to define the neo-Buddhist movement primarily as a conversion movement. It goes beyond the arena of religion and assumes enormous political dimensions. Religious conversion today, more than before, is a symbol of identity formation. As a self-respect movement for a new identity, it has certainly achieved its goal and the Mahars, under Ambedkar's guidance, are no longer prepared to accept their position in society and are willing to fight tooth and nail for what Ambedkar called *manuskichya haka* or the right to humanity. One might say that the neo-Buddhist movement has had its greatest impact on confronting, challenging, and to some extent, changing the received belief in the mind of the Mahar that he is a lesser mortal than those of the higher castes. It would seem that, after Ambedkar, the ideology of inequality cannot any longer have the same grip on the Mahar as it had hitherto.

To sum up, one would argue that while the spiritual aspects of Buddhism and its rites and rituals have not been integrated into the daily lives of rural Mahars, the secular values Ambedkar sought to propagate through the medium of Buddhism have had a significant effect upon the lives of the villagers of Ambegaon.

In view of these new findings of field research, it becomes difficult to follow the optimism of Diwan Chand Ahir who suggests at the end of the commemorative volume (1998a: 201), which was put together on the occasion of the fiftieth anniversary of India's Independence:

Buddhism in India is yet shorn of its ancient grandeur and glory, and is still to be animated with the ever-fresh vitality of a living religion. However, as more and more Indians are seeking refuge in Buddhism in order to enjoy the bliss of Nirvana, to do away with social distinctions, and to caste aside irrational beliefs and customs, the future of Buddhism in India seems bright; and the hopes are that the Buddha-Dhamma will henceforth shine for ever like a Beacon Light in the land of its birth.

Based on observations made over several years, however, I have arrived at the understanding that such general statements are not possible. Buddhists in India today can be appropriately understood only as a diverse multitude of groups, each with its own peculiar characteristics. The New Buddhists were described in the report on the literature above; the larger Buddhist milieu will now be described, illustrated by texts, pictures, and documents.

Here, again, I will not enter into a detailed discussion of the Barua Buddhists who were mentioned in the first footnote of this chapter. Instead, I point to the descriptions given by the Bauddha Dharmankur Sabha (1992) itself in the first part of the book entitled *Hundred Years*, published on the occasion of their centennary celebrations. I also point to an essay by Hemendu B. Chowdhury (1990) on Kripasaran Mahathera (1865–1926), the founder of this society who came from Chittagong, now in Bangladesh. The history of the emergence and development of the Bengal Buddhist Association is quite important for the proper understanding of the Barua and the Chakma Buddhists as supposedly being the direct descendants of the contemporaries of the Buddha. However, far more essential for the international rediscovery of Buddhism in India, in general, is the Maha Bodhi Society, which was founded at the same time (1891) in Ceylon.

CHAPTER TWO

The Maha Bodhi Society

DON DAVID HEWAVITARNE was born on 17 September 1864 in Colombo, Ceylon, as the first child of the furniture manufacturer Don Carolis Hewavitarne and his wife Mallika. The parents were practising Buddhists but, following the custom among the Singhalese bourgeoisie at the time, their son attended the Anglican missionary school in Colombo. After he completed his schooling, he joined the British colonial administration. He was influenced by the Buddhist renewal movement in the country (Bechert 1988: 47ff.) and by close contacts with Colonel Henry Olcott, the well-known theosophist. In 1886, he decided to dedicate the rest of his life to the revival of Buddhism. With the consent of his parents, he quit his post and from then on called himself Anagarika (one who has no home) Dharmapala (protector of the *dharma*). In 1891, shaken by the reports of Sir Edwin Arnold in English newspapers (Ahir, 1994: 95ff.), he travelled to north India to see for himself the wretched state of the sites of early Buddhism. Coming from Sarnath in the company of the Japanese Shingon monk Kozen Gunaratne, whom he had met at a conference of the Theosophical Society, he arrived by train in Gaya on 21 January 1891. He noted in his diary:

> After driving 6 miles (from Gaya) we arrived at the holy spot. Within a mile you could see lying scattered here and there broken statues etc. of our blessed Lord. At the entrance to the Mahant's temple on both sides of the portico there are statues of our Lord in the attitude of meditation and expounding the Law. How elevating! The sacred Vihara—the Lord sitting on his throne and the great solemnity which pervades all round makes the heart of a pious devotee weep. How delightful! As soon as I touched with my forehead the Vajrasana a sudden impulse came to my mind. It prompted me to stop here and take care of this sacred spot—so sacred that nothing in the world is equal to this place where Prince Sakya Sinha gained Enlightenment under the Bodhi Tree. . . . When the sudden impulse came to me I asked Kozen priest whether he would join me, and he joyously assented and more than this he had been thinking the same thing. We both solemnly promised that we would stop here until some Buddhist priests came to take charge of the place. (Ahir, 1994: 107)

IMPORTANT EVENTS OF THE MAHA BODHI SOCIETY OF INDIA

17.09.1864	Anagarika Dharmapala was born in Sri Lanka (Ceylon)
21.08.1884	His first visit to India
22.01.1891	He visited Buddha Gaya for the first time and vowed to restore the great temple
31.05.1891	Founded the Buddha Gaya Maha Bodhi Society
01.05.1892	Founded the Maha Bodhi Journal
11.09.1892	Maha Bodhi Society started its office in Calcutta
18.09.1893	The Anagarika delivered address at the "Parliament of World Religions in Chicago"
06.02.1895	Instituted case to restore the Buddha Gaya Maha Bodhi Temple
06.07.1908	The Society Headquarters opened at Beniapukur Lane, Calcutta
03.04.1915	Maha Bodhi Society became a registered body
26.11.1920	Sri Dharmarajika Vihara, Calcutta was ceremonially opened
13.07.1931	The Anagarika entered ordination at Sarnath and named Siri Devamitta Dharmapala
11.11.1931	Opening ceremony of Mulagandha Kuti Vihara in Sarnath
16.01.1933	Ven'ble Siri Devamitta Dharmapala received higher ordination
29.04.1933	Ven'ble Devamitta Dharmapala passed away in Sarnath
17.09.1991	The Society celebrated its Centenary.

The Great Buddhist Revivalist
ANAGARIKA DHARMAPALA
Founder - Maha Bodhi Society (1891)

1998

Maha Bodhi Society, title page of a calendar for the year 1998.

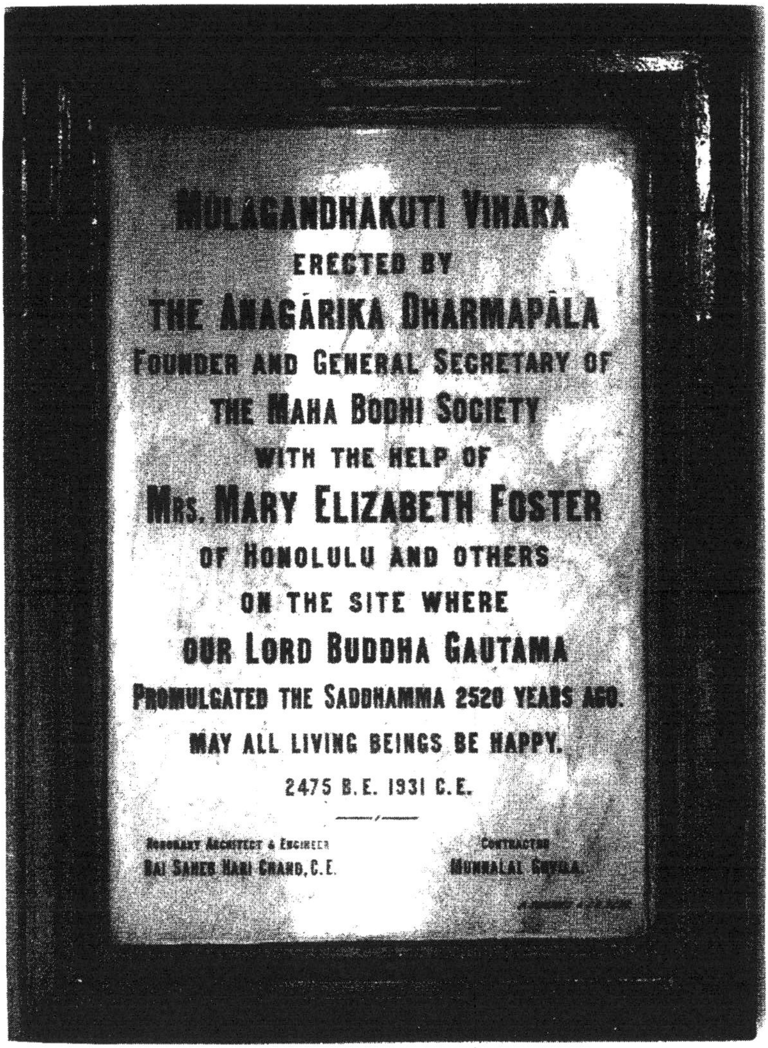

Commemorative plaque at the main entrance to the Mulagandhakuti Vihara in Sarnath.

With this began the history of the 'Buddhification' (Doyle 1997: 16) of Bodh Gaya and the efforts, still going on, to expand the 'place of enlightenment' into a 'Jerusalem for all Buddhists' (Trevithick, 1988) and to give the main temple, which centuries ago had been occupied by the Hindus, over to solely Buddhist responsibility. This history has been traced in the dissertations of Doyle and Trevithick and the process of the socio-religious construction of new realities meticulously documented. Details from this interest us here only inasmuch as they seem important for an understanding of the actual situation.

On 31 May 1891, the Buddha Gaya Maha Bodhi Society was founded in Colombo with Anagarika Dharmapala as General Secretary. It was the goal of the society to regain the Maha Bodhi Temple as soon as possible and to reintroduce Buddhism to India. In 1892, the headquarter of the society was relocated to Calcutta, which at that time was the capital of British India. In the same year, the *Maha Bodhi Journal* was established, an important English voice for the worldwide dissemination of the goals of the society. Anagarika Dharmapala conveyed his goals to the Parliament of World Religions in Chicago in 1893 so effectively that henceforth he could count on international support. The continuous sponsorship through Mrs Mary Foster (1844–1930) of Honolulu, whom he met on board the *Oceanic* on his journey from the USA to Japan, was almost literally a life-saver for him:

> The Parliament of Religions ended on 27 September, 1893. After delivering a few more lectures in America, Dharmapala sailed for India via Japan and China. A chance meeting with Mrs. Mary Elizabeth Mikhala Foster on Board the S.S. Oceanic at Honolulu on 18 October 1893 proved of immense significance both for Mrs. Foster as well as for Dharmapala. Mrs. Foster was born in the far off Hawaii islands in the Pacific Ocean and was a descendent on her mother's side of King Kamehameha the Great of Hawaii. She was married to a wealthy merchant of North America. It is said that she was of an indomitable temper which she was unable to control. As a remedy for this ailment, Dharmapala advised her to cultivate will-power, and to repeat the formula 'I will be good, I will control the rising anger.' These simple words of a practising Buddhist worked wonders. Mrs. Foster was able to get over her temper and gained serenity. She was so deeply impressed by this change that she decided to divert her enormous wealth for the spread of the gospel of the Buddha for which Dharmapala was trying hard. (Ahir, 1989: 17)

In spite of all efforts and international support throughout his life, Anagarika Dharmapala did not succeed in regaining the main temple in Bodh Gaya for the Buddhists. He lost a legal case against the *mahant*

Statue near the Mulagandhakuti Vihara. Inscription: Anagarika Dharmapala, Founder of the Maha Bodhi Society and Pioneer of Buddhist Revival in India. Born in Colombo, Ceylon, 17 September 1864. Died at Sarnath, 19 April 1933.

(abbot) of the Hindu monastery in Bodh Gaya, to whom the main temple, according to common law, had belonged since the end of the sixteenth century.

Anagarika Dharmapala's activities in Sarnath, however, were more successful. With the main support of Mary Foster, a grand Buddhist temple came into existence on the historic grounds of the Deer Park where the Buddha for the first time had passed on his liberating experiences to his first disciples. Construction work for the Mulagandhakuti Vihara began in 1922 and was completed by 1931:

> The foundation stone of Mulagandhakuti Vihara, the life of new Sarnath, was laid in November 1922 by Sir Harcourt Butler, the Governor of the United Provinces. The name 'Mulagandhakuti' has a historic basis. This name was first used for the monastery in which Lord Buddha actually resided. During the archaeological excavations at Sarnath a piece of tablet was found on which this name was inscribed. This discovery prompted Anagarika Dharmapala to name the new Vihara as 'Mulagandhakuti Vihara'. The Mulagandhakuti Vihara cost about Rs. 1,20,000 and the principal donor was Mrs. Mary E. Foster of Honolulu, who is generally called the modern Visakha of the Buddhists.
>
> This magnificent Vihara was opened on November 11, 1931 (Kartik Purnima). On the same day, the sacred relics of Lord Buddha, which were discovered from Taxila, Punjab, in 1913–14 by Sir John Marshall, were presented by the Director General of Archaeology to the Maha Bodhi Society on behalf of the Government of India, and enshrined in this Vihara. (Ahir, 1991: 130)

In the same year, Anagarika Dharmapala joined the *sangha* of monks as the novice Devamitta (friend of the gods) Dharmapala, and it was also here that he was ordained to full monkhood in January 1933. He died three years later, and his body, which was partly paralysed in his last years, was cremated on the temple grounds. Every year, on the full moon in November, the establishment and consecration of the Mulagandhakuti Vihara is commemorated with a celebration (see the activity report).

The letter dated 1925, reproduced as Appendix 2.1, indicates Anagarika Dharmapala's agitational style. A voluminous omnibus volume of his speeches, essays, and letters (Guruge, 1965), published in Sri Lanka, shows that he almost always made similarly polemical remarks about people of other faiths. However, the 'protector of *dharma*' would certainly not have been so effective if he had always and only made polemical remarks. On his journey through Europe, to which he referred in the letter, Anagarika Dharmapala also visited the Buddhist House in Berlin-Frohnau, Germany, which was founded by Paul Dahlke in 1924. His 'kind personality' left a lasting impression there:

MAHABODHI SOCIETY OF INDIA, SARNATH.

ACTIVITES OF THE CENTRE.

From 1st October,97 to 31st January,98.

(1). 66th Anniversary of the Mulagandha Kuti Vihara Celebrated.

The 66th anniversary of the Mulagandha Kuti Vihara was celebrated on the Kattik Fool Moon day- the 14th November,1997. The Programme of the day started with Dhamma Desana in the morning. The Holy Relics Darshan was held in the Vihara in the fore-noon and Sanghadana was given at noon which was participated by hundreds of Ven'ble monks from various Buddhist countries of the world. The Holy Relics - Procession was conducted in the after noon. Besides thousands of Buddhists from different parts of India, Buddhists from different Buddhist countires of the world participated in this procession. In the evening, a Public meeting was held in the campus of the Mulagandha Kuti Vihara to commemorate this historic occasion. Mr. Kalyan Singh, the Hon'ble Chief Minister of Uttar Pradesh, participated as the Chief Guest in this meeting while Mr. K.B.Ratnayake, the Hon'ble Speaker of Sri Lanka participated as the Chief Speaker in this meeting . Mr. Mangala Moonesinghe, High Commissioner for Sri Lanka in India was the Guest of Honour at the meeting. Among the distinguished persons,who participated in this meeting,were Ven'ble Lama Lobzang, member, National Commission for Scheduled Casts and Sceduled Tribes, Government of India, His Excellency Prof. Prabhakar Jha, Ambassador for India in Medagascar, Hon'ble Prof. Om Prakash Singh, Minister of Irrigation and Sugarcane, Government of Uttar Pradesh, Hon'ble Mr. Virendra Singh, Minister of State for Agriculture, Government of Uttar Pradesh, Hon'ble Smt. Saroj, Singh, Mayor of Varanasi. Ven'ble D.Wimala Thero, Bhikkhu-in-charge, Sarnath Centre, welcomed the guests on this occasion and presented the annual report of this centre. The meeting was conducted by Dr. Beni-Madho, Principal, Mahabodhi Inter College, Sarnath as well as Mr. Upali Rupasinghe, Publicity Officer at the Head Quarters of the the Mahabodhi Society of India. The meeting terminated with the blessings by the Bhikkhu Mahasangha.

(2). 49th REPUBLIC DAY OF INDIA CELEBRATED:

The 49th Republic Day of India, coinciding with the Golden Jubilee year of India's Independence, was celebrated under the auspices of the Mahabodhi Society of India, Sarnath. Besides the students

2......

Page 1 of the activity report of the Sarnath Centre of the Maha Bodhi Society, October 1997–January 1998.

> More pleasant and harmonious was a meeting with another important personality who visited the house a few years later: the Venerable Anagarika-Dharmapala. He was with us for eight or ten days, and when in the evenings we sat together in the library, he radiated so much cheerfulness and so much humor that often otherwise serious conversations were interrupted by his or our cheerful laughter. During the day when Dr Dahlke had his consulting hours, he often used to sit in the temple or in the open lobby and recite in a low voice verses in Pali. His tall impressive stature in the yellow robe and his kind personality cannot be easily forgotten. (Fischer, 1974)

It is noteworthy that, in spite of the polemical harshness of Anagarika Dharmapala's letter, it was the only document from his pen that was included in a commemorative volume on the occasion of the centenary of the founding of the Maha Bodhi Society in Bodh Gaya!

Two pages from this volume that appear in Appendix 2.1 characterizes the official objectives of the Maha Bodhi Society. Other material in the Centenary Volume of the *Maha Bodhi* (1992) (also see Appendix 2.1, pp. 75–8), the society's magazine established in 1892 by Anagarika Dharmapala, gives more detail. Perusing this material from the society and examining the following lists of office-bearers, activities, and centres (pp. 67, 77–9) and adding my own field observations, I can give the following picture of the influence of the Maha Bodhi Society on the development and spread of Buddhism, especially on the Buddhists in contemporary India:

- At present, the Maha Bodhi Society has eight centres in north India and collaborates with other groups in affiliated centres in five other places, including two in south India.
- The head office in Kolkata controls the work. The monies for extra-ordinary measures beyond the fixed expenses come from donations, recently mainly from Japan.
- The Maha Bodhi Society sees itself mainly as a missionary society for the dissemination of Theravada teachings. Accordingly, it still recruits its full-time representatives from the Singhalese clergy of Sri Lanka (Ahir, 1998: 59–76), where such missionary work stands in high esteem. The frequent rotation of missionaries, however, results in their speaking Indian languages only inadequately.
- The *bhikkhus* of the Maha Bodhi Society are bound to one place all year round. They act as representatives of the *sangha*, each in his particular *vihara*. Over and above this, they serve mainly in the areas of education and health.

Activities of the Maha Bodhi Society of India

SARNATH CENTRE

- **Maha Bodhi Mulagandha Kuti Vihara –** Development, Maintenance, Pooja and Daily Dhammachakka Sajjhayana.
- **Maha Bodhi Mulagandha Kuti Vihara Library and Reading room –** Free service to readers and students with a vast collection of books.
- **Mahabodhi Book Agency –** Publication and distribution of Books on Buddhism, philosophy with world-wide agencies.
- **Maha Bodhi Inter College –** A complete institution with building and other modern facilities for general higher éducation with government assistance.
- **Dhammapala Bhikkhu and Bhikkhuni Training Centre –** A Centre for teaching Buddhist Philosophy and Sangha Vinaya with preliminary training of Buddhist missionary works.
- **Maha Bodhi Primary School –** A complete body with trained staff to Educate children.
- **Maha Bodhi Girls Junior High School –** An institution for girls education with trained staff which provides service to the girls of the area.
- **Maha Bodhi Birla Dharmashala –** A notable service by the society for pilgrims fully maintained by donations.
- **Maha Bodhi Sangharama --** A hostel for resident monks with free food and other facilities.
- **Dhammapala Museum –** A specially designed place where Anagarika Dhammapala's personal belongings including robes, wheel-chair, arm-chair, walking-sticks, begging bowl, books, personal notes and other important documents are exhibited.
- **Maha Bodhi Hospital (Under Construction) –** This twenty beds hospital is being constructed specially for rendering medical service to the poor patients in this area. The construciton cost is estimated rupees thirty Lakhs in Indian Currency and one hundred thousand U.S. Dollors. The donors and well-wishers are requested to donate generously towards this noble cause and earn the merit.

THE SARNATH CENTRE OF THE MAHA BODHI SOCIETY OF INDIA INVITES YOU FOR YOUR KIND CONTRIBUTION FOR MAINTENANCE OF THE ABOVE INSTITUTIONS

Kindly send your contribution to :

D. Wimala Thero
Secretery and High Priest
Maha Bodhi Society of India
Sarnath, Varanasi (U.P.) India

Description of the Sarnath Centre of the Maha Bodhi Society.

- The hostels of the Maha Bodhi Society in Bodh Gaya and Sarnath are important for the well-being of the many pilgrims from Sri Lanka.
- The journal *Maha Bodhi* (see *A Panorama of Indian Buddhism* under Ahir, 1995a) continues to be important for the international mediation of the activities of the society and the appropriate reflection of the teachings of the Pali canon for English speakers.
- The Singhalese representatives of the Maha Bodhi Society, however, have quite a distant relationship to the New Buddhist movement because they do not accept the new interpretation of the *dhamma* of Dr Ambedkar (1957, 1992) (also see Jatava, 1997: 67-85). On the other hand, the New Buddhist movement does not accept the Maha Bodhi Society because it maintains that the Society represents Bengali high-caste interests (see the lists of members in Appendix 2.1).
- The presence and influence of the Maha Bodhi Society is obvious in the comparatively accessible world of Sarnath. The Mulagandhakuti Vihara with its beautiful frescoes depicting the Buddha's life (donated by B.L. Brownton, an English Buddhist, and painted over a three year period by the Japanese Kosetsu Nosu), as well as the surrounding well-kept park with the remains of the ruins of the monastery and stupas dating back to the classical Golden Age of Buddhism, form a silent retreat that people like to visit. Especially on weekends they also offer to people from all walks of Indian life a welcome change from the noisy narrowness of their living quarters in Benaras. The small administration building of the Maha Bodhi Society has recently been thoroughly renovated, thanks to the donation of a wealthy Japanese woman. With its new roof shaped like a pagoda, a gift from the Indian industrialist G.D. Birla to the society, it now offers an exotic contrast to the neo-classical austerity of the large hostels for pilgrims on the opposite side of the street.
- However, the conditions in Bodh Gaya, the base of the movement for the revival of Buddhism in the land of its origin initiated more than a hundred years ago by Anagarika Dharmapala, are quite different. Here, the formerly single complex of buildings of the Maha Bodhi Society has become overshadowed by booming construction funded by international sources and an uncontrolled growth of bazaars and merchants' shops.

Appendix 2.1

APPENDIX I

Anagarika Dharmapala's Letter to Francis J. Payne, London dated 3.4.1925

NAMO BUDDHAYA

VEN : ANAGARIKA DHARMAPALA
DIRECTOR GENERAL
BUDDHIST MISSION OF INDIA

4/A College Square
Calcutta

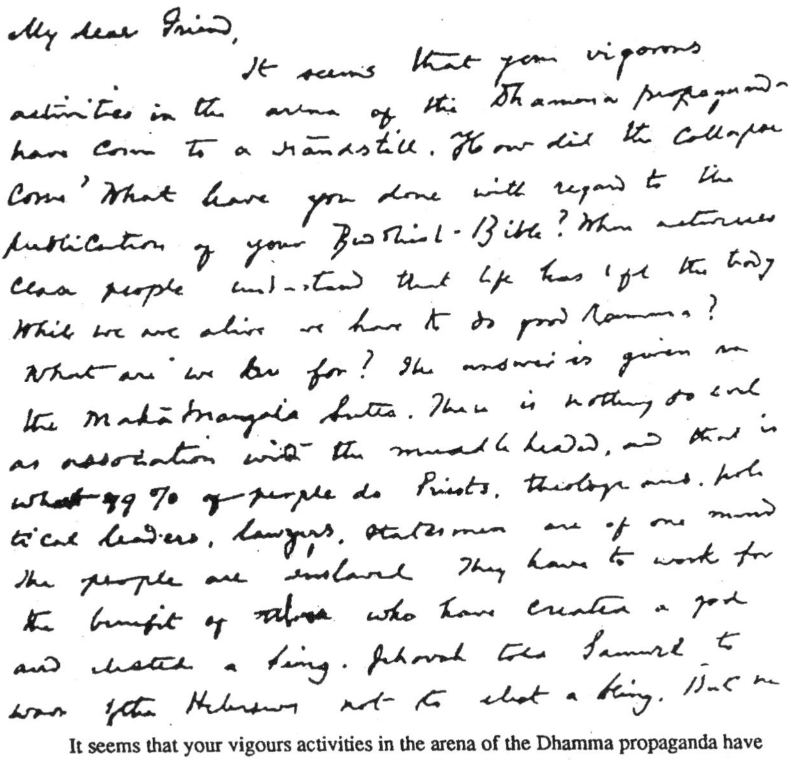
My dear Friend,
It seems that your vigorous activities in the arena of the Dhamma propaganda have come to a standstill. How did the collapse come? What have you done with regard to the publication of your Buddhist-Bible? When activities cease people understand that life has left the body. While we are alive we have to do good Kammas? What are we here for? The answer is given in the Maha Mangala Sutta. There is nothing so evil as association with the muddle headed, and that is what 99 % of people do. Priests, theologians, political leaders, lawyers, statesmen are of one mind. The people are enslaved. They have to work for the benefit of those who have created a god and elected a king. Jehovah told Samuel to warn the Hebrews not to elect a king. But the

It seems that your vigours activities in the arena of the Dhamma propaganda have come to a standstill. How did the collapse come." What have you done with regard to the publication of your Buddhist Bible ? When activities cease people understand that life has left the body. While we are alive we have to do good Kamma ? What are we here for ? The answer is given in the Maha Mangala Sutta. There is nothing so evil as association with the muddle headed, and that is what 99 percent. of people do. Priests, theologians, political leaders, lawyers, statesmen are of one mind. The people are enslaveds. They have to work for the benefit of

Facsimile of a letter cum transcription by Anagarika Dharmapala dated 3 April 1925.

failed to convince the idiots, and gave the tallest of the lot, a donkey-driver, to be made king. The conflict arose between Jehovah and the people's sovereign. Both parties went down when Nebuchadnezzar captured Jerusalem. Jehovah went into a state of suspended animation. The Hebrews went into captivity.

The Dhamma of the Tathagato is little understood in the West. No two scholars agree with the ultimates of the Dhamma. The first requisite necessary to understand the Dhamma is Wisdom (Panna). To have panna one should be armed with the adjuncts of the first two principles of the Noble Eightfold Path. The British people are imbued with the spirit of sensualism, which is a hindrance to enter the Path. Absolute renunciation is too philosophic a requisite to be undertaken by the muddle headed who wish to be governed by the priest and the aristocrat. failing both the wife

Forty years of ceaseless activity has made me

those who have created a god and elected a king. Jehovah told Samuel to warn the Hebrews not to elect a king. But he failed to convince the idiots and gave the tallest of the lot, a donkey—driver, to be made king. The conflict arose between Jehovah and the people's sovereign. Both parties went down when Nebuchad—nezzar captured Jerusalem. Jehovah went into a state of suspended animation. The Hebrews went into captivity.

The Dhamma of the Tathagato is little understood in the West. No two scholars agree with the ultimates of the Dhamma. The first requisite necessary to understand the Dhamma is Wisdom (Panna). To have panna one should be armed with the adjuncts of the first two principles of the Noble Eightfold Path. The British, people are imbued with the spirit of sensualism, which is a hindrance to enter the Path. Absolute renunciation is too philosophic a requisite to be undertaken by the muddle headed who wish to be governed by the priest and the aristocrat, failing both the wife.

Forty years of ceaseless activity has made me

physically weak For 34 years I have spent my life in India in voluntary exile the name of the Lord Buddha was hardly ~~then~~ known 34 years ago by the people of India. Today all India acknowledges Him as their God There was no Vihara in India. no Buddhist publication, no preaching until started by the Maha Bodhi Society- There is a great harvest to be reaped if there are Buddhist workers. The number of Untouchables waiting to be rescued from the Brahmanical despotism is 65 millions. The Brahmans don't want them. they are ~~straightway~~ not allowed by the Brahmans to walk in the same road with them Christians and Moslems wish to convert them, and steps are being taken by both to have them converted. There are 70 million Moslems. If the Untouchables are Converted the number of ~~Moslems~~ will increase to 135 millions Padres will be glad to have the number of Native Christians increased from 3 millions to 68 millions when the Untouchables become Moslems there will be a tough fight between Moslems & Hindus.

physically weak. For 14 years I have spent my life in India in voluntary exile. The name of the Lord Buddha was hardly known 37 years ago by the people of India. Today all India acknowledges hm as their God. There was no Vihara in India, no Buddhist publication, no preaching until started by the Maha Bodhi Society. There is a great harvest to be reaped if there are Buddhist workers. The number of Untouchables waiting to be rescued from the Brahmanical despotism is 65 millions. The Brahmans don't want them. They are not allowed by the Brahmans to walk in the same road with them. Christians and Moslems wish to convert them and steps are being taken by both to have them converted. There are 70 million Moslems. If the Untouchables are converted the number of Moslems will increase to 135 millions. Padres will be glad to have the number of Native Christians increased from 3 millions to 68 millions. When the Untouchables become Moslems there will be a tough fight between Moslems and Hindus.

Indian Christianity is synonymous with butchery & alcoholism. I wish to start a propaganda to carry the Dhamma to the untouchables, but I am now so very weak that the Doctors advise me to take complete rest in a German Sanitarium for 3 months, otherwise I shall be completely break down and be of no use to the Cause

I propose leaving Calcutta next month about the 10 of May and go to Colombo, there to take steamer for Marseilles. After my arrival in Europe I shall let you know. Would it be helpful to the Cause if I visit England

The Buddha Dhamma is too sublime for the barbarian pagans, they do not want to give up alcohol or meat. They are satisfied with the low Caste gods and the fetish priests.

Yours affectionately
The Anagarika Dharmapala

Francis J Payne Esq
London.

Indian Christianity is synonymous with butchery and alcoholism I wish to start a propaganda to carry the Dhamma to the untouchables, but I am now so very weak that the Doctors advise me to take complete rest in a German Sanitorium for 3 months, otherwise I shall completely break down and be of no use to the Cause.

I propose leaving Calcutta next month about the 10th of May and go to Colombo, there to take steamer for Marseilles. After my arrival in Europe I shall let you know. Would it be helpful to the cause if I visit England.

The Buddha Dhamma is too sublime for the barbarian pagans. They do not want to give up alcohol and meat. They are satisfied with the low-caste gods and the fetish priest.

Francis J. Payne Esq.
London.

Yours affectionately
The Anagarika Dharmapala.

GRAM : "BUDDHIST" CALCUTTA PHONE : 32-3591 31-6314

THE MAHA BODHI SOCIETY OF INDIA

(Estd. by Anagarika Dharmapala in 1891)

POST BOX NO. : 12365

4-A, BANKIM CHATTERJEE STREET, CALCUTTA - 700 073 INDIA

MESSAGE

Maha Bodhi Society's main objective was the restoration of Buddhagaya Temple and its vicinity. Hence amongst all activities of Mahabodhi Society during past hundred years Buddhagaya had been main which used to rotate other things and gave impetus to the activities.

The Centenary Celebrations of Mahabodhi Society actually means the **100** years that revolution for restoration of Buddhist prestige in India, which was started from Buddhagaya. This is the most worthy place for the Celebrations, and the Buddhagaya Centre is doing this.

I feel immense pleasure that the year 1991 has rejuvenated most of the Mahabodhi Centres at different places to take on various social and welfare activities. The Buddhagaya has come forward with opeing a hospital, a school, a Bhikkhu Training Centre and—literary organ—which all had been wished by the founder Ven. Dharmapala, for Buddhagaya. It has been brought in action with this Centenary.

I wish all success and I shall co-operate in all of my capacities with its all activities.

Bhavatu Sabba Mangalam.

(Ven. M. Wipulasara Maha Thera)
General Secretary
Maha Bodhi Society of India

Message of greeting from the Maha Bodhi Society, Calcutta, on the occasion of the celebration of the centenary of the founding of the Buddhist revival in Bodh Gaya, 1992.

The Name...

The Maha Bodhi Society derives its name from the tree under which about two thousand five hundred and thirty five years ago, at Buddha Gaya, the Great Being, Gautama Buddha, took his adamantine seat (Vajrasana) and visualised the Truth, The Reality.

This Tree was an Asvattha (Ficus Religiosa), which was sanctified by Siddhartha Gautama's attaining Supreme Knowledge (Bodhi) beneath its shade.

Thenceforth, it became known as the Bodhi-Tree in India and Bo-Tree in Śri Lanka.

Today the word Bodhi has become internationally known term or noun in connection with the Buddhist activities.

The Seal...

The Seal of the Maha Bodhi Society, of which an engraving is printed here, was copied from an alto-redievo tablet in the Indian Museum, Calcutta, and may be seen against the right-hand wall of the large square room, from which one enters the Archæological Sculpture Gallery. It is included in the Gandhara collection made by Major General Sir Alexander Cunningham. It is computed to be more than 2,000 years old, and General Cunningham and most other archæologists believe that it was the seal adopted by the Sangharajas of the greatest Viharas of those days. The Trident in the centre represents the three Gems — Buddha, Dharma, Sangha. The wheel supporting it is the Dharma Chakra or the Wheel of the Law, the Couchant Deer refer to the deer park, Isipatana near Benares, where the Buddha preached his first Great Discourse, entitled the Dhamma Cakkappavattana Sutta, which embodies his doctrines. The two figures typify the celestial hosts in the act of adoration. The Japanese auxiliary of the Maha Bodhi Society (Indo Busseki Kofuku Kwai) has adopted this as their emblem.

The Aim...

Maha Bodhi Society, a true missionary organisation of the type which the founder of the religion had in his mind and carried out literally the direction given by the Buddha in the memorable words :—

> "Go ye, O Bhikkhus, and wander forth for the benefit of the many, for the welfare of many, out of compassion for the worldly beings, for the benefit, good and happiness of men and gods. Do not two of you set forth in the same direction. Proclaim, O Bhikkhus, the doctrine, excellent in the beginning, excellent in the middle and excellent at the end — true in its meaning, true in its letter, preach ye a life of holiness perfect and immaculate".
>
> —Mahavagga Vinaya Pitaka

Description of the Maha Bodhi Society, Calcutta, 1992.

The Maha Bodhi
Founded by Anagarika Dharmapala
First Published in 1892

Centenary Volume

Editor-in-Chief
Venerable Prof. Dr Walpola Sri Rahula Maha Thera
Tripitakavagisvaracarya
B.A.,Ph.D.,D.Litt., LL.D.
Doctor of Sacred Theology
Chancellor, University of Kelaniya, Sri Lanka

Managing Editor
Ven. M. Wipulasara Maha Thera
General Secretary
Maha Bodhi Society of India

Executive Editor
Prof. Dipak Kumar Barua
M.A., P.R.S.,Dip.Lib.,D.Phil.
University Professor and Head of the Department of Pali and Dean Faculty Council for Post-Graduate Studies in Education, Journalism and Library Science, University of Calcutta

Consultant Editor
Santosh Bikash Barua
Formerly of All India Radio (AIR) and Doordarshan
Treasurer
Maha Bodhi Society of India

Editor
Upali Rupasinghe
Senior Journalist — Sri Lanka

Associate Editor
T.B.Dissanayake
Formerly of the Sri Lanka Administrative Service

Printer
Arvind Vajpeyi
Clarion Printing
4/2B, Leonard Road, Hastings
Calcutta 700 022

Published by
Ven. M. Wipulasara Maha Thera
General Secretary and Managing Editor,
'The Maha Bodhi' Journal for the Maha Bodhi Society of India,
4A Bankim Chatterjee Street, Calcutta 700 073

Centenary Volume of the *Maha Bodhi*, 1992.

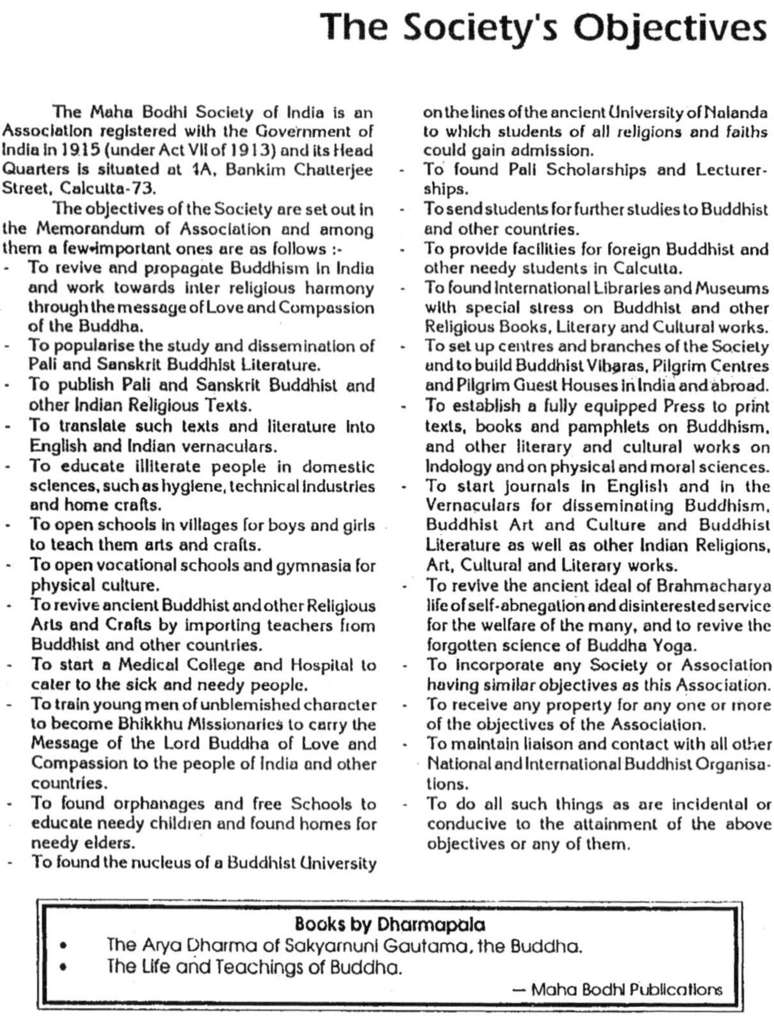
The Society's Objectives

The Maha Bodhi Society of India is an Association registered with the Government of India in 1915 (under Act VII of 1913) and its Head Quarters is situated at 4A, Bankim Chatterjee Street, Calcutta-73.

The objectives of the Society are set out in the Memorandum of Association and among them a few important ones are as follows :-

- To revive and propagate Buddhism in India and work towards inter religious harmony through the message of Love and Compassion of the Buddha.
- To popularise the study and dissemination of Pali and Sanskrit Buddhist Literature.
- To publish Pali and Sanskrit Buddhist and other Indian Religious Texts.
- To translate such texts and literature into English and Indian vernaculars.
- To educate illiterate people in domestic sciences, such as hygiene, technical industries and home crafts.
- To open schools in villages for boys and girls to teach them arts and crafts.
- To open vocational schools and gymnasia for physical culture.
- To revive ancient Buddhist and other Religious Arts and Crafts by importing teachers from Buddhist and other countries.
- To start a Medical College and Hospital to cater to the sick and needy people.
- To train young men of unblemished character to become Bhikkhu Missionaries to carry the Message of the Lord Buddha of Love and Compassion to the people of India and other countries.
- To found orphanages and free Schools to educate needy children and found homes for needy elders.
- To found the nucleus of a Buddhist University on the lines of the ancient University of Nalanda to which students of all religions and faiths could gain admission.
- To found Pali Scholarships and Lecturerships.
- To send students for further studies to Buddhist and other countries.
- To provide facilities for foreign Buddhist and other needy students in Calcutta.
- To found International Libraries and Museums with special stress on Buddhist and other Religious Books, Literary and Cultural works.
- To set up centres and branches of the Society and to build Buddhist Viharas, Pilgrim Centres and Pilgrim Guest Houses in India and abroad.
- To establish a fully equipped Press to print texts, books and pamphlets on Buddhism, and other literary and cultural works on Indology and on physical and moral sciences.
- To start journals in English and in the Vernaculars for disseminating Buddhism, Buddhist Art and Culture and Buddhist Literature as well as other Indian Religions, Art, Cultural and Literary works.
- To revive the ancient ideal of Brahmacharya life of self-abnegation and disinterested service for the welfare of the many, and to revive the forgotten science of Buddha Yoga.
- To incorporate any Society or Association having similar objectives as this Association.
- To receive any property for any one or more of the objectives of the Association.
- To maintain liaison and contact with all other National and International Buddhist Organisations.
- To do all such things as are incidental or conducive to the attainment of the above objectives or any of them.

Books by Dharmapala

- The Arya Dharma of Sakyamuni Gautama, the Buddha.
- The Life and Teachings of Buddha.

— Maha Bodhi Publications

The objectives of the Maha Bodhi Society, 1992.

PAST PRESIDENTS OF THE MAHA BODHI SOCIETY OF INDIA

1891-1911 :	Hikkaduwe Siri Sumangala Pradhana Nayaka Mahasthavira
1911-1924 :	Sir Ashutosh Mukherjea, Kt, Judge, High Court, Calcutta
1925-1942 :	Hon'ble Mr. Justice Manmatha Nath Mukherji
1942-1953 :	Dr. Shyama Prasad Mookerjee
1953-1982 :	H.H. Polden Thondup Namgyal (Maharaj Kumar of Sikkim)
1982-1989 :	Mr. P.K. Thungon, M.P.

The Maha Bodhi Society of India Office Bearers & Members of the Governing Body and Committees

President : The Most Ven. Palipana Dharmakirthi Sri Gunaratana Chandananda Mahanayake Thera.

Vice-Presidents :
i) Ven. L. Ariyawansa Nayake Maha Thera
ii) Ven. Junkai Osada
iii) Mr. Gamani Jayasuriya
iv) Justice Bhagabati Prosad Banerjee
v) Ven. Yuki Washio

General Secretary : Ven. M. Wipulasara Maha Thera

Dy. General Secretary : Ven. Dr. D. Rewatha Thera

Asst. General Secretary : Ven. B. Pannarama Thera

Treasurer : Sri Santosh Bikash Barua

Asst. Treasurer : Sri Anil Kumar Mitra

THESE OFFICE BEARERS AND GOVERNING BODY MEMBERS CONSTITUTED THE CENTENARY CELEBRATIONSCOMMITTEE OF THE SOCIETY.

Members of the Governing Body

Ven G. Prajnananda Thera,
Ven K. Chandaratana Thera,
Ven S. Wijithadhamma Thera,
Ven. D. Wimala Thera,
Ven. U. Ratanapala Thera,
Ven. W. Medhananda Thera,
Ven. M. Suddhammalankara Thera,
Ven. T. Wanaratana Thera,
Ven. M. Wimalasara Thera,
Ven. M. Assaji Thera,
Ven. Saddhananda Thera,
Prof. C.R. Lama,
Ven. Lama Lobzang,
Ven. Lama Sherab Bhaldi,
Ven. Lama Thuplen Jugnes,
Mr. Singha Weerasekera,
Sri Mohan Kumar Mukherjee,
Sri Tara Shanker Banerjee,
Prof. Dipak Kumar Barua,
Dr. Krishna Soll,
Sri Bimal Kumar Ghosh,
Sri Shyamal Baran Chowdhury,
Sri Akhilesh Bhattacharya,
Sri A.K. Bandyopadhyay,
Sri Rahul Suman Chawara,
Mrs. Law Cong Gee,
Smt. Sheela Devi Chaurasia,
Prof. Narain Chand Parashar,
Sri D.T. Rupwate,
Sri Sanal Kumar Dey,
Dr. (Miss) Asha Das,
Sri Ananda Mukherjee,
Prof. Pulin Barua,
Miss Rekha Talukdar,
Sri Sugata Barua,
Sri Mangal Subba,
Sri Ashutosh Dutt,
Sri Indra Bhusan Ghosh,
Dr. C.S. Ma,
Prof. Sanghasen Singh,
Sri Diwan Chand Ahir,
Rev. Dr. Kim Kwan Tae, and
Dr. Sukomal Chowdhuri.

Board members of the Maha Bodhi Society, 1992.

Executive Committee

President (Ex-Officio),
General Secretary (Ex-Officio),
Treasurer (Ex-Officio),
Justice Bhagabati Prosad Banerjee —Vice President,
Ven. Dr. D. Rewatha Thera — Deputy General Secretary,
Ven. B. Pannarama Thera — Asst. General Secretary,
Sri Tara Shanker Banerjee,
Prof. Dipak Kumar Barua,
Sri A.K. Bandyopadhyay,
Dr. Krishna Soft,
Sri Anil Kumar Mitra
Sri Sanat Kumar Dey,
Sri Ananda Mukherjee,
Sri Mohan Kumar Mukherjee,
Sri Akhilesh Bhattacharya.

Finance Committee

Sri S.B. Barua — Treasurer (Chairman),
General Secretary —Ven. M. Wipulasara Maha Thera,
Asstt. Treasurer — Sri Anil Kumar Mitra,
Sri A.K. Bandyopadhyay,
Sri Sanat Kumar Dey,
Sri Mangal Subba,
Sri Bimal Kumar Ghosh,
Sri Tara Shanker Banerjee,
Sri Shyamal Baran Chowdhury,
Sri Ashutosh Dutta,
Ven. Suddhammalankara Thera.

Legal Committee :

Justice Bhagabati Prosad Banerjee
— Vice President (Chairman),
General Secretary — Ven. M. Wipulasara Maha Thera,
Treasurer — Sri S.B. Barua,
Sri A.K. Bandyopadhyay,
Sri Ananda Mukherjee,
Sri Mohan Kumar Mukherjee,
Sri Anil Kumar Mitra — Asst. Treasurer,
Sri Tara Shanker Banerjee.

Religious, Cultural and Educational Activities Committee

Prof. Dipak Kumar Barua — Chairman,
Vice President — Ven. L. Ariyawanse Nayake Thera,
General Secretary —Ven. M. Wipulasara Maha Thera,
Treasurer — Sri S.B. Barua,
Asst. General Secretary — Ven. B. Pannarama Thera,
Ven. Dr. D. Rewatha Thera — Deputy General Secretary
Ven. Suddhammalankara Thera,
Ven. U. Ratanapala Thera,
Ven. G. Prajnananda Thera,
Ven. M. Assaji Thera,
Sri Shyamal Baran Chowdhury,
Smt. Sheela Devi Chaurasia,
Mr. Sugata Barua,
Miss Rekha Talukdar,
Sri Kumud Barua Chowdhury,
Mrs. Law Cong Gee,
Dr. (Miss) Asha Das.

Social Services and Welfare Activities Committee

Sri Sanat Kumar Dey (Chairman),
General Secretary —Ven. M. Wipulasara Maha Thera,
Treasurer — Sri S.B. Barua,
Sri Ashutosh Dutt,
Mrs. Law Cong Gee,
Miss Rekha Talukdar,
Sri Indra Bhusan Ghosh,
Sri Sugata Barua,
Ven. Assaji Thera,
Sri Tara Shanker Banerjee,
Smt. Sheela Devi Chaurasia,
Sri Ananda Mukherjee,
Sri Bimal Kumar Ghosh,
Sri Anil Kumar Mitra,
Sri Akhilesh Bhattacharya,
Sri Shyamal Baran Chowdhury.

The following members were co-opted to this Committee

Sri Manoranjan Barua,
Sri Dipak Kumar Chowdhury,
Dr. Gurupada Sandilya,
Mr. D.L.S. Jayawardena,
Smt. Parul Dey,
Smt. Sukla Daw,
Smt. Usha Bhattacharya,
Ven. Suddhammalankara Thera,
Ven. T. Wanatarana Thera,
Dr. Dipasree Roychoudhury,
Sri Ashok Chatterjee,
Sri Manoj Kr. Sarkar,
Sri Dulal Ch. Biswas,
Sri Gopal Chandra Daw,
Sri Satyen Sarkar,
Sri Krishna Lal Mukherjee,
Sri Bimal Chandra Das.

Members of the committees of the Maha Bodhi Society, 1992.

MAHA BODHI SOCIETY OF INDIA

(Established by Anagarika Dharmapala in 1891)
4-A, Bankim Chatterjee Street • Calcutta 700073
Telephone & Fax: 2415214

OFFICE-BEARERS

PRESIDENT
Kalasuri Ven'ble M. Wipulasara Maha Thero

VICE-PRESIDENTS
Ven'ble G. Prajnananda Maha Thera
Ven'ble Dr. Rashtrapal Maha Thera
His Holiness Kushok Bakula
Most Ven'ble Bishop Kyuse Enshinjoh
Prof. C.R. Lama
Hon'ble Justice Bhagabati Prosad Banerjee

GENERAL SECRETARY
Ven'ble Dr. D. Rewatha Thero

DEPUTY GENERAL SECRETARY
Ven'ble M. Suddhammalankara Thero

ASSISTANT GENERAL SECRETARY
Ven'ble M. Wimalasara Thero

TREASURER
Shri Santosh Bikash Barua

ASSTT. TREASURER
Shri Shyamal Baran Chowdhury

BHIKKHUS-IN-CHARGE OF CENTRES

Buddhagaya :	Ven'ble M. Wimalasara Thero
Sarnath :	Ven'ble D. Wimala Thero
Calcutta :	Ven'ble M. Suddhammalankara Thero
New Delhi :	Ven'ble W. Medhananda Thero
Lucknow :	Ven'ble G. Prajnananda Maha Thero
Bhubaneswar :	Ven'ble Dr. R. Chandaratana Thero
Nowgarh :	Ven'ble Assaji Thero

LEGACIES AND DONATIONS

Are needed by the MAHA BODHI SOCIETY OF INDIA for the maintenance and improvement of the institutions and organisations under the Society. Please correspond with the General Secretary.

ACTIVITIES

CALCUTTA
- Sri Dharmarajika Vihara
- Mahabodhi Library
- Dharmapala Institute of Culture and International Guest House
- Maha Bodhi Ambulance Service
- Maha Bodhi Book Agency
- Anagarika Dharmapala Meditation Centre
- Publications Division
- Jinaratana Memorial Free Homoeopathy Dispensary
- Maha Bodhi Hall

SARNATH
- Mulagandhakuti Vihara
- Maha Bodhi Inter College
- Anagarika Dharmapala International Bhikkhu Training Centre
- Anagarika Dharmapala Museum
- Maha Bodhi Information and Communication Centre
- Maha Bodhi Sangharama
- Maha Bodhi Free Primary School
- Birla Dharmasala
- Maha Bodhi Centenary Memorial Temple
- Maha Bodhi Book Agency
- Maha Bodhi Library
- Maha Bodhi Hall (Seema Mandir)

BUDDHAGAYA
- Maha Bodhi Pilgrims Rest
- Maha Bodhi Library
- Maha Bodhi Free Homoeopathy Dispensary
- Maha Bodhi Information Service
- Maha Bodhi Meditation Centre
- Maha Bodhi Book Agency
- Maha Bodhi Vidyapaith (Free School for Children)
- Maha Bodhi Hall

NEW DELHI
- Buddha Vihara • Maha Bodhi Library
- Maha Bodhi Book Agency

LUCKNOW
- Buddha Vihara • Maha Bodhi Book Agency

BOMBAY
- Bahujana Buddha Vihara

BHUBANESWAR
- Buddha Vihara • Maha Bodhi Free Dispensary
- Maha Bodhi Book Stall

NOWGARH (LUMBINI)
- Buddha Vihara • Pilgrims Rest

Board members of the Maha Bodhi Society and centres in India, 1996.

Maha Bodhi Society of India

HEADQUARTERS

Sri Dharmarajika Vihara, 4-A, Bankim Chatterjee Street, Calcutta-700073, India
Telephone & Fax: 241 5214

CENTRES

BUDDHA GAYA :
Maha Bodhi Society, Buddha Gaya,
Gaya, Bihar
Tel. : 0631 400742 • Fax : 0631 20047

SARNATH :
Mulaganghakuti Vihara,
Maha Bodhi Society, Holy Isipatana,
Sarnath, Varanasi, U.P.
Tel. : 385595 • Fax : 385003

NEW DELHI :
Buddha Vihara, Maha Bodhi Society,
Mandir Marg, New Delhi – 110 001.
Tel.: 3363328

LUCKNOW :
Buddha Vihara, Maha Bodhi Society,
Risaldar Park, Lucknow - 1, U.P.
Tel. : 247657

BOMBAY :
Bahujana Vihara, Maha Bodhi Society,
Buddhist Temple Street,
Parel, Bombay-12

NOWGARH : (Lumbini)
Sriniwasa Ashram,
Maha Bodhi Society, Lumbini Road
Nowgarh

BHUBANESHWAR :
Buddha Vihara, Plot 4 Unit 9,
New Capital, Bhubaneshwar, Orissa.
Tel : 400745

JAPAN :
HEADQUARTERS :
6-5-23, Honkomagome,
Bunkyo-ku, Tokyo 113, Japan.

- Maha Bodhi Society
Japan–Sri Lanka Buddhist Centre
3318, Kogaishima,
Swara-Shi, Chiba-Ken, Japan

- Maha Bodhi Society,
8/1, Kanda, Iwatsuka cho, Nakamuraku,
Nagoya, Japan

KOREA :
Maha Bodhi Society,
Buddhist Acadamy Temple,
537-6 Kilum 1 Dong
Sungduk-KJ, Seoul – Korea

HONG KONG :
The Maha Bodhi Society,
4, Somerset Road,
Kowloon Tong,, Kowloon, Hong Kong.

AFFILIATED CENTRES :

- **Shravasthi :**
Maha Bodhi Society,
Shravasthi, Baharaich, U.P.

- **Bangalore :**
Maha Bodhi Society, 14, 1st Main Road,
Gandhinagar, Bangalore 9, Tel. : 24684

- **Sanchi :**
Chetiyagiri Vihara, Telephone : 39
Maha Bodhi Society,
Sanchi, Bhopal, M.P.

- **Madras :**
Maha Bodhi Society, 17, Kennet Lane,
Egmore, Madras-8. Tel. : 8252458

- **Ajmer :**
Maha Bodhi Ashoka Vihara,
Maha Bodhi Society,
Mayo Link Road, Ajmer, Rajasthan.

- **England :**
The London Buddhist Vihara,
Dharmapala Building
The Avenue, Bedford Park
London W4 IUD

- **America :**
Dharma Vijaya Buddhist Vihara
1147, Crenshaw Blvd, Los Angeles
California 90019
U.S.A. Tel. (213) 737-5084

- **Sri Lanka :**
Maha Bodhi Society,
130, Maligakanda Road
P.O. Box-250, Colombo-10, Sri Lanka,
Tel. : 95093, Telegram : Bauddhaya

Centres and affiliated centres of the Maha Bodhi Society, 1996.

CHAPTER THREE

Bodh Gaya as the 'Central Place' of Buddhism

On 19 June 1949, the Bihar State Government passed the Bodh Gaya Temple Act as Bihar Act 17. Through its publication in the governmental communications dated 6 July 1949, the law for the revision of the temple administration came into force. In the description of the temple by Dipak K. Barua (Barua 1981: 288–308) one can read the text together with the detailed regulations regarding the implementation of the law dated 26 February 1957. The regulations set down in Paragraphs 3 and 4, which concern the composition of the Temple Management Committee installed by the state government of Bihar for a three year period, played a decisive role in future controversies concerning the administration of the temple:

The Committee shall consist of a Chairman and eight members nominated by the State Government, all of whom shall be Indians and of whom four shall be Buddhists and four shall be Hindus including the Mahanth.

Provided that if the Mahanth is a minor or of unsound mind or refuses to serve on the Committee, another Hindu member shall be nominated in his place.

The District Magistrate of Gaya shall be the ex-officio Chairman of the Committee:

Provided that the State Government shall nominate a Hindu as Chairman of the Committee for the period during which the District Magistrate of Gaya is non-Hindu.

The State Government shall nominate a person from among the members to act as Secretary of the Committee.

The Committee shall be a body corporate by the name of the Bodh Gaya Temple Management Committee, having perpetual succession and a common seal, with power to acquire and hold property, both movable and immovable, and to contract, and shall by the said name sue or be sued. (D.K. Barua, 1981: 289–90)

BUDDHA GAYA TEMPLE.

Edited and published by Prof. S. V. Phadnis for Buddha Society Bombay.

JOWELL'S PRINTING PRESS, BOMBAY.

Maha Bodhi Mahavihara, Bodh Gaya.

With the committee of nine people established in this way, it is guaranteed that Hindus will be in the majority. Accordingly, the draft for the alteration of the Temple Management Act introduced in 1992 by the All India Bhikkhu Sangha is mainly directed against this regulation. Below I quote from the Draft Bill of 1992 as placed at my disposal:

> The Government may nominate ten members, all of whom shall be Indian Buddhists to constitute a Committee comprising of a Chairman, a Secretary and eight members on the recommendation of and in consultation with the All India Bhikkhu Sangha and the All India Federation of Buddhist Societies.
>
> The District Magistrate of Gaya shall be an ex-officio Member of the Committee.
>
> The Chairman and the Secretary shall be elected by the Committee from among its Buddhist Members.
>
> The Committee shall be a body corporate by the name of the Bodh Gaya Mahavihara Management Committee, having perpetual succession and a common seal, with power to acquire and hold property, both movable and immovable, and contract, and shall, by the said name, sue or be sued.

The Japanese-born monk Surai Sasai from the centre of the New Buddhist movement in Nagpur introduced in 1992 the 'Liberate Bodh Gaya Movement' to push these changes through. This hit the headlines (Lynch, 1998), but the liberation march met with cautious resistance at Bodh Gaya itself. It was said that the international construction work would not be furthered by spectacular campaigns in the manner of the fundamentalist Hindu movements for the liberation of the Ramjanmabhoomi in Ayodhya. The local elite saw its economic interests endangered, and an attempt at appeasement was made. Collisions between the guardians of peace, mobilized by the government, and the volunteers of the campaign were prevented (Doyle, 1997: 387ff.). Nevertheless, the campaign was effective because, following this, the administration committee was partly changed and the spokesmen of the campaign were nominated as members. Concerning this, D.C. Ahir wrote me a letter from New Delhi dated 19 September 1996:

> As regards the Buddha Gaya Mahavihara Act, there is practically no progress. The Bihar Government have not shown any interest in enacting it and the Court case is just dragging. No date for its hearing has so far been fixed. So the Buddhists are feeling frustrated. The only thing the Bihar Government has done is to reconstitute the Temple Management Committee in which the four Buddhist members are: Ven. Surai Sasai, Ven. Ananda, Ven. Gyaneshwar and Ven. Ananda Deva—the monks who had been leading the Buddhist Agitation.

List of Temples, Monasteries and Buddhist Institutions at Buddhagaya

- *Mahabodhi Mahavihar .*
- *Mahabodhi Society of India .*
- *Burmese Vihara*
- *Chinese Temple*
- *Tibetan Temple of dGeluk School.*
- *Tibetan Temple of Karma School.*
- *Tibetan Temple of Nying - ma School* (Sechen Monastery)
- *Tibetan Temple of Shakya School.*
- *Temple of Bhutan*
- *Temple of Thailand (Wat Thai)*
- *Temple of Sikkim*
- *Temple of Taiwan.*
- *Temple of Korea.*
- *Temple of Bangladesh.*
- *Tamang Monastery*
- *Indo-San Nipponji*
- *Daijokyo Temple & Great Buddha Statue*
- *Temple of Vietnam.*
- *All India Bhikkhu Sangha*
- *International Maditation Centre .*
- *Buddhist Thai Bharat Society.*
- *Root Institute of Culture & Wisdom.*
- *Maitreya Project .*
- *Asian Buddhist Cultural Centre.*
- *Buddha - Vihara - Siddharthanagar.*
- *Tai - Bodhi - Kham - Siddharthanagar.*
- *Trailokya Buddha Centre .*

As a solid-rock is not shaken by the wind, so wise men are not moved amidst blame and praise. - Dham 81

Shivam Printing Works
156, A. P. Colony Gaya

Temples, Monasteries, and Buddhist Institutions in Bodh Gaya in 1998.

There is so far no telling what consequences the new nominations will have for the future work of the administrative committee. Anyhow, in the spring of 1998 the atmosphere seemed less tense. Otherwise, the holding of various mass events would not have been possible at the venue.

Meanwhile, what Sri Krishna Sinha, the Chief Minister of Bihar, had hinted at during the ceremonial takeover of the temple on 28 May 1953, became a reality (Ahir, 1994: 136–7). He said at that time that one could hope that Buddhists from around the world would come in the future and help to fill the dried-up headwaters of Buddhist culture with new life. The following pictures and documents illustrate to what extent Bodh Gaya has since developed as a central place of Buddhism.

- *Sangiti*, the first newsletter of the Buddhagaya Buddhist Cultural Centre which was founded in 1997, gives a 'List of Temples, Monasteries, and Buddhist Institutions at Buddhagaya' which offers an overview of all institutions at the beginning of the year 1998 (see plate on page 84).
- Maps are certainly helpful for visiting the various temples and institutions. In this respect, here are three approaches to the confusing diversity of the place:

  The map from the guidebook for pilgrims, *Middle Land, Middle Way* by S. Dhammika (1992), published in Kandy, Sri Lanka, shows the pure form of Bodh Gaya so to speak, and its central sites (map plate on page 91). A more detailed illustration of the actual conditions is found in the map circulated by Middle Way Travels (no date) (map plate on page 92). However, the most graphic image of the colourful development of the rapidly growing sacred place is given in the Tibetan Map (see map plate on pages 94-5). Though not drawn to scale, it shows all the institutions and temples included in the *Sangiti* report and, besides that, it also suggests a certain planning in the area of new constructions.

- The commemorative volume for the centenary anniversary of the founding of the Maha Bodhi Society published a letter from the ambassador of Belgium regarding the specific problems of the infrastructure of such a rapidly growing sacred place. This letter reads partly like a commentary on the geographical density of the Tibetan Map (see letter on pages 96-7)
- Special events for Bodh Gaya include the annual functions held on the occasion of the Tibetan New Year. The Root Institute for Wisdom

CHAKMA BUDDHIST TEMPLE CONSTRUCTION COMMITTEE
(BODH-GAYA)

c/o Sidhartha Nagar Buddhist Temple
Miya Bigha Buddha-Gaya
Gaya, Bihar, PIN: 824 231
India.

Date: March 28, 1998

AN APPEAL

Dear Dharma friends,

We on behalf of the "CHAKMA BUDDHIST TEMPLE CONSTRUCTION COMMITTEE" (BODH-GAYA) would like to inform all the Dharma friends that we, the ethnic minority Chakma Buddhists, follow the traditional theravada Buddhism and living uprooted in critical existence at different places in Chittagong Hill Tracts (CHT) in Bangladesh and North-Eastern (Assam, Tripura, Meghalaya, Mizoram, Arunachal Pradesh) parts of India.

As traditional Buddhists we have a socio-religious plan to construct a "CHAKMA BUDDHISTS TEMPLE" at the land of enlightenment - Buddha Gaya for the convenient of pilgrims. Accordingly, I alongwith Mr. Rabindra Lal Chakma and some other local Chakma leaders from different Chakma inhabited areas formed a "CHAKMA BUDDHIST TEMPLE CONSTRUCTION COMMITTEE" (Bodh-Gaya) on ad-hoc basis in Tripura state with a joint Bank account in the State Bank of India, Buddha Gaya Branch our A/C No.8147, the A/c holders are Ven. Priya Pal Bhikkhu and Mr. Rabindra Lal Chakma who are the Working Presidents and Acting Secretary of the construction committee respectively. The Construction Committee's prime objective is to raise fund to construct a CHAKMA BUDDHIST TEMPLE in this holyland - Buddha Gaya.

Therefore, we request all the Dharma friends to come forward with monetary assistance to help us to materialize our long cherished goal and to give complete shape to our noble aim in existence constructing a CHAKMA BUDDHIST TEMPLE at highly sacred place – Buddha Gaya.

Kindly if possible any kind of remittances, Bank drafts, money orders, cheques, pay orders, postal orders, donation which absolutely in need now can be send directly to our above mentioned joint Bank Account and all contributions will be gratefully acknowledged. May all beings be in peace.

Rabindra Lal Chakma
Acting Secretary
CHAKMA BUDDHIST TEMPLE
CONSTRUCTION COMMITTEE
(BODH-GAYA)

Priya Pal Bhikkhu
Working President
CHAKMA BUDDHIST TEMPLE
CONSTRUCTION COMMITTEE
(BODH-GAYA)

An appeal for donations for the construction of a Chakma Temple, 1998.

Culture, the California-based branch of the Foundation for the Preservation of the Mahayana Tradition, organized, with the help of donations from all over the world, a 'light sacrifice' that illuminated for several nights the expanded facilities of the main temple with the radiance of thousands of candles (see plates on pages 108–10).

- The time from mid-November until the end of February is called 'the season' by the Indians; it is cooler and thus more tolerable for foreign visitors. During this time all kinds of buses arrive daily with pilgrims and also tourists from all over the world, not just from Buddhist countries. Meanwhile, the Government of India recognized the special attraction of the sacred sites for the Indian upper middle class, and, under the slogan 'On the Buddha's Trail, by Rail!', arranged for a seasonal night train. Since 22 October 1998, this train has been passing in a six-day round trip through stations near the main sites of pilgrimage such as Sarnath, Rajgir, and Bodh Gaya (see plates on pages 106 and 107).
- A special event for the entire Buddhist world was the full ordination of 102 nuns from 25 countries which took place during 15–23 February 1998. It was carried out and was mainly financed by Master Hsing Yun, the founder of the Fo Kuang Shan order of Taiwan, which has spread to all five continents (see plates on pages 101–5).

It is understandable that such a historic event as the attempt to reintroduce the full ordination of women had to take place at the central site of Buddhism in Bodh Gaya. The first international conference of Buddhist women and nuns also took place in Bodh Gaya in the presence of the Dalai Lama in February 1987 (Tsomo, 1991, 1998). However, apart from such grand events, one should also consider the effect they have on the way people view the respective organizations. Thus, the Great Buddha Statue which was consecrated on 17 November 1989 is not just a particular expression of the exaltation of the central place, not just a major attraction next to the main temple, but it also signals the extraordinary means which the Japanese Daijokyo Order in Nagoya quite obviously has at its disposal (see *Daijo Graph* 1990, No. 5).

The interaction between external and internal self-representation of Buddhist organizations may explain why so many different temples exist in Bodh Gaya. One could ask the question: why is the main temple not sufficient for the Buddhists from all over the world as a symbol of the *bodhi* in their life? Or does the diversity of the architectural styles of the new Buddhist installations reflect the Buddhist ecumenical movement?

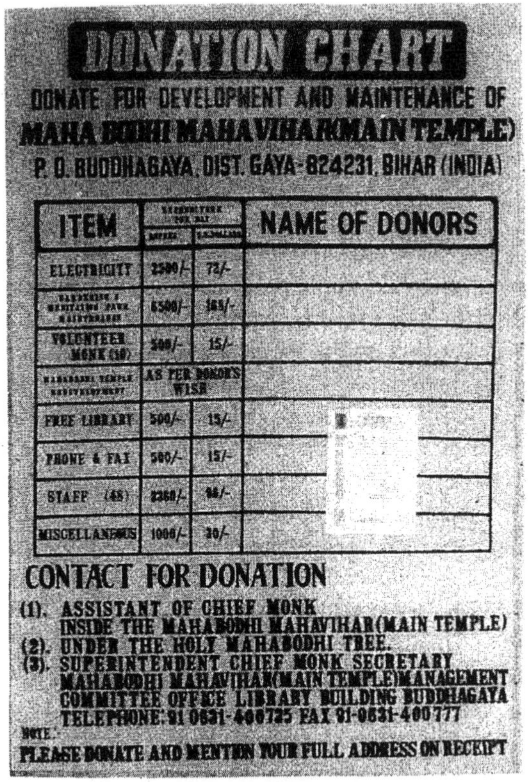

At the entrance to the office of the Temple Management Committee, one finds a request for donations for the fixed daily expenses given in US Dollars for the following: electricity 72; gardens and meditation park 168; ten monks 15; library 15; telephone/Fax 15; 48 employees 96; others 30.

- For the Chakmas and the Marmars from north India and Bangladesh the answer to such speculative questions would be quite simple and literally self-evident. In order to portray their identity as Buddhists from a certain area of origin with a particular and honourable cultural tradition, they too need their own temple with attached hostel for their countrymen. Their request for donations conveys in a nutshell an explanation of the great diversity of the representations of Buddhist culture achieved in Bodh Gaya (see plates on pages 86 and 98–9). For people from South and South-East Asia, this explanation is very easy to understand.
- The main temple in Bodh Gaya, where the revival movement of the place began in 1891, is the central place in the coming and going of pilgrims from all over the world because it is considered especially commendable to give a donation for its continued improvement and for covering the quite considerable daily expenses (see plate on page 88). This has enabled the Temple Management Committee to develop large facilities in a short time to such an extent that the pictures in Janice Leoshko's book, *Bodh Gaya—The Site of Enlightenment*, published in 1988, now seem almost outdated.

However, what significance has the new diversity of Buddhist culture over and above this for Buddhists in India? Or, put in another way: Where indeed would we meet Indian Buddhists here at the central site? Where can they find accommodation?

- The building of the All India Bhikkhu Sangha is centrally located at the intersection of the Main Road and the Temple Street. However, it is not mentioned on most maps, and on the Tibetan map it is shown as being quite small (see map on pages 94–5). The plans for a multi-purpose building unfortunately did not go beyond the foundations; the steel reinforcements are rusting away and testify to the mis-management of funds. Behind this modern ruin, we find a modest low building with four rooms and a small meditation hall. Occasionally pilgrims from Maharashtra can find accommodation here. Otherwise, however, the large grounds give the visitor an impression of a deserted and comparatively neglected place. A monk-secretary from the All India Bhikkhu Sangha looks after it, and he receives enough income for his support only when Tibetan pilgrims set up their tents here for a few days. In addition, a bus with New Buddhists from Maharashtra may occasionally arrive, but these visitors mostly stay only for one day, prepare their food on an open fire, and move on in the evening.

- The Trailokya Baudha Mahasangha Sahayak Gana (TBMSG), the Organization of the Helpers of the Great Buddhist Order of the Three Worlds, which is supported by the Friends of the Western Buddhist Order (and has its centre in Pune), also bought land in Bodh Gaya in order to build a centre there. However, the construction work has not gone beyond the customary surrounding walls, and the land thus enclosed is used for agricultural purposes.
- The Dhamma Bodhi, finally, the meditation centre of the Vipassana movement which was founded by S.N. Goenka, is located behind the campus of the Magadh University. It is still under construction and is managed from Patna. It offers only occasionally rather small courses because the infrastructure so far does not allow adequate care for more than 15 participants.

The TBMSG, the All India Bhikkhu Sangha, and the Vipassana Academy in Igatpuri will be introduced in greater detail later. However, in Bodh Gaya our tour ends with an observation which may be slightly disappointing to some visitors: Here, at the central site of Buddhism, we hardly meet any Indian Buddhists except the exiled Tibetans. So from here we move on to Nagpur, the central place of New Buddhism, located 750 km further to the south and west.

* * * * *

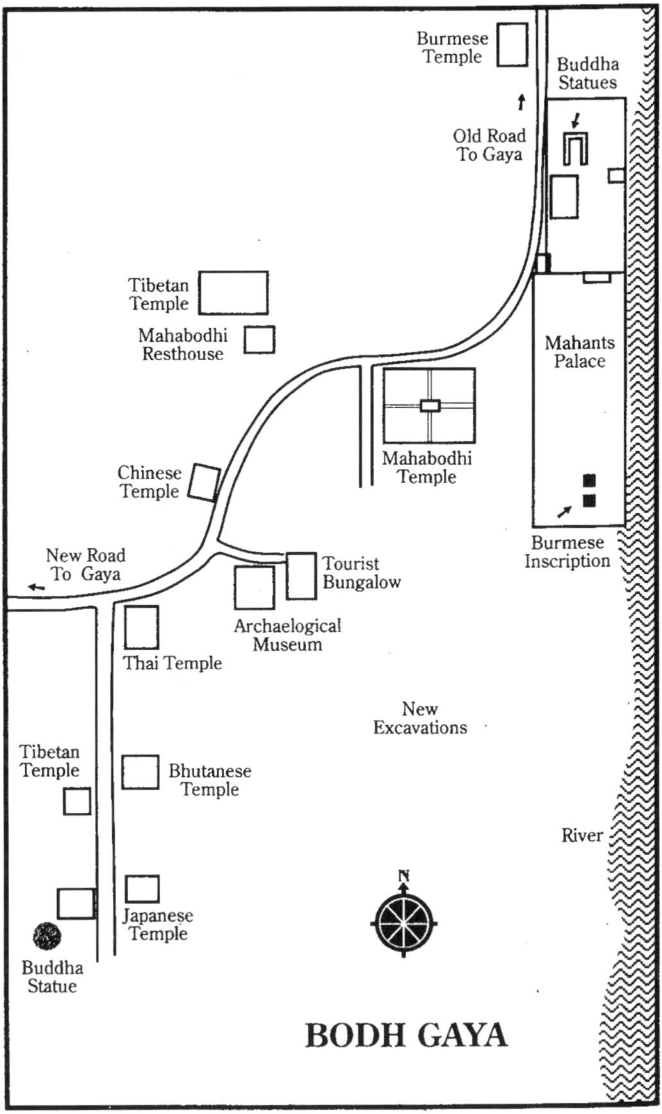

Simplified map from a pilgrim's handbook of the Buddhist Publication Society, Kandy, Sri Lanka

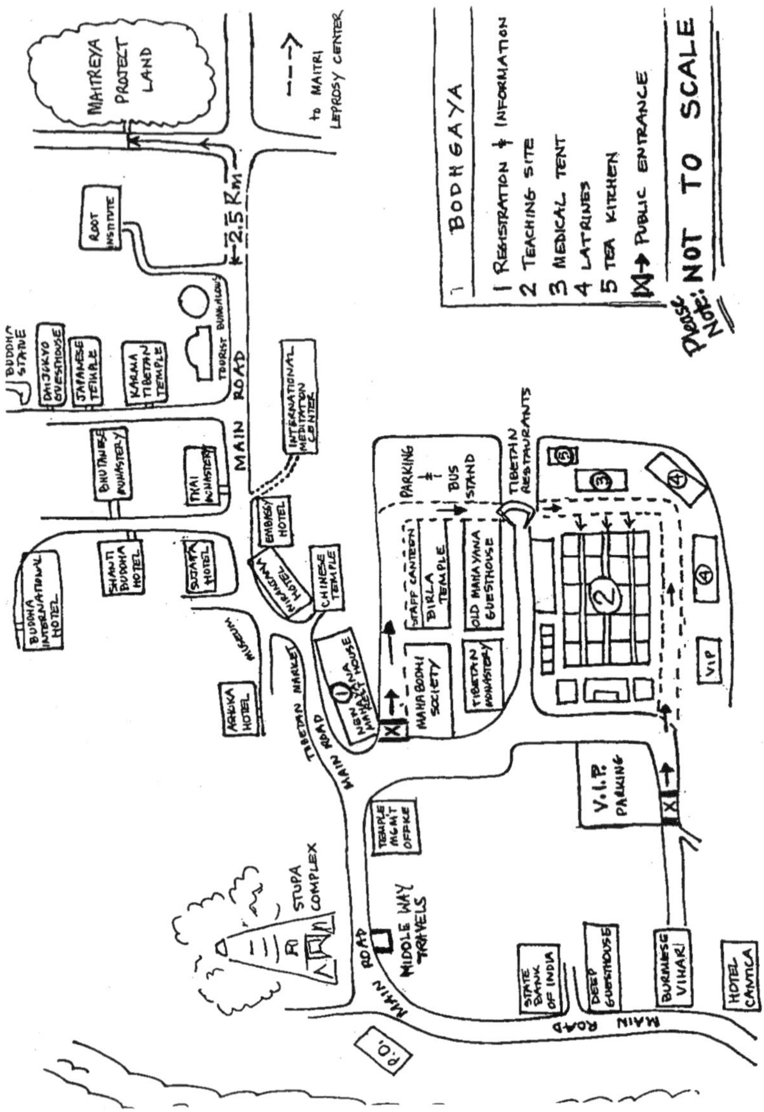

A map distributed by Middle Way Travels on the occasion of a Tibetan instruction.

The Buddha Image and Bodhi Leaves Plates

Devotional objects: Bodhi leaves and a soapstone sculpture of the Japanese Great Buddha.

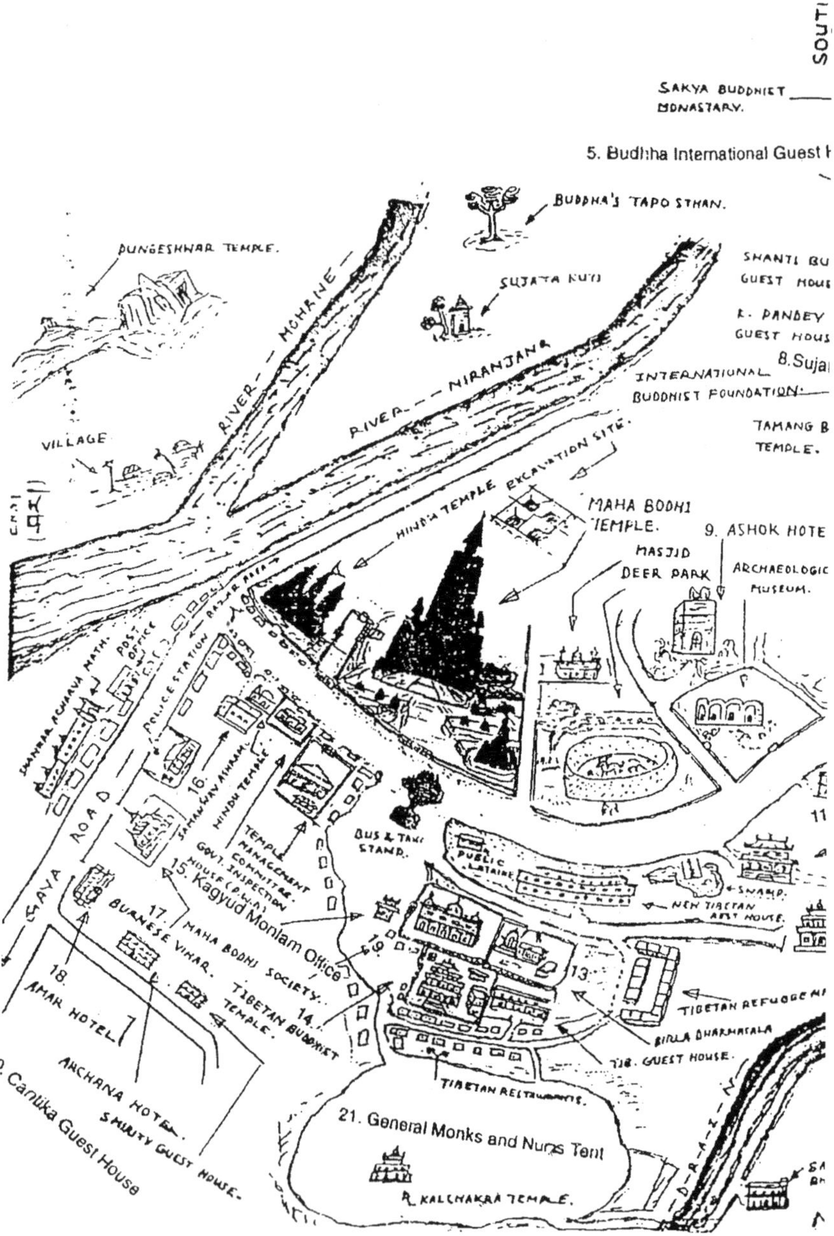

A map of Bodh Gaya distributed by an information stall for Tibetan pilgrims.

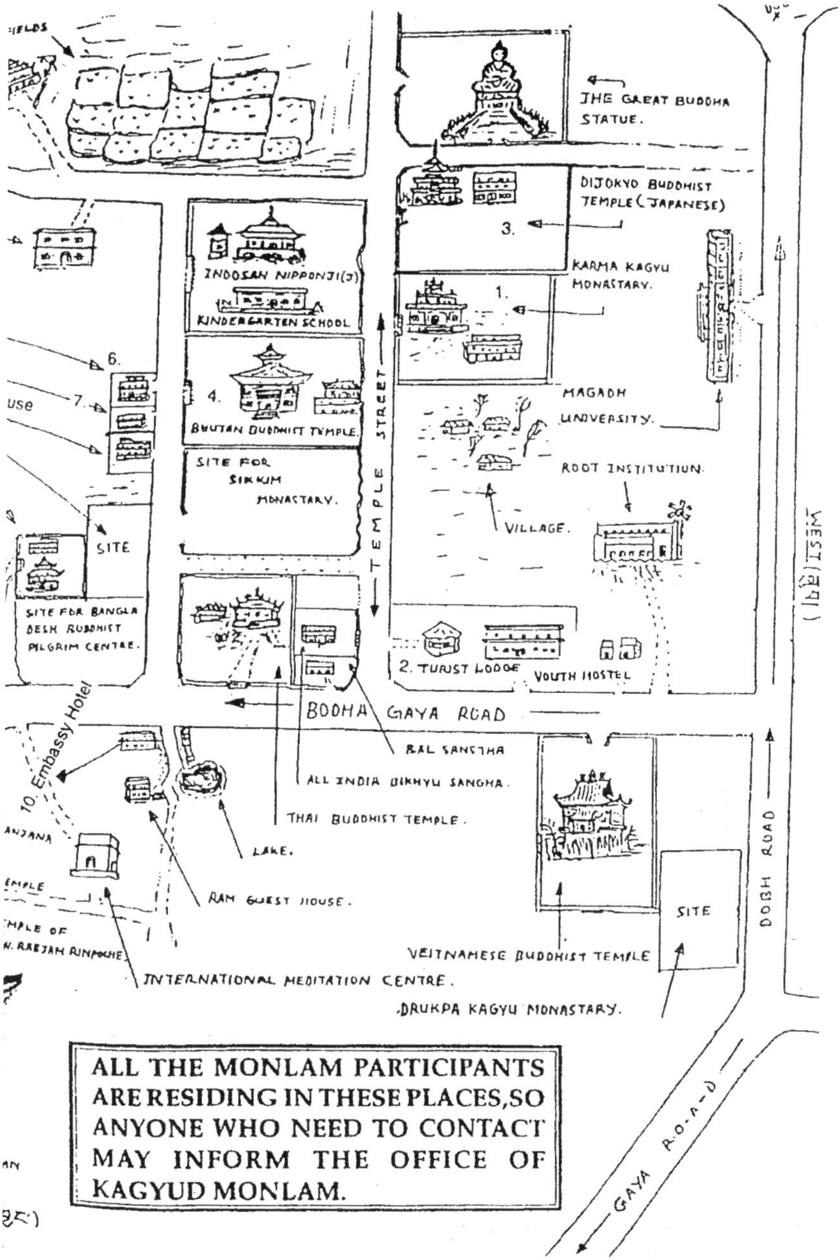

ALL THE MONLAM PARTICIPANTS ARE RESIDING IN THESE PLACES, SO ANYONE WHO NEED TO CONTACT MAY INFORM THE OFFICE OF KAGYUD MONLAM.

RESTORATION OF BUDDHAGAYA

—*K. Godage

After a lapse of 23 years, I visited Bodh Gaya on pilgrimage. The intervening period has seen the erection of the giant Buddha Statue by the Japanese, the pavilions of Japan, Thailand, Bhutan and Tibet. Sri Lanka has a new pilgrim's Rest and the Burmese Pilgrim's Rest has, like the country, deteriorated. Nothing else has changed.

The significance of Bodh-Gaya to Buddhists and to India and Indians of whatever faith cannot be exaggerated, for Bodh-Gaya is, without dispute, the place where India's greatest son achieved enlightenment. His thoughts and his message have influenced millions through a period of over two thousand five hundred years. The Buddha and his message form an eternal bond between Buddhists, the world over and India. It is for the above reasons that India becomes custodian and trustee for Buddhists world over, of the place most sacred to Buddhists.

Firstly, the Buddhist world owes a deep debt of gratitude to that great archaeologist Lord Cunningham, but for whom this great place of worship would yet have been a piece of land, at the same level as the present road, to be built upon by shop keepers or dwellers. Sadly there is no recognition of our gratitude to Lord Cunningham, for Bodhgaya has neither a monument nor a statue of him. It is particularly ironic that, this country, which erects statues for all manner of people, thas not erected a monument to a man to whom India and the world, owe so much. Buddhist countries which have erected pavilions, statues at great cost have also failed to erect a monument to this great man. They seem to have forgotten that the first act of the Buddha, after attaining enlightenment, was to stand before the Bodhi Tree to show his gratitude, even to a tree, for it had given him shade and protecton at the time of his enlightenment.

Serenity : A word synonymous with the Buddha, captured in statues of the Buddha which adorn living rooms even of non-believers (only because of the serenity which the Buddha face exudes) is sadly lacking in Bodh-Gaya. There is no appropriate ambiance. The mood of the place is furthest from the serene. Immediately outside the Vihara premises is a bustling market place, where all manner of trade and services are being conducted. It is also teaming with beggars and touts pickpockets and conmen.

It is ironic that, at a time when the Hindus of India are protesting the unspreing of the birthplace of Lord Ram, the Hindus had put a 'lingam' inside the main shrine room at Gaya. Hindus (particularly the Brahmins, after having reconverted the Buddhists of the Asokan era to Hinduism) conveniently sought to incorporate the Buddha as the ninth avatar of God Vishnu and to deify him. Not only did the Buddha very categorically and lucidly denounce Gods, rituals and beliefs of Hinduism but he also attacked the very basis of its social system. Ironically almost vertically opposite the Maha Vihar is a sign post, indicating that the

*Ambassador of Belgium.

Buddha, in debate with a Hindu Sankaracharya had stated, (at that spot), that contr to the Hindu belief that a man is born a Brahmin because of his karma and is also condemned to be an untouchable because of his karma, that by deed alone does one become a 'brahmin' or an 'untouchable' and not by birth. He challanged the religous and social systems of Hiduism. Therefore, the Buddha's message was/is contrary to the Hinduism particulay of the Sankarachary and the Brahmins. Therefore a fundamental differences between Hinduism and Buddhism and it is, therefore, not acceptable that the temple erected originally by the Buddhist emperor Ashoka, to respect the memory and venerate the Buddha, should have at the centre of shrine room, a 'lingam' ! This would have been considered a desecration but the fact the 'lingam' is worshipped by the Hindus.

Another incongrous feature of Buddhagaya are the hundreds of structures which have been erected in its precincts.

In the context of all that has been aforesaid may I therefore, make the followng suggestions for the consideration for the authorities :

(a) foremost architects town planners of India, perhaps in consultation with counterparts in 'Buddhist countries' re-plan the town of Buddhagaya with the objective of ensuring that it be restored to what it may been like during and after the time of the Buddha. Keeping in mind the foremost fact that it is a place of worship and should, therefore, have an absolutely serene atmosphere.

(b) The shops, boutiques and dwellings that now surround the area should be removed to a point at least half a mile away from the main temple.

(c) The 'lingma' inside the temple should be removed and placed in another temple which should be erected near the river and a pipal tree, to respect the beliefs of those who consider the Buddha as the tenth avatar of Lord Vishnu.

(d) All structures, of no relevance to the Buddha's presence within the prsent precincts, should be removed and placed at a site outside the main Temple. The main premises would threrefore only have the places of special significance in the Buddha story.

(e) The Government of India should declare an area of half a mile from the main temple, as a sacred area no structures permanent or semi-permanent should be permitted within this area, other than perhaps a statue of. Cunningham.

(f) The Government of India may consider setting up an international fund which would enable Buddhist countries in the neighbourhood and Buddhists the world over, to be associated in the restoration of Buddhagaya.

> *Everywhere flow the currents of craving. It sprouts like creeper and stands. Cut the root thereof with (the weapon of) wisdom as and when you see it springs up.*
>
> DHAMMAPADA, TANHA VAGGA-7

Suggestions for the restoration of Bodh Gaya.

An Appeal

Dear Devotees to "Sadhamma."

All of you know that "THE LORD BUDDHA" has attained the ENLIGHTENMENT under the Bodhi tree at BODH-GAYA and from that very time the place is being treated as a sacred one to the followers of BUDDHA. Gradually now a days it has become an International Pilgrimage Centre to, the world Buddhists. The Government of India and Bihar State Government has EARMARKED the said Holy place as one of the best Tourist Spots of India. In every year thousands and thousands of visitors are coming there from different parts of India and abroad with various purposes. Some of the visitors step up to this Holy place as a tourist, some of them to perform their religious rites and some others for Learning Meditation in the International Meditation Centre at BODH-GAYA So from that point of views the place has got a great importance which is un-countable to the world Buddhists.

Due to the importancy of the place the Buddhist Nations of the world like Ceylonese, Mayanmaris, Thaise, Chinese, Japanese, Tibbetans, and Taiwanis have their own Temples and Rest Houses for the pilgrims of their own countries. But it is a matter of great regret that the CHAKMAS and the MARMAS who are being the Traditional Buddhist in India and Bangladesh have no Temple and Rest house for the pilgrims of their own Communities at BODHGAYA. Consequently, the CHAKMA and MARMA pilgrims from Bangladesh and within India suffers a lot for want of Temples and Rest house of their own.

Inorder to focus our entity and identity as CHAKMAS and MARMAS are the Traditional Buddhist to the other Buddhist Nations of the world and also to facilitated the pilgrims of our own communities one Temple and another Rest house are badly needed for construction at BODH-GAYA. Keeping the idea in mind I took the initiative with very few persons and formed a "CHAKMA AND MARMA BUDDHIST TEMPLE CONSTRUCTION COMMITTEE (BODH-GAYA) on Ad-hoc basis in TRIPURA STATE. A full-fladged Committee will be formed later on to this end after extending our activities with our fellow brothers and sisters of MIZORAM, ARUNACHAL PRADESH, ASSAM, WEST BENGAL, BANGALADESH and other persons residing in the foreign countries.

In view of accomplishing the sacred task i.e. construction of a Temple and a Rest house a huge amount of money will be required to give the complete shape to this noble cause. It is also fact that it is not possible on the part of the few persons to get the plan implemented without the generous financial assistance of others. With a view to achiving the plan A CONSTRUCTION FUND estimating approximately Rs. 25 Lacs was created for collection of Donation where myself is the acting Secretary.

It is a matter of great delight that some pious Devotees to Tripple GEMS (Buddha, Dhamma & Sangha) have in the mean time committed to donate Rupees One Lac Ten thousand for the aforesaid purpose Moreover, During my visit to Bangladesh I have got an opportunity to discuss the matter with some prominent personalities like babu Krishna mohan Khisa, Niharbindu Chakma, Sinode Chakma and others. They have also whole heartedly appreciated the plan and expressed their willingness to donate in our fund. Receipt books have been distributed to the collectors of the respective areas from the office for collection.

So, I Personally and on behalf of the Committee appeal to the Lovers of SADHAMMA to extend their generous financial help to us with purity of mind and best abilities and also share with us in this noble task.

"BHABATU SABBA MANGALANG."

Dated, Abhoynagar
the 26th March'96.
AGARTALA.

Mr. Rabindra Lal Chakma.
(RETD. TRIPURA CIVIL SERVICE OFFICER.)
Secretary.
CHAKMA & MARMA BUDDHIST TEMPLE CONSTRUCTION FUND
(BODH-GAYA.)

An appeal to support a planned temple of the Chakmas and the Marmars.

News reports from a German newspaper, *Buddhayana Zeitung*, July 1998: 6, 7, on the ordination of monks and nuns in Bodh Gaya:

The Historic International Ordination of Monks and Nuns in Bodh Gaya, India

Bodh Gaya, 21 February (1998)—For the first time in hundreds of years Buddhist leaders from various schools and traditions came together for the higher ordination of 102 nuns and 30 monks from 23 different countries.

This ceremony in the country of the Buddha's birth had a special significance. The striving of some Buddhist leaders is characterized by trying to establish again the order of nuns on an international plane. In 1996, 10 Buddhist nuns received higher ordination in Sarnath—for the first time after almost eight hundred years. The Maha Bodhi Society in India organized this ceremony.

This time, the ceremony was performed by Master Hsing Yun of the Fokuangshan order in Taiwan. Leading monks from Cambodia, India, Taiwan, Korea, Sri Lanka, Mongolia, Thailand, and Nepal participated.

One of the nuns who had just received the higher ordination died under the Sri Maha Bodhi tree on the campus of the Bodh Gaya Mahavihara. The honourable Karma Ghopel Dremma was a Spanish nun who lived as a disciple of Lama Yeshi in Scotland. During the puja she became unconscious and died a few minutes later. Lama Yeshi declared that her death occurred under auspicious circumstances. This was the first time in the 2,542-year history of the Buddha Gaya Vihara that a Buddhist had died during a puja. Hundreds of Buddhist leaders who had gathered for the ceremony held a special puja for the departed nun in order to share their merit with the deceased.

Buddhayana Zeitung, July 1998: 6

Sangha of Sri Lanka does not recognize the Bhikkhuni order

Colombo, 12 April—The main monks of the four great Nikayas (teaching schools) in Sri Lanka do not agree with the new establishment of the *bhikkhuni* (nuns) order. It was called 'newly established' because of the higher ordination of a number of Singhalese women recently in Bodh Gaya. Since no Theravada land has an existing order of nuns, they explain, it is according to the Vinaya impossible to ordain a nun. Nobody is able to newly establish an Order which ceased to exist about a thousand years ago.

Buddhayana Zeitung, July 1998: 7

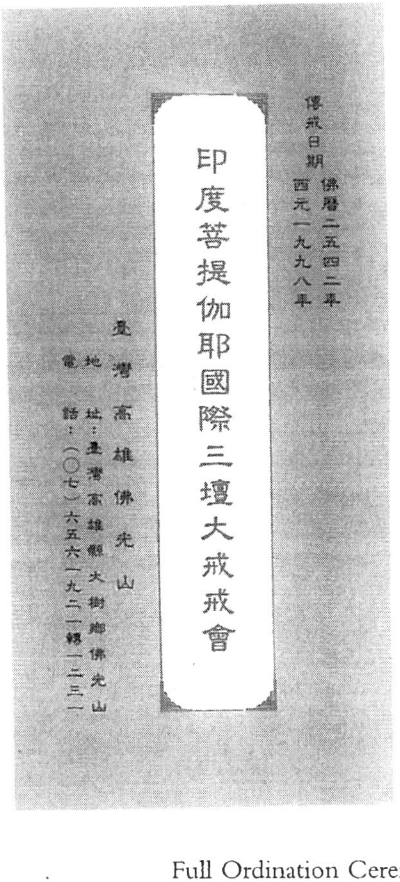
傳戒日期 佛曆二五四二年
西元一九九八年

印度菩提伽耶國際三壇大戒戒會

臺灣高雄佛光山
地址：臺灣高雄縣大樹鄉佛光山
電話：（○七）六五六一九二一轉一二三一

BODHGAYA INTERNATIONAL FULL ORDINATION CEREMONY

February 15 to 23, 1998

Objectives

Buddhism originated in India. The formation of the Sangha Order can be traced back more than twenty-five centuries ago when the Lord Buddha ordained his first five followers - the elder Kaundinya (Pali: Kondanna) and four others. This establishment of the bhiksu order was followed by the bhiksuni order five years later when Mahaprajapati Gautami, the Buddha's foster-mother, took her full ordination together with five hundred companions. Thus, was completed the monastic orders - bhiksu, bhiksuni, sramanera and sramanerani.

The bhiksu and bhiksuni orders formed in India were carried to Sri Lanka by the elder Venerable Mahinda and Venerable Sanghamitra, the son and daughter of King Asoka. These orders were subsequently brought to China during the 3rd and 5th century respectively.

To Buddhism, the bhiksu and bhiksuni orders are like the legs of a person or the

Full Ordination Ceremony for Bhikshuni.

wings of a bird. Through generations, they have played an important role to facilitate the propagation of Dharma around the world. However, the bhiksuni order in her motherland was interrupted by foreign invaders. In Sri Lanka, it also ceased to exist with the fall of Anuradhapura during the 11th century. Thus, Buddhism has lost half of its propagational force.

Today, as we face the challenge of the twenty-first century, it is crucial for Buddhists to return to the epoch of the Buddha and to strengthen the spread of Buddhism. Thus, to repay their gratitude, all the Sangha members must work in cooperation to restore the bhiksuni order in India and Sri Lanka.

From May 5 to 9, the 4th International Monastic Seminar was held at Fo Kuang Shan in Taiwan. During the seminar, participants - monastic and lay, from the Theravada, Mahayana and Vajrayana traditions jointly requested by signature to invite Venerable Master Hsing Yun, the founder of Fokuangshan Buddhist Order to hold a higher ordination for bhiksuni in Bodhgaya, India.

In gratitude for having received the bhiksuni lineage from Indian and Sri Lankan's missionaries, the Chinese feel that it is their duty to return the lost bhiksuni lineage to their ancestral lands. As such, Fo Kuang Shan has accepted the invitation to sponsor a higher ordination at the most sacred place in India - Bodhgaya. This, thereore, will allow nuns living in such countries as India, Sri Lanka, Nepal, Bhutan, Thailand, western conutries and so on to have the opportunity to take higher ordination.

The ordination at Bodhgaya will be in accordance with one of the original Indian traditions, abiding by the Dharmagupta Pratimoksa. Nuns will take dual ordination from both orders.

Full ordination Ceremony for Bhikshuni.

Eligibility

Buddhist novices between the ages of 20 to 55 who have full use of their six sense organs and have right thought and clear understanding are welcome to apply.

Application Requirements

(1) Filled out application form.
(2) Photocopy of passport or official identity card.
(3) Two recent passport-sized photographs.
(4) Medical reports from a doctor or hospital showing that you are in good health.
(5) Upon approval, notification letter will be sent to you.

Expenses

(1) Three robes (kasaya), alms-bowl, meals and accommodation during the ordination are provided free by the sponsors. (You may bring your own traditions robe if you so desire).
(2) Bear your own airfare. (Candidates who have financial problems may apply for sponsorship of airfare. Acceptance of such a request will be informed separately).
(3) Arrange your own visa application.

Date of Ordination
February 15 to 23, 1998

Venue of Ordination

The Chinese Temple, Bodhgaya, Gaya, Bihar, India

Date of Application

Now opened till October 31, 1997

Correspondence Address

Attn: Ven. Bhiksuni Chueh Men

Bodhgaya International
Full Ordination Organizing Committee
c/o Asian Buddhist Cultural Center
Temple Street, Bodhgaya, Gaya,
Bihar, India

Tel:91-631-400478
Fax:91-631-400824

Note:

The ceremony will be conducted in Chinese with English interpretation. Senior Acaryas from both Theravada and Mahayana traditions are invited to witness the ceremony, and also to give advice and blessings.

Invitation to participate in the Full Ordination Ceremony.

Posters on the fence of the Chinese Temple with information on the reintroduction of the nun tradition.

Posters on the fence of the Chinese Temple with information on the reintroduction of the nun tradition.

INDIA

Hit the Buddhist trail on the tracks of divinity.

BAUDDHA PARIKRAMA

TOURIST TRAIN

Let the divinity in you come out as you follow the trail of the Buddha's footsteps in his own land.
On board the Bauddha Parikrama Special Train - a joint venture between Indian Railways & India Tourism Development Corporation.
Starting its exciting journey from Howrah Station every Thursday w.e.f. 22nd October '98, the train will take you along the Buddhist Circuit - Gorakhpur, Varanasi, Rajgir, Gaya & then back to Howrah.
What's more, the 5 nights & 6 days journey includes unforgettable sightseeings, guided visits to historical monuments & delicious meals in-between. All these for an attractive all inclusive tariff of US $ 379 onwards or equivalent per person!

Announcement by the Indian Railways of the introduction of a seasonal special train called 'Bauddha Parikrama' going to the Buddhist sites.

GRAND INAUGURATION

by

Shri Nitish Kumar,

Hon'ble Minister for Railways

9:00 pm on 23rd October 98

at

Gorakhpur Railway Station, North Eastern Railway.

Chief Guest : **Shri Madan Lal Khurana,**

Hon'ble Minister for Tourism & Parliamentary Affairs.

Guest of Honour : **Shri Kalraj Misra,**

Hon'ble Minister for Public Works Department & Tourism, Government of U.P.

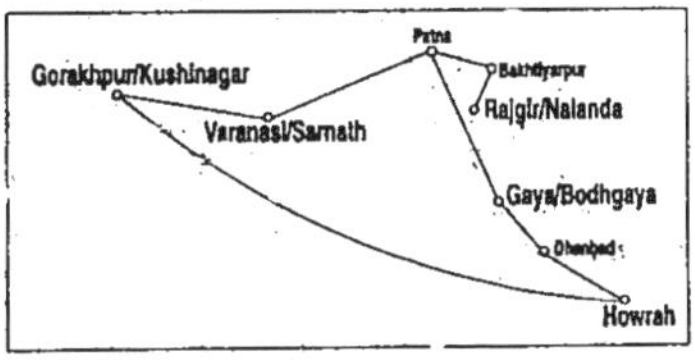

Howrah	Dep. 1200 hrs	(1st day)
Gorakhpur	Arr. 500 hrs – Dep. 2200 hrs	(2nd day)
Varanasi	Arr. 500 hrs – Dep. 2200 hrs	(3rd day)
Rajgir	Arr. 500 hrs – Dep. 2230 hrs	(4th day)
Gaya	Arr. 430 hrs – Dep. 2100 hrs	(5th day)
Howrah	Arr. 500 hrs	(6th day)

TRAIN DEPARTURE DATES :-

22nd & 29th October '98 • 5th, 12th, 19th & 26th November '98 •
3rd, 10th, 17th, 24th & 31st December '98 • 7th, 14th, 21st & 28th January '99
4th, 11th, 18th & 25th February '99 • 4th, 11th, 18th & 25th March '99 • 1st, 8th & 15th April '99

For reservations, please contact :-
Ashok Travels & Tours,
India Tourism Development Corporation
3rd Floor, New Delhi House, 27, Barakhamba Road, New Delhi-110001, India
Tel. : 91-11-3313233/3715917/3325035, Fax : 91-11-3324905
Website : http : // www.indiatourism.com, E-mail : reservation@indiatourism.com

INDIAN RAILWAYS

On the Buddha's trail. By rail !

Announcement by the Indian Railways of the introduction of a seasonal special train called 'Bauddha Parikrama' going to the Buddhist sites.

"All comfort,
happiness and peace
in this world are received
by making offerings
to the triple gem"

- Kshitigarbha Sutra

Root Institute
for Wisdom Culture

P.O. Bodhgaya
Distt. Gaya
Bihar 824231
India
Tel.: 00 91 631 400714
Fax: 00 91 631 400548

Foundation for the Preservation
of the Mahayana Tradition

(Approved by FPMT Board Remote Meeting)

One Million Lights
at Losar

Those who offer one thousand lights
or 1000 blue Utpali flowers or make the
pinnacle of a stupa, or who make
the holy form will be reborn when
Maitreya Buddha shows the deed of
gaining enlightenment
and receive his first Dharma teaching

- Arya Maitreya Sutra

Foundation for the Preservation of the Mahayana Tradition.

During the first 15 days of Losar, Shakyamuni Buddha performed a host of miracles to increase the faith of his followers. Any virtuous action performed at this time is increased one hundred thousand times.

Each Losar, Root Institute for Wisdom Culture celebrates this event with an offering of over one million lights at the seat of enlightenment, the Great Stupa of Bodhgaya. We also perform Shakyamuni

pujas, Tara pujas , Guru pujas and Protector pujas with the monks of the Bodhgaya Gelugpa Gompa.

The merit created by this vast offering and pujas will be dedicated in the following way...

"May the sponsor's of this offering, their families and all sentient beings never be separated from the pure complete path admired by the Buddhas and may they achieve every happiness and perfect enlightenment.

May His Holiness the Dalai Lama, Lama Thubten Zopa Rinpoche, Lama Tenzin Osel Rinpoche and all our holy Gurus have long lives and remain to teach us until samsara ends."

The dedications and sponsors' names will be read daily at the Bodhgaya Stupa during the offering.

We invite you all to participate in this great event. Please see the attached form for details of how to sponsor Lights and Pujas.

Any donations remaining after the costs of the offering have been covered, will go towards supporting Root Institute for Wisdom Culture, Lama Zopa Rinpoche's centre in Bodhgaya.
Root Institute is a socially engaged Dharma centre offering free medical aid and education to the under privileged of Bihar, India's poorest region.

Appeal of the Foundation for the Preservation of the Mahayana Tradition to Support the Losar Light Puja.

To sponsor lights or pujas, please send cheque or money order in US $ or credit card details with the attached form to:

FPMT Central Office
P.O. Box 1778
Soquel CA. 95073 USA
Fax: 001 408 476 4823

NB. Forms should be forwarded to arrive before February 8th

Requested sponsorship rates in US $

1000 lights	$20
7000 lights	$80
21,000 lights	$200
54,000 lights	$400
108,000 lights	$700
Pujas	$30 each

This year Losar offering February 8th - 22nd

Wishing you a
Very Happy Losar

To FPMT Central Office

I would like to sponsor .... lights this Losar, as well as

☐ Tara Puja ☐ Shakyamuni Puja
☐ Guru Puja ☐ Protector Puja

Name ....
Address ....
....
Country ....
Enclosed is my cheque / money order
for US $ ....
Please charge my credit card
VISA / AMEX / MASTERCARD
Number..
Signed..
Expires..

(Multiple Sponsors
please attach list of names)
....
....

Specific dedication (if any)
....
....
....
....
....

Appeal of the Foundation for the Preservation of the Mahayana Tradition to Support the Losar Light Puja.

CHAPTER FOUR

Nagpur as the 'Central Place' of New Buddhism

On 13 October 1935, Dr Ambedkar declared for the first time (Ahir, 1988: 14) that he would not die a Hindu: 'Unfortunately, I was born a Hindu. It was beyond my power to prevent that, but I solemnly assure you that I will not die a Hindu.'

In 1954, Dr Ambedkar made the final decision to declare his faith in Buddhism formally and to seek refuge publicly in 1956, the 2500th year after the Buddha entered into Mahaparinirvana (according to the Theravada tradition at the full moon in May 544 BC), which was celebrated worldwide as Buddha Jayanti. He came to this decision in Mandalay, which he visited on the occasion of his participation in the Third Conference of the World Fellowship of Buddhists in Rangoon. As the date he chose 14 October, Vijaya Dashami:

> This day was chosen as it was the auspicious day of 'Dhamma Vijaya', the day on which Asoka the Great had embraced Buddism in B.C. 262 and had declared that henceforth he would conquer the people by love and persuasion instead of by force. (Ahir, 1988: 106)

Nagpur was chosen as the place for this historic event because the Nagas were in Ambedkar's opinion the ones who more than others helped to spread Buddhism in India. He said in this respect:

> Those who have studied the Buddhist history of India know that the people who worked in the beginning for the propagation of the religion of Buddha were the 'Nagas'. It were the Nagas who spread the religion of the Buddha throughout the world. These people were predominantly the inhabitants of Nagpur. Through the soil of this city there flowed a river named the 'Nag'. It appears that the Nagas lived on the banks of this river. This is mainly the reason for selecting Nagpur for this great occasion. (Ahir, 1988: 107)

Sangharakshita has given us a detailed analysis of the ceremony and its surroundings (1986: 127–44). Here, however, I will follow the short report of another eyewitness, who describes it in this way:

> On the bright morning of Sunday, 14 October 1956, lakhs of people, men and women, who had been pouring into the Nagpur city by train and bus from all parts of Maharashtra or had trekked on foot hundreds of miles, prepared themselves for the ceremony wearing white clothes. Procession after procession of white-clad men and women with Buddhist flags in their hands made their way to the Deeksha Bhoomi or the Initiation Ground. By 9 a.m. they had reached the site and turned into a vast ocean of humanity.
>
> When Babasaheb Ambedkar, accompanied by his wife, and N.C. Rattu, his private secretary, reached the pandal, the vast crowd lustily cheered their uncrowned king. Wearing the white silk dhoti and white coat, he was seated at the dias next to the Venerable U Chandramani Maha Thera, the oldest and seniormost Buddhist monk in India. Seated in the second row were Devapriya Valisinha, General Secretary of the Maha Bodhi Society of India, Venerable monks, and some leading members of the Buddhist Society of India founded by Babasaheb. About four lakhs of people witnessed the auspicious ceremony which began at 9.40 a.m. The 80-year old Ven. U Chandramani of Kushinagar administered in Pali to Dr. Ambedkar and his wife, the Tisarana (Triple-Refuge). Standing solemnly before the shining image of Lord Buddha, they recited three times, 'Buddham saranam gacchami, Dhammam saranam gacchami, Sangham saranam gacchami'. The three Refuges were followed by the Five Precepts (Panca-Sila). They repeated the same in Marathi. Then they bowed thrice with clasped hands before the Buddha image and offered white lotus flowers before it. With this, the conversion ceremony was over. When Dr. Ambedkar's entry into Buddhism was announced, the vast concourse of humanity gathered there gave thunderous applause and raised full-throated cries of 'Victory to Lord Buddha', 'Victory to Babasaheb Ambedkar'. Thereafter, Dr. Ambedkar was profusely garlanded by D. Valisinha and other dignitaries present there.
>
> The historic Nagpur ceremony marked the end of a pilgrim's journey. Addressing the vast gathering, Dr. Ambedkar, now a Buddhist, said in an emotional voice: 'I started the movement of renouncing the Hindu religion in 1935 and since then I have been continuously struggling. This conversion has given me enormous satisfaction and pleasure unimaginable. I feel as if I have been liberated from hell.' (Ahir, 1989: 145-6)

After Ambedkar and his wife publicly took refuge, the mass conversion followed: several hundred thousands rose and repeated the Threefold Refuge and the Five Shila that Ambedkar had just recited. Then, however, they also repeated the twenty-two vows composed by Ambedkar (see page 26) in order to emphasize that for him as well for as his followers the turning towards Buddhism at first meant a turning away from Hinduism.

Trailokya Bauddha Mahasangha Sahayak Gana and Bahujan Hitay celebrate DR. AMBEDKAR CENTENARY YEAR APRIL 14th, 1990 – APRIL 14th, 1991

Dr. Ambedkar's conversion to Buddhism in 1956

Guided by U. Chandramani, Dr Ambedkar and his wife take refuge in the Buddha, the *dhamma*, and the *sangha*.

On the next day, 15 October 1956, again more than one thousand people, who on the previous day had not reached Nagpur in time for the ceremony, followed their Babasaheb and repeated the refuges and the twenty-two vows. Afterwards, Ambedkar gave an improvised talk lasting more than three hours (for excerpts in English translation see Ahir, 1997: 115–33). In this speech, Ambedkar marked the path of suffering for himself and his caste brothers and sisters, a path that all other Untouchable Hindus had to walk before they were finally born 'new' as Buddhists.

Four weeks after this spectacular mass conversion, Dr Ambedkar participated in the Fourth Conference of the World Fellowship of Buddhists, 15–21 November, in Kathmandu, and addressed the delegates who enthusiastically honoured him as the new founder of Buddhism in India. He spoke to them about Buddhism and Communism, an up to date topic during the Cold War (for the text see Ahir, 1997: 135–43). On his way home, on 23 November 1956, he visited Bodh Gaya—for the first time as a Buddhist pilgrim. However, he continued his journey on the same day by train to Sarnath. There, he stayed three days and visited the Buddhist memorials and the Mulagandhakuti Vihara. More than 150 monks from various countries in Asia had gathered for his visit, and he urged them to become aware of their new task of conveying the *dhamma* to India. On 27 November, he flew from Sarnath to Gorakhpur and from there visited the Mahaparinirvana temple in Kushinagar. On 29 November, he returned to Delhi where he died in the early morning of 6 December 1956. His body was taken to Bombay (Mumbai) and was cremated there on 7 December in accordance with Buddhist rituals:

> More than 500,000 people joined the funeral procession, the biggest such procession ever seen in the city of Bombay, and it took nearly four hours to cover a two mile distance from Rajgraha, his residence, in Dadar to the local burning ghat, near Shivaji Park. Babasaheb had planned a mass conversion ceremony in Bombay on 16 December. To fulfill this wish, about 100,000 people insisted that they be admitted into the fold of Buddhism. Hence, an impromptu conversion ceremony was organised at the cremation ground, and they were administered the Three Refuges and Five Precepts on the spot by Bhadant Anand Kausalyayan. (Ahir, 1989: 150–1)

Soon after his death, the followers of Ambedkar requested that a memorial honouring him and the historic event of the mass conversion be erected in Nagpur. On 30 May 1961, Y.B. Chavan, Chief Minister of Maharashtra, entrusted the 12-acre area on which the ceremony of conversion had taken place to the Dr Babasaheb Smarak Samiti of Nagpur so that the work on the memorial could begin:

In 1963, a bust of Dr. Ambedkar was installed at the historic site standing where he had embraced Buddhism, and given a clarion call to his people to do so. The grand Memorial Stupa which had been under construction at Deeksha for more than 30 years has since been completed, and is the greatest land mark in the architectural heritage of Nagpur. Dr. Babasaheb Memorial College established at Deeksha Bhoomi in 1964 has since become a premier educational institution.

The Deeksha Bhoomi also has a Buddha Vihara, Bhikkhu Niwas, and a flourishing Bodhi Tree, all established by Bhadant Anand Kausalyayan, a Punjabi Buddhist monk, who stayed at Deeksha Bhoomi from 1969 to 1982, and greatly made Deeksha Bhoomi a living religious centre.

Nagpur, the capital of neo-Buddhist movement initiated by Dr. Ambedkar in 1956, has now over 40 Buddha Viharas. (Ahir, 1998: 1992–3)

Thus, Nagpur became the central place of the New Buddhist movement. Looking back, it is understandable that Buddhists from Maharashtra—and only there does one meet Buddhists in today's India in significant numbers—rarely travel to distant Bodh Gaya in the state of Bihar. In 1991, Bihar had 86.3 million inhabitants of whom merely 3,518 were Buddhists. In 1971, the number had been 4,806 Buddhists (see the chart on page 20). The name Bihar still reminds one of the time when the area was home to many *viharas*, but today the name stands for economic backwardness and deprivation. Here we find gangs of 'landed gentry' which can perform acts of retaliation against Untouchables should they dare to demand legal rights. On 1 December 1997, the massacre of Lakshmanpur-Bathe took place where, under cover of darkness, the quarters of the Untouchables were destroyed and more than 70 people were murdered (*Dalit International Newsletter*, Vol. 3, No. 1, February 1998).

Bodh Gaya is generally worshipped as a holy place of Buddhism; however, the centre of the new religious identity of New Buddhists lies in Nagpur. Here began the rebirth of the followers of Babasaheb.

It must be added that the educational institutions run by the People's Education Society, founded by Dr Ambedkar in 1945, enabled their social rise. The impressive story of the founding and the success of the People's Education Society has been described by D.L. Ramteke (1983: 221–6) and recently also by Jayashree Gokhale (1993: 195–205). Here I want to refer to the short description given in 1991 by R.R. Bhole as president of the society on the occasion of the centenary celebrations of Dr Ambedkar's birth on the campus of the Milind College of Science, called Nagasena Vana, of the Milinda Mahavidyalaya in Aurangabad (see pages 121-3).

Birth Centenary
of
Dr. Babasaheb Ambedkar

Founder, People's Education Society, Bombay

14th April 1891 **14th April 1991**

Photo of Dr Ambedkar, *c.* 1954.

After creating the first higher educational institutions for the specific advancement of members of the backward classes and the Scheduled Castes in Bombay, Ambedkar decided that Aurangabad should become a new centre for the educational work of the People's Education Society. Aurangabad was situated at that time in a region ruled by the Nizam of Hyderabad, and was considered especially backward. However, Ambedkar's decision was also based on the fact that Aurangabad was a centre of the glorious past of Buddhism in Maharashtra. It is not far from the world famous cave temples of Ellora and Ajanta, and only 8 km north of the city are twelve less-known but nevertheless impressive rock monasteries created between the second and the seventh centuries AD which testify to the former influence of Buddhism (Ahir, 1988: 56–8) in the surrounding areas.

The foundation stone for the Milinda Mahavidyalaya was placed on 1 September 1951 by Rajendra Prasad, the first President of independent India. The name Milinda Mahavidyalaya was inspired by the Greek king Milinda, whose skeptical questions to the Buddhist monk Nagasena belong to the classical Pali canon. The students of the new university on the Nagasena Vana campus were to be educated in this same critical spirit (see the *Milindapanha*, 1985). In his celebratory address, Dr Ambedkar commented on the central role of education:

> Coming as I do from the lowest order of the Hindu Society, I know what is the value of education. The problem of raising the lower order is deemed to be economic. This is a great mistake. The problem of raising the lower order in India is not to feed them, to clothe them and to make them serve the higher classes as the ancient ideal of this country. The problem of the lower order is to remove from them that inferiority complex which has stunted their growth and made them slaves to others, to create in them the consciousness of the significance of their lives for themselves and for the country, of which they have been cruelly robbed by the existing social order. Nothing can achieve this purpose except the spread of higher education. This is in my opinion the panacea of our social troubles. (Ramteke, 1983: 223–4)

Today, Babasaheb Ambedkar is worshipped by some of his followers as a Bodhisattva, even on the campus of the Milinda Mahavidyalaya (see plate on p. 118). However, for professors as well as students, the message of 'Educate, Agitate, and Organize' (see plates on pages 123 and 124) is possibly even more important than his instructions for religious emancipation from the fetters of Hinduism.

Entirely in this spirit, official India too celebrated Dr Ambedkar. In 1990, he was posthumously awarded the highest national award, the

पीपल्स एज्युकेशन सोसायटी (मुंबई) चे
संस्थापक

भारतरत्न बोधिसत्व डॉ. बाबासाहेब आंबेडकर

M.A.,Ph.D.,D.Sc. (London), L.L.D. (Columbia), D.Litt. (Osmania), Barristor-At-Law.

जन्म
१४ एप्रिल १८९१

महापरिनिर्वाण
६ डिसेंबर १९५६

Bharat Ratna Bodhisattva Dr Babasaheb Ambedkar, born on 14 April 1891, Parinirvana on 6 December 1956.

Bharat Ratna (Jewel of India) as chief architect of the Indian Constitution, and on the centenary of his birth, on 21 April 1991, a life-size bust was unveiled in the central hall of the Parliament in New Delhi. A brochure of the Ministry of Information and Broadcasting was published later which shows how Dr Ambedkar has been integrated into the semi-official historiography of the nation (see pp. 125-34). The special challenge which he represented to the nation as the founder of a new religious movement was pushed into the background in this way. But how did he himself see the future role of the *sangha*? How is the *sangha* organized today? How far do the members do justice to the new duties which Ambedkar wanted them to undertake?

Dr Ambedkar hands over the Constitution of independent India to the President, Rajendra Prasad.

MR. R. R. BHOLE,
Chairman,
PEOPLE'S EDUCATION SOCIETY, BOMBAY.

Till 1956

At the time when Babasheb passed away in 1956 our Society was conducting the following Institutions and building the Foundation of the Democratic and Socialistic set up our country by making the unprivileged aware of their self respect, human rights and liberties :

1. Siddharth College of Arts & Science, Bombay.
2. Siddharth College of Commerce and Economics, Bombay
3. Siddharth College of Law, Bombay.
4. Milind Mahavidyalaya Aurangabad.
5. Milind Multipurpose High School, Aurangabad.
6. Siddharth Night High School Bombay.
7. Sant Gadge Maharaj Vidyarthi Vasatigriha, Pandharpur.

After 1956 Institutions and our own Buildings

After 1956 our Society continued its activities to the weaker and Backward people of our country and has now added more Institutions all over Maharashtra as well as at Banglore and are running Colleges in many buildings controlled by us of many faculties, Vocational Courses, High Schools, Hostels, Laboratories, Libraries etc. and has also purchased large areas of Land for the purpose at different places. After the Mahaparinirwan of Dr. Babasaheb Ambedkar we have, among other assets, added after purchase and construction at high costs the followings :

Bombay

1. Siddharth College of Mass Communication, Bombay.
2. Siddharth Institute of Industry and Administration, Bombay.
3. Dr. Ambedkar College of Commerce and Economices, Wadala, Bombay.
4. Dr. Ambedkar College of Law Wadala, Bombay.
5. Siddharth English School, Wadala, Bombay.
6. Siddhartha Vihar Hostel, Wadala, Bombay.

New Bombay

1. Dr. Babasaheb Ambedkar Public School in an acquired high cost building
2. PES's Jr. College of Education
3. PES's Marathi Medium Secandary School and Jr. College in another required high cost big building
4. PES's Marathi Medium Primary School.

Educational Institutions of the People's Education Society.

Aurangabad

Were Baba wanted the Capital to be because it is Central and more secure :

1. Milind College of Science
2. Laboratory Building for Milind College of Arts
3. Dr. Babasaheb Ambedkar College of Arts and Commerce, Aurangabad : Constructed is Hostel Library and Canteen buildings and Residential Quarters for its staff members.
4. Hostel for Working Women
5. Dr Ambedkar College of Law
6. College of Physical Education with all Gymkhana arrangements.
7. Matoshri Ramabai Ambedkar High School after acquiring large area of land and constructing a building :
8. College Girls Hostel
9. Rang Bhavan Auditorium
10. Milind Primary School

Mahad

Where Baba burnt to ashes Manusmriti, which enslaved the untouchables; and where Baba first fired the gun for struggle of human liberty for Untouchables by drinking water in the Common Tanks :

1. Dr. Babasaheb Ambedkar College of Arts, Science and Commerce with its Hostel building
2. Subedar Sawadkar Vidyarthi Ashram.

Pune

Where Baba signed the Poona Pact with Mahatma Gandhi which were then recognised for first time the Scheduled Castes as a separate entity and their right to separate seats reserved in Legislature first time in thousands of years in Federal India :

1. Dr. Ambedkar College of Arts and Commerce
2. PES's Pre-Primary, Primary and Secondary School

Nanded

1. Nagsen Vidyalaya and Jr. College
2. Negsen Primary School

Pandharpur

Blessings from Ghatge Maharaj.

1. Gautam Vidyalaya

Banglore

Where Baba desired to establish Buddhist Seminary and Institute for spreading Buddhism in India :

1 Nagasena Vidyalaya
2 Seminary and Institute of Research (Foundation laid)

All this service is dedicated to the sacred cause of Baba by us with the active and dedicated assistance of all the Heads of the Institutions and their staff.

Educational Institutions of the People's Education Society.

An Appeal

April the 14th, 1891 will remain a GOLDEN LETTER DAY in the annals of Indian history. It was on this day that Dr. B. R. Ambedkar, popularly known to millions as Dr. Babasahab Ambedkar was born to give the millions of oppressed masses of India a new vision of self-respect, self-reliance and self-identity which was denied to them for centuries.

A political leader, a social revolutionary, a religious evangelist. Dr. Babasaheb Ambedkar has left the impress of his powerful personality on several spheres of activity. As the first Law Minister of Free India, he was the architect of the Constitution of India which is a permanent monument to his legal genius.

He played many important parts on the stage of life. His popular image as an iconoclast represented only a part of his personality; for he was also a constructive statesman, who regarded education as a nation-building activity.

With the true vision of a sage, he founded the People's Education Society on the 8th of July 1945, the purpose of which he set out is as follows :

> "The People's Education Society's objective is not merely to give education, but to give education in such a manner as to promote intellectual, moral and social democracy. This is what modern India needs and this is what all well wishers of India must promote."

He firmly believed that education was the only effective lever for the uplift of the down-trodden.

As an educationist, Babasaheb has carved an abiding niche for himself in the temple of fame. He firmly believed that it was only through education the suffering Indian masses could be made conscious of their rights as human beings. He said to his people :

> "My final words of advice to you is educate, agitate and organise, have faith in yourself. With justice on our side, I do not see how we can lose our battle. It is a battle for freedom. It is a battle for the reclamation of the human personality."

Under its well-spread umbrella, People's Education Society runs 12 University affiliated Colleges, 6 of which are affiliated to the University of Bombay, 5 to the Marathwada University and one to University of Pune imparting University education to as many as 30,000 students of whom over 15,000 belong to the under privileged Classes. Besides these, the Society runs many High Schools, Diploma Institutes and Hostels.

Ambedkar's legacy to the youth: 'Educate, Agitate, and Organize'.

Ambedkar's legacy in Hindi as postcard.

Ministry of Information and Broadcasting
(Government of India) Brochure:
Bharat Ratna Babasaheb Dr Bhimrao Ambedkar as architect of social justice from the official point of view.

Bharat Ratna Dr Bhimrao Ambedkar

In 1990, the Bharat Ratna was presented to late Dr Bhimrao Ambedkar, chief architect of the Indian Constitution. The same year Dr Ambedkar's life-size portrait was also unveiled in the Central Hall of Parliament. The period from 14th April, 1990 to 14th April, 1991 was observed as 'Year of Social Justice' in the memory of 'Babasaheb', the champion of the poor and downtrodden.

Genius Par Excellence

Dr Bhimrao Ambedkar was born on 14th April, 1891 in Mahu Cantt in Madhya Pradesh. He was the fourteenth child of his parents. Young Bhimrao's father, who was serving in the Indian Army at the time, constantly encouraged his children, specially Bhimrao to pursue his studies.

The life of Dr Bhimrao Ambedkar was marked by struggles but he demonstrated that every hurdle in life can be surmounted with talent and a firm determination. The biggest barrier in his life was the caste system of Hindu society for which the family in which he was born was considered as 'untouchable'.

In the year 1908, young Bhimrao passed the Matriculation examination from Bombay University with flying colours. It was a unique and rare accomplishment for an 'untouchable' child, which led to his being felicitated at a public meeting.

Four years later, he graduated in Political Science and Economics from Bombay University and got a job

Ministry of Information and Broadcasting
(Government of India) Brochure.

in Baroda. Around the same time his father passed away. Although in a sad state of mind, Bhimrao decided to accept the opportunity to go to U.S.A. for study at Columbia University for which he was awarded a scholarship by the Maharaja of Baroda. This achievement was unprecedented but he did not let matters rest there. He was of the firm view that knowledge was power and without this power he could not break the shackles which forced millions of 'untouchables' to live in virtual slavery. By this time he had personal experience of this and had realized that these shackles were quite formidable.

Bhimrao remained abroad from 1913 to 1917 and again from 1920 to 1923 and when he finally returned to India he was thirty two years old. During this period he had established himself as an eminent intellectual. Columbia University had awarded him the Ph. D for his thesis which was later published in a book form under the title "The Evolution of Provincial Finance in British India". But his first published article was "Castes in India - Their Mechanism, Genesis and Development." He presented this paper at a seminar on Anthropology. During his sojourn in London from 1920 to1923, he also completed his thesis titled "The Problem of the Rupee" for which he was awarded the degree of D.Sc. Before his departure for London he had taught at a college in Bombay and also brought out a Marathi weekly whose title was, 'Mook Nayak' (meaning 'Dumb Hero').

By the time he returned to India in April 1923, Dr Bhimrao Ambedkar had equipped himself fully for waging a war against the practice of untouchability on

Ministry of Information and Broadcasting
(Government of India) Brochure.

behalf of the 'untouchables' and the downtrodden. In the meanwhile the political situation in India had undergone substantial changes and the freedom struggle in the country had made significant progress. From then onwards till the achievement of Independence in 1947, Dr. Ambedkar's life is intricately linked to the history of modern India.

Saviour of the downtrodden

While Bhimrao was an ardent patriot on one hand, he was also the saviour of the oppressed, women and poor on the other. He fought for them throughout his life. In 1923, he set up the "Bahishkrit Hitakarini Sabha" (Outcastes' Welfare Council) which was devoted to spreading education and culture amongst the downtrodden, improving their economic status and raising matters concerning their problems in the proper forums to focus attention on them and finding solutions to them.

The problems of the downtrodden were centuries old and difficult to overcome. Their entry into temples was forbidden. They could not draw water from public wells and ponds. Their admission in schools were prohibited. Between 1927 and 1932 Dr Bhimrao launched a non-violent but resolute movement to secure the right of entry into places of worship and for drawing water from public wells and ponds. Two of these agitations were noteworthy. In 1927, he led the Mahad march at the Chowdar Tank in Colaba, near Bombay, to give the 'untouchables' the right to draw water from the public tank where he burnt copies of the "Manusmriti" publicly. This marked the beginning of

Ministry of Information and Broadcasting
(Government of India) Brochure.

the anti-caste and anti-priest movement. The temple entry movement launched by Dr. Ambedkar in 1930 at Kalaram Temple, Nasik is another landmark in the struggle for human rights and social justice.

In the meantime, Ramsay McDonald announced the 'Communal Award' as a result of which in the following year several communities including the 'depressed classes' were given the right to have separate electorates. This was a part of the overall design of the British to divide and rule. Gandhiji wanted to defeat this design and went on a fast unto death to oppose it.

On 24th September, 1932 Dr Ambedkar and Gandhiji arrived at an understanding which became the famous Poona Pact. According to this pact, in addition to the agreement on electoral constituencies, reservations were provided for 'untouchables' in Government jobs and legislative assemblies. The provision of separate electorates was dispensed with. Commenting upon the circumstances under which he had to accept this compromise Dr. Ambedkar said in one of his books, "I had two options before me. One was to protect the 'untouchables' and the rights granted to them by the British Prime Minister, Ramsay McDonald in the Communal Award and the other was to save the life of Mahatma Gandhi as a member of human society. I accepted the voice of humanity and saved the life of Mahatma Gandhi by agreeing to such modifications in the Communal Award as would satisfy him". Despite this, Dr. Ambedkar was misunderstood and maligned by both supporters and detractors of the Communal Award.

Ministry of Information and Broadcasting
(Government of India) Brochure.

Thus the Communal Award was modified by the Poona Pact which carved a clear and definite position for the downtrodden on the political scene of the country. It opened up opportunities of education and government service for them and also gave them the right to vote.

Dr Ambedkar criticised British rule and made relentless efforts to remove social, economic, educational and legal bottlenecks for the benefit of the downtrodden. He was convinced that the interests of the downtrodden can be protected only by creating separate constituencies even if it was only for a limited period. This was the cause of his conflict with Gandhiji and the Congress party. In 1932 these differences came into the open and were eventually resolved in the Poona Pact.

Dr Ambedkar attended all the three Round Table Conferences in London and, always, forcefully projected his views in the interests of the 'untouchables'. He exhorted the downtrodden sections to raise their living standards and to acquire as much political power as possible. He was of the view that there was no future for 'untouchables' in the Hindu religion and they should change their religion, if need be. In 1935, he publicly proclaimed "I was born a Hindu because I had no control over this but I shall not die a Hindu". He, thus, hinted at his desire for conversion to Buddhism. The same year he was appointed principal of Government Law College, Bombay. It was also the year that he lost his wife.

Formation of Independent Labour Party

After a while Dr Ambedkar organised the

Ministry of Information and Broadcasting
(Government of India) Brochure.

Independent Labour Party, participated in the provincial elections and was elected to the Bombay Legislative Assembly. During these days, he stressed the need for abolition of the 'Jagirdari' system, pleaded for workers' right to strike and addressed a large number of meetings and conferences in Bombay Presidency. In 1939, during the second world war, he called upon Indians to join the army in large numbers to defeat Nazism which, he said, was another name for Fascism.

In 1947, when India became independent, the first Prime Minister, Shri Jawaharlal Nehru, invited Dr Ambedkar, who had been elected as a member of the Constituent Assembly from Bengal, to join his cabinet as Law Minister. The Constituent Assembly entrusted the job of drafting the Constitution to a Committee and Dr. Ambedkar was elected Chairman of this Drafting Committee. While he was busy with drafting the Constitution, India faced several crises: The country had been partitioned and Mahatma Gandhi had been assassinated.

Architect of Constitution

In the beginning of 1948 Dr Ambedkar completed the draft of the Constitution and presented it before the Constituent Assembly. In November 1949 this draft was adopted with very few amendments. Many provisions have been made in the Constitution to ensure social justice for scheduled castes, scheduled tribes and backward classes. In this context Articles 15, 16, 27, 46, 332, 335, 338 and 340 are significant.

Dr Ambedkar was of the opinion that traditional religious values should be given up and new ideas be

Ministry of Information and Broadcasting
(Government of India) Brochure.

adopted. He gave special emphasis on dignity, unity, freedom and rights for all citizens as enshrined in the Constitution.

Dr Ambedkar advocated democracy in every field: social, economic and political. For him social justice meant maximum happiness to the maximum number of people. He gave utmost importance to individual dignity in his concept of democracy.

Dr Ambedkar wanted more powers to be given the Centre to strengthen the unity and sovereignty of the country. He wanted to safeguard the territorial integrity of India. He said that Indian society is divided not only by castes and communities but, also, there are regional, linguistic, traditional, cultural and ideological differences. Therefore, for territorial integrity and administrative discipline, a strong Centre is absolutely essential.

Dr Ambedkar favoured small linguistic states as opposed to multi-lingual states. He wanted the creation of linguistic states to be governed by certain conditions like (1) there should be only one language in the state, (2) linguistic states should be economically viable, (3) the official language of every state should be Hindi and as long as Hindi is not capable of attaining this status English should continue.

In the pages of history Dr Ambedkar is remembered as the chief architect of the Constitution. His life size statue in Parliament would always keep his memory alive in this role.

Re-exponent of Buddhism

Dr Ambedkar had differences of opinion with the

Ministry of Information and Broadcasting
(Government of India) Brochure.

Government over the Hindu Code Bill which led to his resignation as Law Minister. On 24th May, 1956 on the occasion of Buddha Jayanti, he declared, in Bombay, that he would be ordained into Buddhism in October. On October 14, 1956 he embraced Buddhism along with many hundred thousands of his followers. The same year he completed his last writing "Buddha and his Dhamma". He devoted many years to the writing of this book and studied numerous scriptures on Buddhism. In this book he presented the teachings of Buddhism in their original form in a scientific way. This book has been translated and published in several Indian and foreign languages.

In a detailed analysis of the caste system Dr Ambedkar observed that it is neither based on the principle of division of labour nor on natural talents. Caste allocated work to people according to birth and not on the basis of their training and abilities. Caste of a person is determined by birth and the social status of the parents. The obnoxious principles on which the caste system is based breeds prejudice which inhibits change of vocation according to changing circumstances and, consequently, it generates unemployment. It also fosters the wrong notion that destiny is supreme and progress through hard work is impossible. He gave solid arguments to prove that the four 'varnas' and the caste system has handicapped a very large segment of India's population.

Dr Ambedkar's patriotism started with the uplift of the downtrodden and poor. He fought for their equality and rights. His ideas about partiotism were

Ministry of Information and Broadcasting
(Government of India) Brochure.

not only confined to the abolition of colonialism, but he wanted freedom for every individual. For him, freedom without equality means democracy is incomplete and equality without freedom could lead to absolute dictatorship. Therefore, he wanted a system that offered guarantee of both equality and freedom.

On 6th December, 1956 Baba Saheb Dr Bhimrao Ramji Ambedkar attained 'Mahaparinirvan'.

विदृप्रनि
davp

Designed and produced by the Directorate of Advertising and Visual Publicity, Ministry of Information and Broadcasting, Government of India, Printed at Gowardhan Kapur & Sons, New Delhi-110 064

No. 1/41/93 - PP III English 20,000 Nov. '93

CHAPTER FIVE

The Trailokya Bauddha Mahasangha Sahayak Gana

THE HISTORY of the development and the influence of the Friends of the Western Buddhist Order (FWBO) is sufficiently known (Dharmachari Subhuti, 1983) and need not be described here. What is interesting in the present context is the specific expression which the committed Lay Buddhism of the FWBO in the form of the TBMSG (Union of the Helpers of the Buddhist Great Order of the Three Worlds) helped to bring forth in India (for a recent and detailed study on this, see Alan Sponberg, 1996).

The charismatic attraction that Sangharakshita and the FWBO, which he founded in 1967 in London, still continue to have, particularly in the state of Maharashtra, goes back to the beginnings of the New Buddhist movement. Sangharakshita's description of his three meetings with Dr Ambedkar, however, also explains more easily a few of my own critical assessments concerning the position of the Maha Bodhi Society (see pages 60ff) which is still controlled by the Singhalese from Sri Lanka and by Hindus from north India. I will quote later a few longer passages from Sangharakshita's book (1986).

Sangharakshita was born as Dennis Lingwood in 1925 in London and came to India in 1944 as a lance corporal in the British army. Before this he had already declared his faith in Buddhism, and so, in 1945, he remained in India and began as a wandering *saddhu* his search for teachers. In 1949, he was accepted by U. Chandramani, the senior Theravada monk in India, as a novice and was fully ordained under the name Sangharakshita (protector of the *sangha*) in 1950. Following the advice of another teacher, the Ven. Jagdish Kashyap, a Professor of Pali at Benaras Hindu University, he moved to Kalimpong in order to do missionary work among the Nepalese Newars. He lived there for fifteen years and was, in addition to the Theravada tradition, initiated into the order of the Vajrayana. Before returning to England, he was thoroughly grounded in Tibetan Buddhism by Geshe Dhardo Rimpoche.

dr ambedkar & buddhism

In 1956, following the example of their great leader Dr Ambedkar - who was himself born an 'untouchable' - many ex-untouchables converted to Buddhism in order to leave behind the Hindu caste system. This decisive act inaugurated the movement of peaceful social and spiritual uplift within which Karuna is working today. Dr Ambedkar chose Buddhism because it has always been totally opposed to caste, has no place for blind belief or superstition, and encourages self-respect and compassion as the basis of a just and humane society.

One of Dr Ambedkar's key supporters was the English Buddhist Sangharakshita. After Ambedkar's sudden death in 1956, Sangharakshita became a leading figure in India working for the emancipation of the ex-untouchables. Karuna was set up as a partnership between Western and Indian disciples of Sangharakshita, all members of an international Buddhist order known in the West as the Western Buddhist Order.

BUDDHIST ACTIVITIES AND EFFECTIVE SOCIAL CHANGE
Karuna's work does not promote conversion to Buddhism and it is freely available to benefit Hindus, Muslims, Christians and Buddhists. However, following the example of Dr Ambedkar there are now over ten million Buddhists in India. Unfortunately, the vast majority have little or no opportunity to study and practise their new religion and culture – important if they are not to slip back into old caste attitudes. For those supporters of Karuna who agree, a proportion of their contribution goes towards funding specifically Buddhist activities.

The Mahavihar, Pune

RURAL RETREAT CENTRES
With the help of Buddhists and others from around the world Karuna has raised the funds for two retreat centres, one between Pune and Bombay, and the other near Nagpur in central India. These give men and women the chance to spend time in beautiful and peaceful settings away from the slum conditions they usually live in, and to gain inspiration from Dr Ambedkar's vision and the practice of Buddhism.

Dr Ambedkar's Buddhism and Sangharakshita's assistance.

In 1952, Sangharakshita met Dr Ambedkar for the first time. At that time he was still a young Theravada monk who had just completed a rather extensive work on Anagarika Dharmapala for the Maha Bodhi Society in Calcutta. He visited Dr Ambedkar in his office in Dadar, an area of Bombay, and had to wait a little until Dr Ambedkar had said goodbye to a group of petitioners:

When the delegation had departed Ambedkar seated himself behind his desk and, after we had exchanged the usual amenities, fixed me with an unfriendly stare, and demanded belligerently, 'Why does your Maha Bodhi Society have a Bengali Brahmin for its president?' The word Brahmin was not only emphasized but pronounced with such contempt and scorn that the whole Brahmin caste, as well as any organization so misguided as to have a Brahmin for its president, was at once consigned to a kind of moral dustbin. Realizing that Ambedkar took me for one of the Bhikkhus (mostly Sinhalese) who ran the Maha Bodhi Society's various pilgrim-centres, I hastened to make my position clear. It was not *my* Maha Bodhi Society, I explained. Though I was happy to help the Society in whatever way I could, I did not actually belong to it, and one of the reasons I did not belong to it was that it had a Brahmin for its President, as well as a Governing Body that was dominated by Caste Hindus who had no real interest in Buddhism. Some of the Buddhist members of the Society, I added, were no more satisfied with the present state of affairs than he was and both they and I hoped that before long we would be able to do something about it. This explanation appeared to mollify Ambedkar, and the fixed stare became less unfriendly. For my part, I not only sympathized with his question but knew why he had asked it with so much feeling. Not only was the President of the Maha Bodhi Society a Bengali Brahmin, but that Brahmin was also a former President of the Hindu Mahasabha, a right-wing Caste Hindu organization. (Sangharakshita, 1986: 18)

The second meeting again took place in Bombay and was much more relaxed. This time, Sangharakshita visited Dr Ambedkar in the rooms of Siddharth College in the centre of the city and had to give detailed information regarding the formalities for conversion to Buddhism. What was more, at the end of the conversation Ambedkar asked him as an official representative of the *sangha* to confirm him and his wife during the planned public celebration as Lay Buddhists:

We met in his office on the top floor of Buddha Bhavan, and on entering the book-lined room I found him seated behind his desk, with Mrs. Ambedkar standing beside him. He did not look very well and apologized for receiving me sitting down. He was suffering from arthritis, he explained, and this made standing up difficult. Whether because he was in pain, or for some other reason, he was much quieter and more subdued than he had been on the occasion of our first meeting, and seemed to have lost much of his belligerence. In the course of our discussion, in which Mrs. Ambedkar also joined from time to time, mainly in order to reinforce a point made by her husband, Ambedkar explained to me at length his plans for the revival of Buddhism in India, adding that he intended to devote the rest of his life to Buddhism. But though he had, as it seemed, made up his mind that he and his followers should embrace Buddhism, he appeared to be uncertain as to exactly how this was to be done. At any rate, he questioned me closely on the subject and I explained that formal conversion to Buddhism consisted in 'going for Refuge', as it was called, to the Three Jewels, i.e. the Buddha, the Dharma, and the Sangha, and in undertaking to observe what were known as the Five Precepts, or five basic principles of ethical behaviour. It was as simple as that. One could 'take' the Refuges and Precepts from any Buddhist monk.

By this time Ambedkar and I had been talking a good while, and a feeling of warmth and confidence had sprung up between us, as though we were members of the same family. I was therefore not surprised when he asked me if I would be willing to administer the Three Refuges and Five Precepts to him and his followers. To this I replied that I would certainly be willing to administer them, but that their conversion would probably be taken more seriously by the Buddhist world if it took place at the hands of the oldest and seniormost monk in India, who to the best of my knowledge was U Chandramani of Kusinara, from whom I had received my own Shramanera ordination. At the time Ambedkar seemed not to pay much attention to this suggestion, but he must have given it further thought, for it was from U Chandramani that, ten months later, he took the Three Refuges and Five Precepts. Before we parted he did, however, ask me to write to him recapitulating everything I had said on the subject of conversion. He also asked me to speak to his followers and explain to them what conversion to Buddhism really meant. (Sangharakshita, 1986: 19–20)

At the third meeting at the beginning of November 1956 in New Delhi, Ambedkar looked so frail that Sangharakshita could not imagine how he would still be able to travel to the Conference of the Fourth World Fellowship of Buddhists in Kathmandu.

During the great mass conversion on 14 and 15 October 1956, Sangharakshita was not present due to other obligations. Therefore, he gladly accepted the invitation to visit Buddhist friends in Nagpur on his way back to Calcutta. As chance would have it, he arrived in Nagpur only a few hours before the news of the demise of their leader reached the New Buddhists. His following report on the memorial service (1986: 25–7) at Nagpur is still a moving description and clearly shows how liberating the Untouchables felt their new birth as Buddhists under the leadership of Ambedkar to be and how intense, therefore, was their shock that he had to leave them a few weeks later:

I found a crowd of some 2,000 excited ex-Untouchables waiting on the platform to receive me. After being profusely garlanded I was escorted to the house of the friend with whom I had arranged to stay and then left to rest there and recover from my journey. Less than an hour later, when I was still settling into my new quarters, there was a sudden disturbance outside and three or four members of the Indian Buddhist Society burst into my room with the news that 'Baba Saheb—as Ambedkar's followers respectfully and affectionately called him—had died in Delhi the previous night. The speakers seemed utterly demoralized. What was more, they reported that the Society's down-town office was being beseiged by thousands of grief-stricken people who, knowing that I had arrived in Nagpur, were demanding that I should come and speak to them. Pointing out that it would be impossible for me to address so many people without a microphone and loudspeakers, I told my visitors to organize a proper condolence meeting for seven o'clock that evening. I would address it and do my best to console people, who from the accounts that now started coming in were frantic with grief and anxiety at the sudden loss of their great leader.

A condolence meeting was therefore held in the Kasturchand Park at the time indicated. When I arrived it was quite dark and the long columns of mourners were still converging on the place from all directions. They came clad in white—the same white that they had worn for the conversion ceremony only seven weeks earlier—and every man, woman, and child carried a lighted candle, so that the Park was the dark hub of a wheel with a score of golden spokes. Partly because of their demoralized state, partly because there had been so little time, the organizers of the meeting had been able to do little more than rig up a microphone and loudspeakers. There was no stage and, apart from a petromax or two, no lighting other than that provided by the thousands of candles. By the time I rose to speak—standing on the seat of a rickshaw, and with someone holding a microphone in front of me—about 100,000 people had assembled. By rights I should have been the last speaker but as things turned out I was the first. In fact I was the only speaker. Not that there were not others who wanted to pay tribute to the memory of the departed leader. One by one, some five or six of Ambedkar's most prominent local supporters attempted to speak, and one by one they were forced to sit down again as, overcome by emotion, they burst into tears after uttering only a few words. Their example proved to be contagious. When I started to speak the whole of the vast gathering was weeping, and sobs and groans rent the air. In the light cast by the petromax I could see grey-haired men in convulsions of grief at my feet.

It would have been strange if I had remained unaffected by the sight of so much anguish and so much despair, and I was indeed deeply moved. But though I felt the tears coming to my eyes I realized that for me, at least, there was no time to indulge in emotion. Ambedkar's followers had received a terrible shock. They had been Buddhists for only seven weeks, and now their leader, in whom their trust was total, and on whose guidance in the difficult days ahead they had been relying, had been snatched away. Poor and illiterate as the vast majority of them were, and faced by the unrelenting hostility of the Caste Hindus, they did not know which way to turn and there was a possibility that the whole movement of conversion to Buddhism would come to a halt or even collapse. At all costs something had to be done. I therefore delivered a vigorous and stirring speech in which, after extolling the greatness of Ambedkar's achievement, I exhorted my audience to continue the work he had so gloriously begun and bring it to a successful conclusion. 'Baba Saheb' was not dead but alive. He lived on in them, and he lived on in them to the extent to which they were faithful to the ideals for which he stood and for which he had, quite literally, sacrificed himself. This speech, which lasted for an hour or more, was not without effect. Ambedkar's stricken followers began to realize that it was not the end of the world, that there was a future for them even after their beloved 'Baba Saheb's' death, and that the future was not devoid of hope.

In the course of the next four days I visited practically all the ex-untouchable 'localities' of Nagpur and made more than forty speeches, besides initiating about 30,000 people into Buddhism and delivering lectures at Nagpur University and at the local branch of the Ramakrishna Mission. Wherever I went I repeated, in one form or another, the message that I had given in Kasturchand Park: Ambedkar was not dead and his work—especially the work of conversion—must continue. When I left Nagpur I had addressed altogether 200,000 people and the members of the Indian Buddhist Society assured me that my presence at such a critical juncture was a miracle and that I had saved Nagpur for Buddhism. Whether or not I had saved Nagpur for Buddhism it was difficult to tell, but there was no doubt that during those five memorable days I had forged a very special link with the Buddhists in Nagpur and, indeed, with all Ambedkar's followers.

In the following ten years, Sangharakshita was frequently active as a teacher for the New Buddhists. When he said goodbye to them on the tenth anniversary of Dr Ambedkar's death in Nagpur, 1,00,000 followers came to hear him one more time: 'In future, I told them, I would be dividing my time between England, the country of my birth, and India, the country of my adoption, and hoped to spend six months in each of them alternatively.' (ibid. p. 170)

These hopes could not be realized directly, but were realized indirectly through Dhammachari Lokamitra (Jeremy Goody, born in 1947 in England), one of the closest disciples of Sangharakshita. Again chance came into play. During a study trip, Lokamitra was visiting friends of Sangharakshita in Nagpur, when, on 14 October 1975, the anniversary of the mass conversion was celebrated:

Traveling across India, he arrived in Nagpur, quite by chance, on the day of the twenty-first anniversary of Ambedkar's conversion. Immediately drafted by some

Educational aid in the name of the Buddha and Ambedkar.

of Sangharakshita's ex-Untouchable friends to join the speakers at a memorial service, he soon found himself addressing a half-million new Buddhists who had converged at the *diksha-bhumi* site. That experience and the enthusiasm for Buddhism that Lokamitra experienced among the ex-Untouchables over the next few days had a profound effect, he reports, leading rapidly to his decision to commit his life to Dharma work among the Ambedkarites. Within a matter of months after arriving back in England he had settled his affairs there, and he soon returned to India to begin working with the ex-Untouchable Buddhists. TBMSG was officially inaugurated a few months later by Sangharakshita on a visit to India that also included the ordination of several of his earlier Indian followers into the Trailokya Bauddha Mahasangha (TBM), the new Indian wing of the WBO. Although Lokamitra began his work as a saffron-robed *anagarika*, after his first several years as a TBMSG organizer he found the monastic persona increasingly limiting, both socially and administratively. This led him to give up his monastic vows and eventually to marry into the ex-Untouchable community, a change of status he found personally as well as culturally more appropriate since most of the new Indian order members were also married householders. (Sponberg, 1996: 89)

In the following years, two other persons from England Dharmachari Virabhadra (Dr William Stone) and Dharmacharini Padmashuri (Hilary Blakiston) (see Blakiston, 1990) supported Dhammachari Lokamitra in setting up a public health service (but nowadays the Government of India is more concerned about the long-term temporary residence permits given to foreigners and neither could stay for a long period). Lokamitra succeeded, with increasing annual donations from England and recently also from Taiwan, in building an impressive spiritual and administrative centre in Dapodi, a suburb of Pune. Moreover, he managed to initiate and control from here Buddhist-inspired educational and social work in other parts of the country as well (see the plates on pages 147 and 148). Since 1982, this work has been supported continuously by Karuna, a society that was founded specifically for this kind of Buddhist development assistance. Karuna gave assistance in these amounts: 361,914 in 1994, 487,006 in 1995, and 598,951 in 1996 (amounts in Pounds Sterling. See the financial statement of the Karuna Trust).

These measures are certainly helpful in every individual case (Beltz 1997); however, according to the evaluation of the members of the order, more important for the deepening and expansion of the content of the Buddhist teachings among New Buddhists over a long period of time is the gradual training of men and women for Buddhist social work. Meanwhile, they support, professionally and full-time, measures in the health sector, kindergartens, hostels, campaigns for programmes against

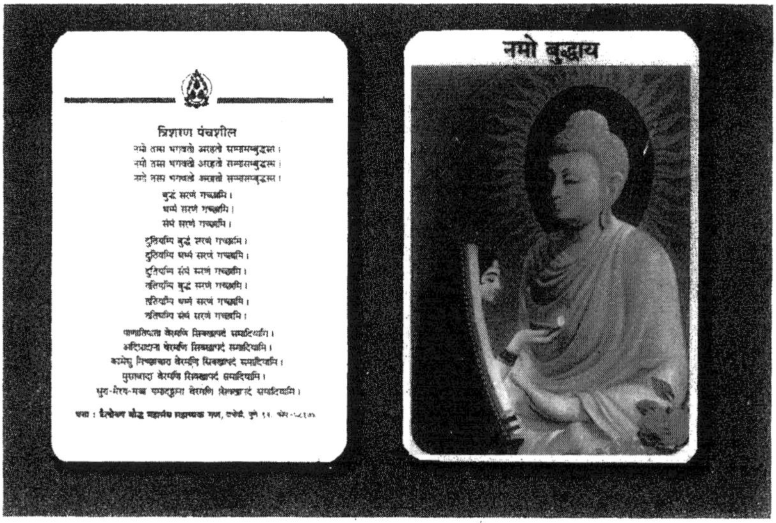

Front and back page of a coloured "vade mecum",
6 × 9 cm, welded together in plastic:
Devotional praise of Buddha as the Supreme
Enlightened One (repeated three times),
the Threefold Refuge to Buddha, Dhamma and Sangha,
and the Five Shilas as norm of daily conduct.
These are the world-wide used formula
in classical Pali, but here in Devanagari script.

illiteracy, and lay theatre groups for the development of new forms of communication. The TBMSG distinguishes three steps of approaching the inner circle, which at present comprises approximately 180 *dharmacharis* and *dharmacharinis*.

- As a *sahayak* (helper), one is in sympathy with the work of the TBMSG and attends various meetings, but does not yet intend to make a further commitment to the movement.
- As a *dhamma mitra* (friend of the *dhamma*), one declares one's deep interest in the work and, following specific invitations, one attends regularly training courses and also meditation courses.
- As a *dharmachari* or *dharmacharini*, one has been trained for several years under the guidance of two *kalyana mitras* (noble friends) and one has visited special retreats for candidates. Until a few years ago, however, Ven. Sangharakshita was the only one who could grant admission to an individual seeking membership into the order. But since he has withdrawn from the daily business of the immediate management of the order, there is a team of (British) elders of the order who can perform the ritual of admission.
- Four Indian members of the order have gone even a step further and have taken the vow of an *anagarika*: They live in celibacy and have dedicated their lives entirely to the work of the order.

Recently, at a seminar at the University of Pune, Lokamitra (1997: 7) outlined the inner structure of the worldwide brotherhood and sisterhood of the Friends of the Western Buddhist Order (FWBO) and the special forms of their influence within the TBMSG in the following way:

> The heart of the TBMSG is a Sangha, the Trailokya Bauddha Mahasangha (TBM). It is not a monastic Sangha, but nor is it a lay Sangha in the usually understood sense of the word. It is based on going for Refuge to the Buddha, Dhamma, and Sangha and ten precepts or principles of skilful action, speech and mind. Some live in communities and work in right livelihood situations, while others live at home with their families and work in worldly jobs. Members come from about 30 different countries. Of about 700 members world-wide about 180 come from India and these come from about 9 different caste backgrounds. Whilst most of the members in the West come from U.K., and most of those in India come from the ex-Mahar community, the TBM is beginning to provide a situation in which one's predominant experience of oneself and others in the Sangha is not in terms of caste or nation, but in terms of a human being going for Refuge to the Buddha, Dhamma and Sangha.

TBMSG cannot be a mass movement in that there is so much emphasis on training and individual commitment, and anyway, although it is open to all who want to make that commitment, not all are going to want to do so. That does not mean to say others will not be benefitted by the Sangha. Venerable Sangharakshita defined it as the nucleus of the new society. The members of the Sangha need to keep up contact with the wider group who, being receptive to the Dhamma will be influenced by its teaching. From the wider group come support and new members. We are not as active as we perhaps could be in this way, held back by some of the constraints that hold back the rest of the Buddhist movement, especially the increasing consumerism and old caste conditioning. Increasing consumerism seems to lead to less mobility and less inspiration. The young need to be approached in different ways. In India TBMSG is predominantly made up of one community and this seems to have a perpetuating effect in that few outsiders are inclined to join, and we tend to stick to people with whom we are familiar. It is only when we get many more members from other communities that we will be able to effectively break down the old caste identity.

The TBMSG creates a similar experience of a community approach that transcends Indian caste barriers with their courses in both their meditation centres:

Dhamma *shibirs* concentrating on meditation and study in ideal surroundings are conducted from two large retreat centres at Bhaja near Pune, and at Bor Dharan near Wardha. There is a publications wing known as Triratna Grantha Mala which besides books on Buddhism (mainly by the Venerable Sangharakshita) brings out quarterly magazines known as *Buddhayan* in Marathi, Hindi and Gujarati. Most of those who participate in Maharashtra are from the ex-Mahar community, although in Kolhapur a number of people from the Matanga community have converted to Buddhism and are involved in TBMSG activities. Elsewhere members of other dalit and backward class communities have shown some interest but this has not so far been taken far. Recently in Mumbai and Pune, attempts have been made to contact members of other communities who are interested in Buddhist meditation. (Lokamitra, 1997: 5)

In his discussion of Gopal Guru's (1991) criticism of the alleged appropriation of Ambedkar's approach by the TBMSG, Lokamitra (1991: 1304) tried to clarify the effect of a *dhamma shibir* (session of meditation and classes) by pointing out that liberation from the traditional rituals and cults of Hinduism can only be achieved through such continuous practices of self-reflection:

The sad fact is that many Buddhists still worship the old gods, thus unwittingly maintaining the old religious conditioning. In the last 12 years perhaps several thousand people have attended Dhamma shibirs organised by TBMSG, where they both learn meditation and study a Buddhist text or something written by

Ambedkar on Buddhism (the atmosphere is far from 'restrictive' as implied in Gopal Guru's note, but is pervaded by a joy and a sense of meaningfulness that few have experienced before). Perhaps the most universal experience for those who have attended such a shibir for the first time is understanding how Ambedkar could say in the 22 vows, 'Now I have taken a new life, Buddhism becomes meaningful to them as never before. They begin to understand how through Dhamma practice they can lead much more creative lives than hitherto they had thought possible, and thus develop a confidence in it that many did not have before. Most of them will go home and throw out the pictures and murtis of the old gods, having eradicated their psychological dependence on them.

It remains to be seen whether the TBMSG will one day be in a position to finance its manifold programmes and the corresponding personnel expenses with its own resources. However, this is not just an Indian problem. Social work does not pay its way; it is supported from outside. Thus, the early begging order (*bhikkhu/ni* = male/female beggar) of Buddhism, which at that time was actively involved in preaching, was also dependent on the support of the society at large for their food, clothing, medicine, and accommodation (though only during the rainy season, for otherwise empty shelters and shady trees should suffice).

In my report on the literature in the first chapter, I had asserted in closing that the TBMSG forms a special type of Buddhism in India and that one could not yet judge how far the measures of social work, which were supported by meditation training, would have a multiplying effect beyond a narrow circle of its members and attenders. This conclusion coincides with the self-assessment reported here.

Finally, however, one must also emphasize that more than 180 *dharmacharis/charinis* were trained by the TBMSG; they represent a new type of Buddhist missionary who takes the Western experiences of the FWBO as a model. It does not necessarily speak against the approach and the work of the TBMSG that these missionaries have not yet succeeded in building patterns of communication within Indian society that transcend the boundaries of their own origin. Instead, this once again points towards the overriding integral power and persistence of Indian caste society.

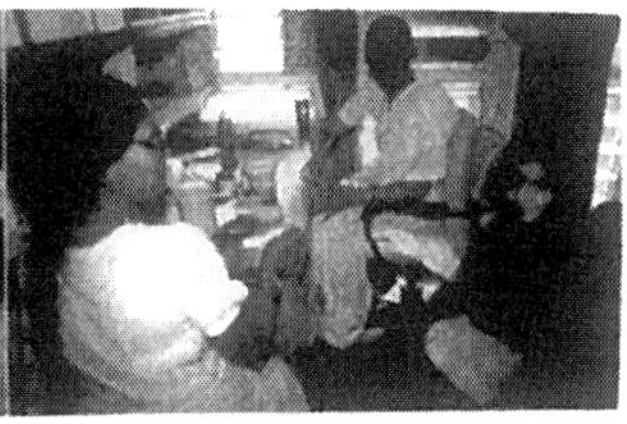

Education Index

47 kindergartens for 1400 children
7 after-school study classes for 240 children
4 literacy classes for 80 women and girls
Creche for 30 children
School for 200 children of Tibetan refugees
19 hostels in 5 Indian states allowing 915 boys and girls to continue their education.

Health Index

Primary health care in 8 of Pune's slum districts serving a population of 12,000.
Clinic in the Dapodi district of Pune treating 30 patients a day.

the karuna index

Projects currently supported by karuna

Costs Index

Some examples of expenditure in 1995:
Construction of purpose-built hostel for 80 boys or girls: £70,000.
Direct cost of supporting a child at a hostel: £8 a month.
Direct cost of supporting a kindergarten for 30 children: £240 a year.

A number of Karuna supporters agree for part of their donation to go towards Buddhist activities. These include 2 Rural Retreat Centres and Meditation and Buddhist Classes within urban slum communities.

Activities of the TBMSG in various sectors and regions.

Sports and Cultural Index
7 karate classes for 240 boys and girls
Asvagosha cultural project
After-school sports and arts activities
Library in Dapodi, Pune.

Sustainability Index
9 sewing classes for 145 women
3 shops
Handicrafts business
2 horticultural/agricultural projects
Social work training schemes for up to 40 men and women each year.

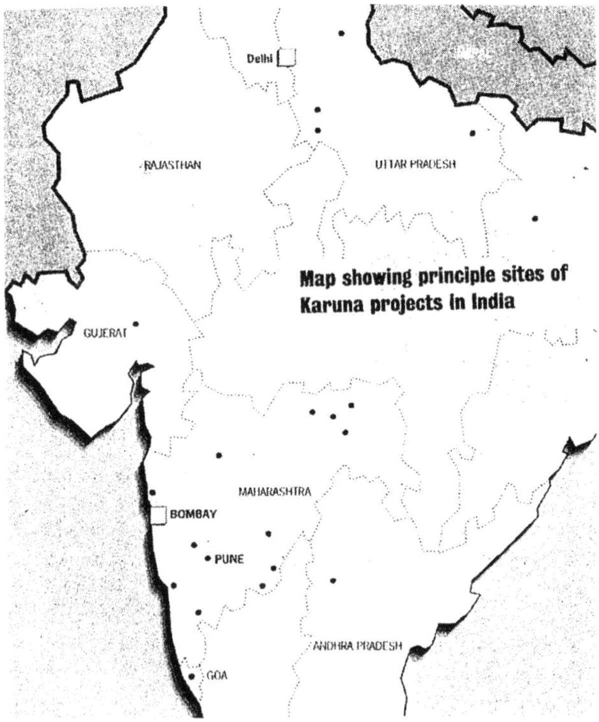

Activities of the TBMSG in various sectors and regions.

find out more

The Karuna Trust
St Marks Studio
Chillingworth Road
LONDON
N7 8QJ
Great Britain
TELEPHONE 0171 700 3434
FAX 0171 700 3535
E-MAIL 100420.3457@compuserve.com

If you'd like to find out more about the Karuna Trust and its work, you may like to consider these videos and books, which are available from the Karuna office:

Videos

A Peaceful Revolution
Introduces the social and Buddhist background to the projects supported by Karuna in India.

For the Welfare of the Many
Highlighting Karuna's educational work, particularly the hostels, and the opening of the major Mahavihara complex in Pune.

With the Snow Lions of Tibet
An uplifting and entertaining view of the ITBCI school for Tibetan refugee children in Kalimpong, which Karuna supports.

All £9.95 including post and packing.

Books

Jai Bhim
Dispatches from a Peaceful Revolution
by Terry Pilchick, £5.95
A colourful and moving account of the work and the people that Karuna is involved with in India.

Ambedkar and Buddhism
by Sangharakshita, £5.95
The social, religious and personal background to Dr Ambedkar's 'peaceful revolution', which has transformed the lives of millions in modern India.

But Little Dust
by Hilary Blakiston, £5.95
Hilary tells how she helped set up Bahujan Hitay's health care projects in Pune and taught 'ex-untouchable' women about their newly adopted religion – Buddhism.

Description concerning the work of the Karuna Trust in India.

CHAPTER SIX

The All India Bhikkhu Sangha

On 18 March 1956, Dr Ambedkar spoke at a mass gathering in Agra on the future prospects of his movement and the special demands which it would place upon individual groups. Quite firmly he also discussed the role of the monks. In order to reintroduce Buddhism into India, the new monks would not be able to retire into monasteries and work on books and commentaries, but would have to go from door to door, just as in the Buddha's time, in order to reach the masses of the New Buddhist movement:

> Buddhism is a great religion. The founder of this religion Tathagata Buddha has propagated this religion and due to its good aspects it could reach every nook and corner of India. After its great fame, this religion became extinct in 1213 AD. There are many reasons for this. One of the reasons is also that the Buddhist Monks became addicted to living a luxurious and restful life. Instead of moving from place to place for propagation of the religion, they started taking rest in Viharas and indulging in writing books in praise (of Kings). Now for re-establishing this religion, they will have to work hard. They will have to move from door to door. We have very few monks in the society. Therefore, the common good people should also propagate the religion and perform its rites. (Ahir, 1997: 111)

As we saw in the previous chapter, at first Sangharakshita and later the TBMSG picked up on this appeal of Dr Ambedkar and developed a new kind of Buddhist social worker. However, the approximately 180 *dharmacharis/dharmacharinis* of the movement have not become active on a large scale, since their contacts, though professional and experienced, remained limited to a special group located in the rather narrow social milieu of the movement.

As one of the guests of honour in the front row, Devapriya Valisinha (1904–68) took part in the mass conversion in Nagpur on 14 October 1956. After the death of Anagarika Dharmapala in 1933, he had become the General Secretary of the Maha Bodhi Society. Two weeks after the celebrations, Dr Ambedkar asked him in an urgent letter dated 30 October 1956 for the support of the Maha Bodhi Society in the future training of monks:

> Thank you very much for your letter of 25th October 1956. It certainly was a great event and the crowd that came forward for conversion was beyond my expectation. Thank the Buddha it all went well.
>
> I am glad you realize that having begun the task well we have to look to its continued progress in the future. We have to consider ways and means of imparting knowledge of Buddhism to the masses who have accepted His Dhamma and will accept it on my word. We should no doubt train a large number of workers to teach the Dhamma to the people, but the best agents for carrying out the same are the Bhikkhus. They would carry a great deal of prestige with them which no layman could do.
>
> The Bhikkhus in my judgement ought to be very happy to find out that a large task awaiting them has been done. The only difficulty with the Bhikkhus is that they don't care to learn the language of the people. I am afraid the Sangha will have to modify its outlook and instead of becoming recluses they should become like the Christian missionaries social workers and social preachers. As I told you, today they are neither Arhants nor useful members of the Society. This fact must be hammered into them and make them realize that they could serve the Buddha well by becoming preachers of His Dhamma.
>
> I like your idea of opening a sort of a logical seminar where Bhikkhus and non-Bhikkhus could be taught the fundamentals of Buddhism and made to learn the different languages of India so that they could be sent to the different parts. (Ahir, 1989: 147-8)

Indeed, Devapriya Valisinha frequently supported the New Buddhist movement. Through his connections, for example, a woman from Darjeeling gave a substantial donation so that on 14 April 1957 the laying of the foundation stone for the first *vihara* (place of Buddhist worship and *bhikkshus*' residence) in Nagpur became possible. Shortly afterwards, he opened an assistance account, the Indian Buddhist Fund, which financed the production and free distribution of brochures of Buddhist texts in the Hindi and Marathi languages. However, the seminar that Ambedkar mentioned at the end of his letter was realized only indirectly (Ahir 1989: 34): 'Over a dozen persons from among the new Buddhists were also ordained and given training at Sarnath with the help of this fund. Valisinha continued to help in various ways the new movement in subsequent years also.'

The first and so far only comprehensive attempt to systematically train the New Buddhist monks took place at the invitation of Phra Debvisuddhimoli, the main abbot of the Thai Temple, from 1–30 November 1972 in Bodh Gaya (see the plates on pages 163 and 164). At this time it created its Constitution (see plates on pages 160–1). The All India Bhikkhu Sangha had stated its objectives and membership at the meeting of the general body held in the Thai monastery in Bodh Gaya from 3–6 July 1970, which included the organization of a Sangha (see plates on pages 165–70). The Sangha was registered on 15 October 1971.

Almost all members (at that time numbering ten) of the governing body of the All India Bhikkhu Sangha came from the ethno-Buddhist background of the Barua and the Chakma Buddhists of Bengal and Assam (see the biographies of Ven. Ananda Mitra, Ven. Dharmapal, and Ven. Dhammaviriya in Ahir, 1998: 99f.). However, Bhikkhu Jagdish Kashyap (1908–76), who was the *Sangha Nayaka* (President), was a rare type of erudite north Indian monk. He came from the educated middle class in Bihar. After finishing his Sanskrit studies, he went to Ceylon in 1933 and was ordained as a monk in 1934 (see Ahir, 1989: 89–100). He gained lasting credit for the new dissemination of the *dhamma* in India through taking care of the 41 volumes of the Pali canon in the Devanagari script literally day and night, from 1956 until 1961. The first specimen of this complete edition was handed over to Prime Minister Jawaharlal Nehru in Sarnath during a grand ceremony in December 1961.

If today one looks back at these promising beginnings and talks to elder representatives of Buddhism in India about the further development of the *sangha*, then one generally receives a negative judgement even from the members of the *sangha* themselves:

- 'The new monks do not want to receive training at all. As young people, they never held money in their hands. Thus, they now roam about and try to receive donations for all kinds of projects.' (Ven. Sasanarashmi Mahathero, General Secretary of the Sangha, Sarnath, February 1998.)
- 'The Thais think that we Indian monks are all poor beggars.' (Ven. Gurudhamma Thera, Treasurer of the Sangha, Sarnath, February 1998. He lives, like Ven. Sasanarashmi, in the Thai Temple in Sarnath, which is sponsored by the Thai foundation in Bangkok. During the season, groups of pilgrims from Thailand arrive regularly at the guest house of the Thai Temple.)
- 'If I may say so: we in our family are pre-Ambedkar Buddhists.' (Dr A.K. Narain, former Professor of Religion at the University of Wisconsin, and nephew of Bhikkhu Jagdish Kashyap at his home in Varanasi, March 1998.) (Also see Narain, 1994.)

- 'The new Bhikkhus do not work at all for the society.' (Dr J.S. Sardar, lecturer at the Milind College of Science in Aurangabad and a committed Ambedkar Buddhist, March 1998. He has organized several times meditation courses for his students, including one in the summer of 1996 with the American Yogavacara Rahula in the Buddhist rock caves in Aurangabad.)
- 'Right now it is unfortunately the case that we do not have outstanding monks any more like Anand Kausalyayan, Jagdish Kashyap, or Ariyawansa. We have to wait and hope.' (D.C. Ahir at his home in New Delhi, March 1998.)
- 'So far we have approximately sixty young monks in India, many of whom came from Arunachal Pradesh, supported by training stipends. But they all have disappeared again.' (Mrs Sasithorn Thananart, Vice President of the Mrigadayavana Mahavihara Foundation, April 1998 in Bangkok. This foundation sponsors, as mentioned above, the Thai Temple in Sarnath.) In the same conversation, Mrs Thananart told me, though with some reservation, that it had also become quieter in the great Wat Mahadhatu monastery in Bangkok. In the past, almost 550 monks or rather *sramanerans* (novice) had lived in the monastery, but today there were only slightly more than 300. And in the northern provinces of Thailand one would already consider inviting young monks from Burma to fill the local monasteries or rather to keep them functioning at all.

According to the estimates of my informants, supposedly no more than 75 Buddhist monks existed in all of India in 1977, most of whom lived in Bengal and Assam. For 1998, however, one may assume that there are 1,250 monks. Of these, about 150 are supposedly Chakmas, about 60 to 80 Baruas, and 1,000 Ambedkar Buddhists. No more than ten monks come from the formerly higher Hindu castes.

In February 1998, 574 monks were registered with the All India Bhikkhu Sangha, most of whom had a postal address in Maharashtra. However, the Sangha is not an order in the classical sense but is an attempt to create a group representing the interests of all monks and performing educational and informative work. On the application form for admission (see the plate on page 171) potential members simply show where they were ordained into monkhood. Clause 12 of the *Rules and Regulations* of the All India Bhikkhu Sangha, states:

A Bhikkhu or a Sramanera above the age of 20, in agreement with the aims and objects of the Sangha shall submit an application with the recommendation of a member of the Governing Council and addressed to the General Secretary, paying a subscription of Rs. 6 per annum and admission fee of Rs. 2 shall be enrolled as a General Member.

The General Secretary examines the application, and then an identity card is issued (see plates on pages 173-5) which shows that the applicant is a member of the *sangha*. This identity card confirms the monkhood of its holder, but the *sangha* itself cannot ordain monks and thus cannot exercise any great influence on the standard of their education and behaviour.

In this context, one has to realize that, perhaps for the first time in the history of the Buddhist order of monks in India, an attempt is being made to build a Buddhist community *from below*, so to speak, without the (as was often in the past) active support of rulers and rich merchants *from above*. For the contemporaries of the Buddha, as for himself, the path into the order was indeed a way into homelessness. Men as well as women left behind their property and status in their search for liberation from the weariness of life, which often was caused by an abundance of material wealth. The patchwork robe of the *bhikkhus* and *bhikkhunis* was in that sense truly a symbol of their renunciation of the world. Today, however, for many New Buddhists it is rather a symbol for embracing the world. They do not leave the palace behind, but they leave behind the poor conditions in the narrow huts of the settlements of the Untouchables. An empty cell or even a room in a *vihara* under construction, with regular meals provided by the laity, is in many cases already more than they had ever experienced before!

My experiences in the New Buddhist environment are quite patchy, and I cannot combine them into general statements about the *sangha*. However, measured against my observations in Sri Lanka and Thailand, in India I often had to think of the detailed instructions for behaviour and decorum which the Buddha had given to the *sangha* in his day, so that the *bhikkhus* and the *bhikkhunis* could be ambassadors of a simple yet well-mannered life. Today, such rules are urgently needed again, but seem to be unknown to most of the new *bhikkhus* who do not behave any differently than their countrymen around them. They are equally noisy, chatter about the daily events of politics and society, are careless about the disposal of garbage, bargain while shopping in the bazaar, like to sleep and meditate, if at all, at official occasions only.

When I communicated my amazement about these and many other observations to Gurudhamma, the Treasurer of the All India Bhikkhu Sangha, who was trained for fifteen years as a monk in Thailand, he almost laughed and said: 'Please, do not forget the Indian conditions!' In other words: Please accept an Indian way of life also within the *sangha*.

It is part of this 'Indian way of life' that the Buddhist monks have no special status and are not particularly noticeable in a colourful Indian society of *saddhus* and self-declared holy men. In Sri Lanka or Thailand, the robe alone demands respect, even at a distance, but in India it is not commonly known as a special kind of clothing of a particular order. For example, during a train ride from Varanasi to Gaya, Gurudhamma had to explain at great length to our fellow travellers that he was not just a run-of-the-mill *swami* but a Buddhist monk. What is more, it had to first of all be communicated and then explained that the Buddha was not a deity of the Hindu pantheon and was not the ninth incarnation of Vishnu. The Hindu counter-reformation centuries ago had conveyed this idea very successfully (see in this context the letter of the All India Bhikkhu Sangha dated 23 February 1996 to the Prime Minister of India, reproduced on page 156).

However, such clarifying attempts are hardly of any use. For most Indians, a *bhikkhu* is and remains a *swami* or a *baba*, just as the Hindu pilgrims in Bodh Gaya worship the Buddha himself as a *baba*. They do not make their pilgrimage to the Buddha in the magnificent Thai Temple but to the *nau lakh ka baba*, i.e. to the *god* whose golden statue once, in the 1960s, had cost the unimaginable sum of *nau lakh*, i.e. Rs 9,00,000. It was brought from Bangkok to Gaya on an American military transport vehicle which was made especially available for this occasion. And the Buddha in the Japanese temple indeed is the *japani baba*, not more (but also not less!) than a further manifestation of the many variants on the search for *moksha*.

This short description and evaluation may suffice to indicate the surroundings within which the All India Bhikkhu Sangha is active. The invitation to the twenty-eighth general assembly of the Sangha in April 1998 in Dhulia (Maharashtra), which is reproduced on pages 176–7 and translated later, gives an overview of the questions and problems with which the All India Bhikkhu Sangha at present is concerned as does the material presented here which records the proceedings of the Sangha's assembly. The list of the new members of the board shows that the All India Bhikkhu Sangha today is ruled almost exclusively by New Buddhists from western India. Only Ven. Dharmapala from Kolkata and Ven. Medhankar Mahathero as President (see the short biography in Ahir, 1998: 101–4), a disciple of the well-known monk and scholar Anand Kausalyayan (1905–88), represent the founding phase of the Sangha.

All India Bhikkhu Sangha (Regd.)

(DELHI-STATE)

Office :
Nav Nirman Buddha Vihar,
Sector-3, R. K. Puram,
NEW DELHI - 110022

Ref No. AIBS-727/96

Dated 29.2.95

MEMORANDUM

To

Shri P.V. Narasimha Rao
The Prime Minister of India
South Block,
New Delhi

I would liketo draw your kind attention to the News item appeared in "The Hindustan Times" weekly Entertainment Guide" Friday dated 26.1.96 regarding picturising of the tele-film "Buddha" produced by the Padmalaya Tele-films of Andhra and sold to Sony Entertainment Television. The Sony Entertainment Television has telecasted this Tele serial on 11th, 14th & 16th Feb.,1996 from Singhapore. Shri Arun Govil has been shown to act as Buddha in the same ways as he acted as lord Ram in TV serial "Ramayana". Lord Buddha has been depicted as Incarnate of Lord Vishnu. Eminent Buddhist scholar have expressed deep anguish on picturising this Tele Serial "Buddha" as it is against the principle of Buddhism. In past also no permission was granted by the Govt. and nobody can act as Buddha. The serial on Lord Buddha is also against the precepts as contained in the pious books of Buddhism. Copies of the protest letters from eminent Buddhist organizations and scholars are being received.

I would like to add that this tele-film will not only hurt the religious feelings of Buddhists in India & abroad, but may also cause law and order problems as Buddhists in India and abroad will strongly resent this. Secondly, its acceptance may distort peace and harmony among different communities. Buddha's presentation as a sectarian God and mythological figure may distort the very concept of secularism which his teaching of peace, harmony and goodwill embodies. As you know, the Buddha was never a mythological figure as Rama & Hanuman but very much a historical figure. Therefore, to show Buddha as a mythological figure is deeply resented by the millions of ardent followers of the Buddha's Teaching in India as well as all over the world.

I on behalf of All India Bhikkhu Sangha request your honour to intervene in this matter and take up with the Govt. of Japan go give directions to Sony TV not to screen on mass media to avoid world vide violance.

Yours

Dhamma Jyoti.
(President)

Letter of protest by Ven. Dhamma Jyoti.

The following notes deal with the individual points of the agenda of the General Assembly, 1998:

- A new plot of land belonging to the All India Bhikkhu Sangha, additionally purchased near Maghad University, is very conveniently located at the new main road to Gaya. It urgently needs to be surrounded by a new wall, since otherwise one must fear that squatters will appropriate it or that it will be used for agricultural purposes. The income of the Sangha from the membership fees, however, is so small that it cannot pay for any significant building. So they are dependent on donors and have to try to find suitable *bhikkhus* to serve as fund raisers.
- The secretary in the head office for Bodh Gaya is responsible for many irregularities and for the obvious mismanagement. Moreover, physical violence between monks occurred on the grounds of the All India Bhikkhu Sangha.
- Regarding the question of the release of the main temple in Bodh Gaya (which is pictured in the logo on the stationery of the All India Bhikkhu Sangha—see the plate on page 176), the Sangha has tried again and again to become a partner in talks with the provincial government (see the letter of Ven. Dhammaviriyo on page 158; as a Buddhist representative in the National Commission for Minorities from 1990–6, he had a certain influence in New Delhi). The radical leaders of the Liberation Campaign for the Main Temple in Bodh Gaya were expelled from the All India Bhikkhu Sangha in 1993.

In my opinion, the chances of the All India Bhikkhu Sangha's achieving a change in the composition of the Temple Management Committee are slim. Bodh Gaya as a centre of the growing international tourism of pilgrims is a very important resource, so the main temple as the religious centre of the place cannot be handed over to the particular interests of the New Buddhist movement. Also, the worldwide community of Buddhists, which is often called upon in the campaign, is mainly interested in ensuring that law and order in Bodh Gaya are guaranteed. Neville Kanakaratne, High Commissioner of Sri Lanka in Delhi, recommended to his government in an internal report that restraint be exercised in this 'inner-Indian' matter, the background of which is difficult for outsiders to understand. 'In this sensitive and complicated area, it is my view that the Sri Lankan government, should, at least for the present, refrain from

2.1/95

4/2, Multy Storey Flats,
Shahjahan Road,
New Delhi 110011
Tele.No.389452
384664

Dear Shri Bommai,

I am very glad to enclose herewith a letter from Shri Vishwanath Pratap Singh, Former Prime Minister of India and Shri Ram Vilas Paswan, senior leader of Janata Dal for your kind information and necessary action.

We have several times met Shri Laloo Prasad Yadavji, Chief Minister of Bihar and explained the problems of Bodh Gaya Temple Management Act 1949 for suitable amendment. He has gives assurances but till now no notification has been issued in this regard. The Election of ~~Bihar~~ is on the card. The Bodh Gaya movement has already begun and many rallies are going to be organised against this Act in the near future. I am sure this is going to be one of the major issue before the Janata Dal Government. The Election in Bihar has been deferred. I believe this is the high time for you to write to Laloojі for suitable amendment in the Bodh Gaya Temple Management Act. We have already sent the draft Act last year to the Bihar Government for suitable amendment. Till today no notification has been issued by the Bihar Government which I am sure will hurt the sentiments of Buddhists and other weaker sections of the community.

With regards,

Yours sincerely,

(VEN.DHAMMAVIRIYO)

Shri S.R.Bommai,
Member of Parliament(Rajya Sabha)
10, Lodi Estate,
NEW DELHI 110003

Letter from Ven. Dhammaviriyo to a member of the Rajya Sabha concerning the Bodh Gaya Temple Management Act

involving itself in what, to the outside world will be purely an internal domestic problem of the Indian state.'

Tara Doyle (1997: 394) complements this remark with the comment that the representatives of other countries with a Buddhist population have also strikingly restrained themselves and do not comment upon the Liberation Campaign.

Whether the All India Bhikkhu Sangha will succeed in communicating the urgency of the building needs in Bodh Gaya to the New Buddhist members in Maharashtra is also questionable. For them, as we have seen, the central site in the Buddhist diaspora from Bihar is not Bodh Gaya, but Nagpur. There the liberation began, and there one may meet at least 18 Buddhists among every 100 inhabitants.

The New Buddhists of Maharashtra, moreover, made it possible for meeting halls and *viharas* to be constructed everywhere in their areas. And up to 900 *bhikkhus* are being supported. Though they mostly do not correspond to foreign ideas as far as their way of life is concerned, perhaps just because of this they are suited for the ritual needs and financial possibilities of the believers for whom there is no Karuna Trust in England to subsidize special programmes, personnel, and meditation centres.

However, the headquarters of the All India Bhikkhu Sangha is partly supported by funds from abroad, since the home of the General Secretary and the Treasurer is the Thai Temple in Sarnath. They are thus not dependant on donations from the Hindu regions surrounding Sarnath for their work in the administration of the Sangha. This explains why the business of the All India Bhikkhu Sangha is carried out from a "camp office" in Sarnath (see the letterhead on page 176) and not from Bodh Gaya, where the organization is registered. It remains to be seen whether one day the centre of the movement will remain in Nagpur or move to Bodh Gaya in a new building of the Sangha.

CONSTITUTION

OF

ALL INDIA BHIKKHU SANGHA

IN COMMEMORATION

of the

Training Indian Bhikkhus

&

The Third Conference

of

All India Bhikkhu Sangha

at

WAT THAI BUDDHA GAYA.

[THAI MONASTERY, BODH-GAYA]

FROM 1ST NOVEMBER TO 30TH NOV. B·E·2515 / A·D·1972

Preface to the Constitution of the All India Bhikkhu Sangha.

PREFACE

We are glad to publish this Constitution of the All India Bhikkhu Sangha, organized under the patronage of the Venerable Lord Abbot, Phra- Debvisuddhimoli of the Thai Monastery, Bodh-Gaya. The Bhikkhu members of this Sangha hail from all parts of India mostly from Bihar, Bengal, Uttar Pradesh, Punjab, Delhi, Assam and Maharastra. There may be other organizations of the Bhikkhu Sangha; but there is none such in this part of the country. If there be some, we look upon them as our brother missions and we hope that they will give us their best co-operation in our effort towards the enhancement for the cause of the Dharma. We have no sectarian or provincial bias. We welcome all alike to join us and give their best service.

Preface to the Constitution of the All India Bhikkhu Sangha.

This constitution is open to revision in the response to the changing times and occasions, subject to the approval of our father patron, the Lord Abbot of the Thai Monastary, Bodh-Gaya.

Sabbe satta bhavantu sukhitatta.

BHIKKHU J. KASHYAP
SANGHA NAYAKA.

ALL INDIA BHIKKHU SANGHA,
NAVA NALANDA MAHAVIHAR,
NALANDA,
INDIA

25. 10. 2515 (1972)

Preface to the Constitution of the All India Bhikkhu Sangha.

BHIKKHU TRAINING CENTRE OF ALL INDIA BHIKKHU SANGHA

Programme of special Training for the head of Bhikkhu, from all India, to be held at Thai Monastery, Bodh-Gaya, Bihar, from Ist to 30th November B. E. 2515 (1972) under patronage of the Thai Buddhist Sangha, led by Venerable Phra Debvisuddhimoli, the Lord Abbot of Thai Monastery, Bodh-Gaya, Gaya, Bihar in co-operation with All India Bhikkhu Sangha.

AIMS AND OBJECTS

1. **Canthadhura Field** (Canonical study) :—

A. Dhamma, from Tripitaka.

B. Vinaya, from Tripitaka.

C. Sutta, from Tripitaka Buddhist history.

(1) Buddhism in India.

(2) The development of Buddhism in other countries

(3) Spirit of Buddhism (Dhammaniti)

Training programme, 1–30 November 1972, at the Bhikkhu Training Centre, Bodh Gaya.

2. Vipassanadhura Field (Practical) —

A. Samatha-Bhavana.
B. Vipassana-Bhavana.
C. The supreme goal of Buddhism.

3. Buddhist Ceremonial Field :—

A. The form and tradition of Buddhist respects (Samicikamma and Garavata).
B. Buddhist ceremony for Bhikkhus.
C. Method and activity as Buddhist act to other religious faith.

4. Buddhist Propagation Field :—

A. Practices and etiquettes of Buddhist monks and laymen.
B. To know the kindheart, gratefulness, forgiveness mercy, blamelessness, unity and Co-operation among the Buddhist people.
C. To raise standard of living of Buddhist according to economic condition and the 4 neccessities(Paccaya)
D. To lay the foundation and the development for Buddhist.
E, To work for Buddhist propagation for Buddhist.
F. To work for Buddhist propagation for the world.
G. To avoid the problem of conflict between creed of the world.
H. To study comparative religions for peace of the world

5. Ceremonial Practice :—

A. Morning Chanting in sima (Chapter House).
Evening Chanting in Main Temple, Bodh-Gaya everyday.
B. To exercise Chanting Sutta and Paritta in the evening.

—o—

Training programme, 1–30 November 1972, at the Bhikkhu Training Centre, Bodh Gaya.

ALL INDIA BHIKKHU SANGHA
BUDHGAYA THAI TEMPLE
P. O. BUDHGAYA, GAYA,
BIHAR, INDIA.

Registration Act No. 21-1860, Dated 15th October 1971.
Vide No. 37-1971-72.

Resolution of the General Body (General Council) of the
ALL INDIA BHIKKHU SANGHA.

We the office bearers and Counsellers of the Governing council of the 'All India Bhikkshu Sangha' hereby confirm that the following is a true copy of the resolution passed by the General body of All India Bhikkhu Sangha held in the Thai Monastery on 3-7-1970 to 6-7-1970. B. E. 2531, which was inaugurated by Shri D. P. Rai, the Chief Minister of Bihar.

Name :--	Signature
1 Bhikkhu J. Kashyap	Sd/ J. Kashyap
2 Ven. Anand Mitra Mahathero	Sd/ Anand Mahathero
3 Ven. Prajna Jyoti Bhikkhu	Sd/ Prajna Jyoti Bhikkhu
4 Ven. Dharmapal Bhikkhu	Sd/ Dharmapal Bhikkhu
5 Ven. Dhammaviriyo Bhikkhu	Sd/DhammaviriyoBhikkhu
6 Ven. M. Pannanandsri	Sd/ M. Pannanandsri
7 Ven. Santarakkhita	Sd/ Santarakkhita

Founding assembly of the All India Bhikkhu Sangha, 3–6 July 1970.

[2]

1. Name of the Society :-All India Bhikkhu Sangha.

2. Head office of the Society :-Bodh Gaya, P. O. Bodh Gaya District :-Gaya within the state of Bihar.

3. Objects of the Society shall be as follows:-

[a] to organise a Sangha of Buddhist devotees inclusive of monks and lay persons.

[b] to organise and conduct training Centres for inparting knowledge and training to persons believing in Buddha and his Dhamma.

[c] to organise and conduct meditation Centres at Buddha Gaya and other places on the basis of Buddhistic traditions.

[d] to construct and to encourage construction of Buddhist Temple and shrines wherever possible.

[e] to establish libraries and to promote study and research in Buddhism.

[f] to possess and run printing press.

[g] to publish books, Magazines and pamphlets etc. relating to Buddhist thought and culture.

[h] to establish and encourage establishment of charitable Hospitals and Dispensaries.

[i] to provide aid and render services to individuals and communities in distress.

[j] to foster good will, harmony and pleasant living amongst the individuals, communities and nations.

[k] to inculcate the Buddist principles of love, piety compassion and peaceful co-existence etc.

[l] to promote and propagate the knowledge and practice of Buddhist Philosophy, religion and culture.

Founding assembly of the All India Bhikkhu Sangha, 3–6 July 1970.

[3]

[m] to acquire funds and properties both movable and immovable by securing donations, gifts endowments exchange or purchase for the fulfilment of the objects.

[n] to manage, administer and control the funds and properties.

[o] to devote the funds and properties both movable and immovable for the purposes of any or all the objects aforesaid.

[p] to do all other lawful acts in furtherance of the aforesaid objects.

4. Names, addresses and occupations of the members of the Governing body to whom by the rules of the society management of its affairs is entrusted.

Name	Post	Address	Occupation.
1 Bhikkhu J. Kashyap Mahathero.	Sangha Nayaka. [President]	Nava Nalanda Mahavihara.	Govt. Servent
2 Ven. Anand Mitra Mahthero.	Anu Nayka [Vice President]	Bodh Gaya, Bihar.	Buddhist monk.
3 Ven. Jinaratan Mahathero.	Genal. Secy.	Buddhist Temple Shillong, Assam.	Buddhist monk.
4 Ven. Dharmapal	Counseller.	Bengal Buddhist Temple Cal-12.	Buddhist monk.
5 Ven. Sasanabangsa.	Counseller,	P. O. Salapather Sibsagar, Assam	Buddhist monk.

Founding assembly of the All India Bhikkhu Sangha, 3–6 July 1970.

[4]

6 Ven. M. Pannana-ndsi.	Counseller,	Main Temple, Bodh Gaya, Bihar.	Buddhist monk.
7 Ven. Sugata Nand.	Treasurer.	Buddhist temple Madho Jong, Pratapgarh. U.P.	Buddhist monk.
8 Ven. Guna-chara.	Counseller,	Buddhist temple Tipam Phakeal, P. O. Tipam, Assam	Buddhist monk.
9 Ven. Prajna-Jyoti.	Counseller,	Bengal Buddhist 1, Bengal Bud-dhist. St. Cal.-12	Buddhist monk.
10 Ven. Dham-maviriyo.	Secretery.	Jagajyoti Budd-ha Bihar. Sant-nagar, New Delhi-24.	Buddhist monk.

5. We the persons whose names and addresses and occupations are mentioned hereafter are desirous of being formed into a society in pursuance of the memorandum of the society.

Name	Address	Occupation	Signature
1 Bhikkhu J. Kashyap	Nava Nalanda Maha Nalanda [PATNA] Bihar	Govt. Servent	Sd/J.Kashyap

Founding assembly of the All India Bhikkhu Sangha, 3–6 July 1970.

[· 5]

2 Ven. Anand Mitra Maha-thero.	Bodh Gaya, Bihar.	Buddhist monk.	Sd/ Anand
3 Ven. Prajna Jyoti Bhikkhu	Bengal Budd-hist temple, Cal-12	Buddhist monk.	Sd/ P. Jyoti
4 Ven. Dhar-mapal Bhikkhu	Bengal Buddh-ist temple, 1 Bengal Buddhist St. Cal.-12	Buddhist monk.	Sd/ D. Bhikkhu
5 Ven. Dham-maviriyo	Jogajjyoti Buddha, Sant-nagar New Delhi-24.	Buddhist monk.	Sd/ Dhamma-viriyoh Bhikkhu
6 Ven. M. Pannana-ndsri	Bodh Gaya, Bihar	Buddhist monk.	Sd/ M. Panna-nandsri
7 Ven. Santara-kkhita	Ambedhar Bhavan, Rani Jhasi Rd. New Delhi.	Buddhist monk.	Sd/ Santarakk-hita.

6. Certified that the above persons have signed in my presence

Founding assembly of the All India Bhikkhu Sangha, 3–6 July 1970.

[6]

Name	Address	Occoupation	Signature.
U. Mahar-athi	No. 9, Gardnier Patna-1	Govt. Service Deputy Dir-ctor of Industries, Govt. of Bihar & Director, Institute of Industrial Desings.	Sd/ U. Maha-rathi. 10-6-71

—: o :—

Founding assembly of the All India Bhikkhu Sangha, 3–6 July 1970.

॥ सुखा संघस्स सामग्गी समग्गानं तपो सुखो ॥
चरथ भिक्खवे चारिकं बहुजन हिताय बहुजन सुखाय लोकानुकम्पाय

सदस्यता आवेदन-पत्र

सेवा में, दिनांक ....

मानानीय महासचिव महोदय,
अखिल भारतीय भिक्षु संघ,
अस्थायी कार्यालय :
थाई बुद्ध विहार (वट् थाई)
सारनाथ, वाराणसी

मान्यवर,

प्रार्थी ....(भिक्षु / श्रामणेर) पूज्य भिक्षु ....द्वारा स्थान / सीमा... दिनांक..............................को उपसम्पन्न / प्रव्रजित किया गया था। प्रमाण प्रतिलिपि संलग्न है। मैं अखिल भारतीय भिक्षु संघ की सदस्यता के लिए आवेदन करता हूँ।

मैं घोषित करता हूँ कि अन्य किसी संस्था का सदस्य नहीं हूँ और अखिल भारतीय भिक्षु संघ के विधान के प्रति निष्ठावान रहकर उसका पालन करूँगा।

अपनी अनुकम्पा बनाये रख कर कृपया मुझे संघ का सदस्य बना लें।

मैं आवेदन पत्र के साथ देय धन व सूचना दे रहा :—

१. प्रवेश शुल्क .... रू० १०.००
२. वार्षिक सदस्यता शुल्क .... रू० २०.००
३. परिचय-पत्र शुल्क .... रू० १०.००
४. जन्म-तिथि.. राष्ट्रीयता ....
५. जन्म-स्थान..
६. शैक्षिणिक योग्यता ....
७. पत्र-व्यवहार का पता ....
८. अनुमोदनकर्ता का नाम व पता ....

हस्ताक्षर संघ की कार्यकारिणी का सदस्य
महासचिव/सचिव (मुख्यालय) धम्म की सेवा में—

उपरोक्त प्रार्थी को सदस्यता प्रदान कर दी जाये।

हस्ताक्षर हस्ताक्षर प्रार्थी

Application for admission into the All India Bhikkhu Sangha.
See translation on page 172.

The All India Bhikkhu Sangha
(Emblem)

Happiness is the Sangha's unity; happiness is the striving of the united. Walk, O Bhikkhus, the path to salvation of many people and to the blessings of many people, out of compassion for the world.

Application for Admission

c/o The All India Bhikkhu Sangha — Date:
Temporary Office:
Thai Buddha Vihara (Wat Thai)
Sarnath, Varanasi

Respected Sir,

The applicant . . . (Bhikshu/Shramanera) has been ordained by the Honourable Bhikshu . . . on . . .(Date) in . . . (place) as a Bhikshu (*upasampanna*) / accepted into the order (*pravrajjita*). A certified transcript is attached. I herewith apply for the membership of the All India Bhikkhu Sangha.

I herewith declare that I do not belong to any other organization and that I will respect and follow the charter of the All India Bhikkhu Sangha.

Please kindly accept me as a member of the Sangha.

Together with this membership application I pay the due fees and state my personal data:

1. Membership fee — 10.00 Rupees
2. Yearly contribution — 20.00 Rupees
3. Subscription of the circular letter — 10.00 Rupees
4. Date of birth . . . — Nationality: . . .
5. Place of birth . . .
6. Education . . .
7. Address for correspondence . . .
8. Name and address of the sponsor of this application: . . .

Signature — Member of the Board
General Secretary/Secretary (Centre) In service of the Dhamma

The application of the applicant mentioned above may be submitted.

Signature — Signature of the applicant

Translation of Application for Admission into the AIBS.

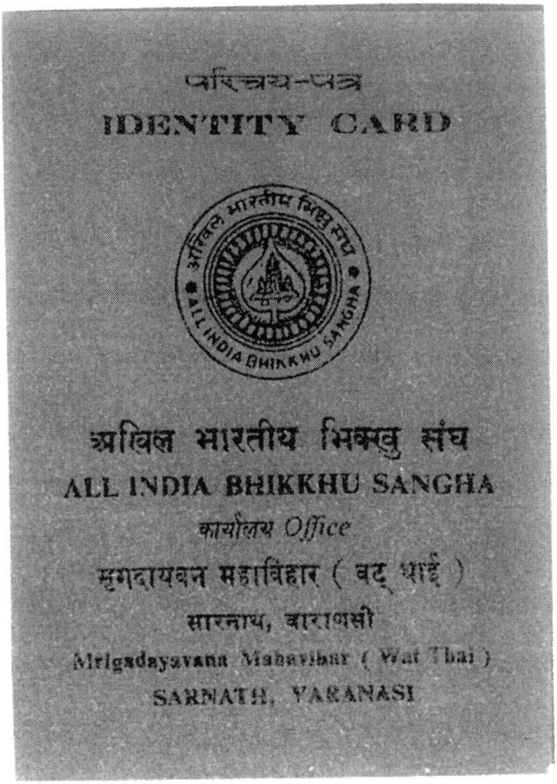

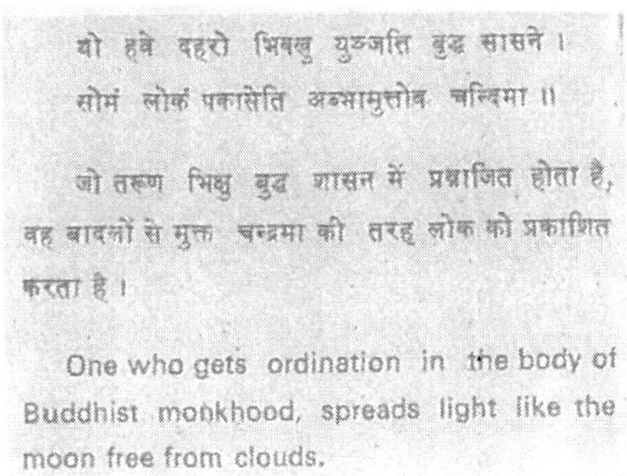
यो हवे दहरो भिक्खु युञ्जति बुद्ध सासने ।
सोमं लोकं पकासेति अब्भामुत्तोव चन्दिमा ॥

जो तरुण भिक्षु बुद्ध शासन में प्रव्राजित होता है, वह बादलों से मुक्त चन्द्रमा की तरह लोक को प्रकाशित करता है ।

One who gets ordination in the body of Buddhist monkhood, spreads light like the moon free from clouds.

Identity card of the All India Bhikkhu Sangha, original size, with the motto on the last page.

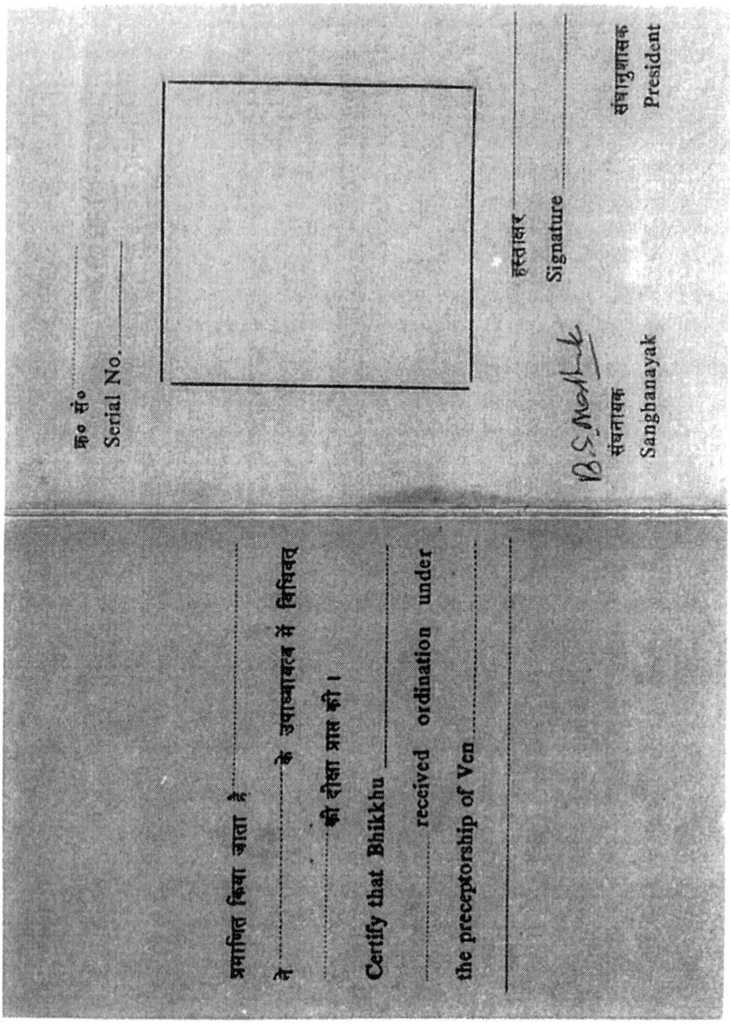

प्रमाणित किया जाता है ....
ने .... के उपाध्यायत्व में विधिवत
.... की दीक्षा प्राप्त की।
Certify that Bhikkhu ....
.... received ordination under
the preceptorship of Ven ....

क्र० सं० ....
Serial No. ....

हस्ताक्षर ....
Signature ....

संघनायक
Sanghanayak

संघानुशासक
President

Identity card, pages 2 and 3.

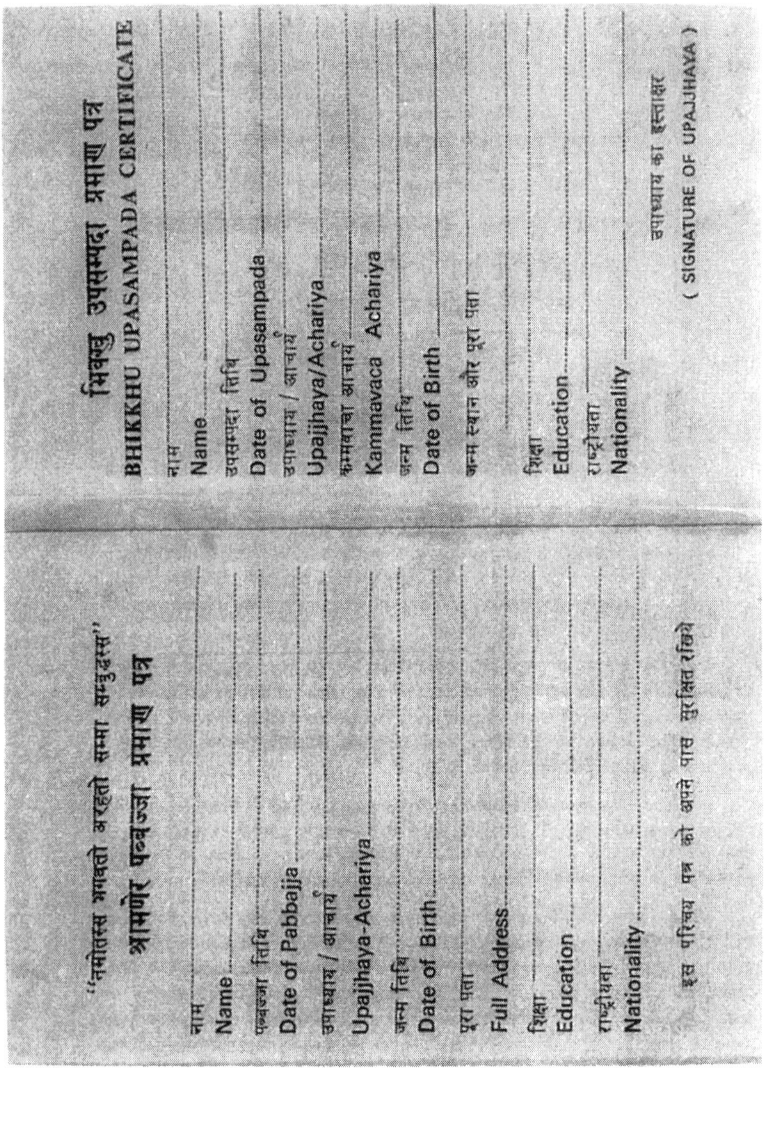

Identity card, pages 4 and 5.

All India Bhikkhu Sangha
Camp office:
Wat Thai
Sarnath, Varanasi
Phone : 385001, 385744

अखिल भारतीय भिक्खु संघ
अस्थायी कार्यालय : थाई बुद्ध विहार
सारनाथ, वाराणसी
फोन : ३८५००१, ३८५७४४

॥ सुखा संघस्स सामग्गी समग्गानं तपो सुखो ॥
चरथ भिक्खवे चारिकं बहुजन हिताय बहुजन सुखाय लोकानुकम्पाय
Registered Under Act XXI of 1960
Vide No. 37-1971-72 dated 10th Oct. 1972

अखिल भारतीय भिक्खु संघ का 28वाँ वार्षिक अधिवेशन

अप्रैल 25-26, 2541/1998

स्थानः— धुलिया (महाराष्ट्र)

सूचना एवं सविनय निवेदन

धर्म बन्धुओं,

आप को सूचित करते हुए हमें अपार हर्ष हो रहा है कि अखिल भारतीय भिक्खु संघ का 28वाँ वार्षिक अधिवेशन श्रद्धा सम्पन्न उपासक-उपासिकाओं के निमंत्रण एवं अनुरोध पर धुलिया (महाराष्ट्र) में अप्रैल 25-26, 2541/1998 को आहूत किया जा रहा है।

इस अधिवेशन से पूर्व जितने भी वार्षिक अधिवेशन हुए हैं, उनमें उपस्थित होकर आप सभी ने संघ की एकता को दर्शाया है। इन अधिवेशनों में संघ के कार्य का ब्यौरा आप के सामने रखा जाता रहा है और आप सभी एकजुट होकर समस्याओं को सुलझाने के लिए सुझाव देते रहे हैं और प्रस्ताव पारित करते हैं। लेकिन अनेकानेक बाधाओं के कारण उन पर आंशिक रूप से ही कार्यान्वयन हो पाता है।

बन्धुओं! अ० भा० भि० संघ इस वर्ष अपने 28वें वर्ष में प्रवेश कर चुका है। इन अट्ठाइस वर्षों की अवधि में जो कुछ भी कार्य हुए हैं, आप सभी उससे अवगत हैं। विशेषकर बुद्ध गया का भवन-निर्माण कार्य हुआ है। वह आपके संगठन से ही हो पाया है। अपनी क्षमतानुसार आप जहाँ भी जिस क्षेत्र में धर्म प्रचार का कार्य एवं हमारे समाज के लिए रचनात्मक कार्य कर रहे हैं वह प्रशंसनीय हैं। अ० भा० भि० संघ को गर्व है कि भिक्खु संघ के सदस्य अपनी क्षमता के अनुरूप बहुजन हिताय कार्य कर रहें है।

संसार का कोई ऐसा समाज नहीं है, जिसमें विध्वंसात्मक तत्व (व्यक्ति) नहीं हैं। स्वार्थवश ही संगठन का कोई तत्व अहितकारक कार्य करता है। हमारा भिक्खु संघ भी इस तथ्य का अपवाद नहीं है। किन्तु ऐसे सदस्यों की संख्या नगण्य होती है। इसके बावजूद वह हमारा धर्मबन्धु है, उसे मैत्री-चित्त से समझा-बुझाकर हमें ही सामूहिक प्रयास से ठीक करना है। चित्त परिवर्तन के बाद वह संघ की रचनात्मक कार्य पद्धति में सहायक हो सकता है।

वार्षिक अधिवेशन ही एक ऐसा माध्यम है जिसमें दायक-दायिकायें एकत्रित होकर अ० भा० भि० संघ को देखते हैं। आपको संगठित देखकर लोग प्रसन्न होते हैं। जो एक दो लोग संघ के सदस्यों के अहित कार्यों से अप्रसन्न होते हैं, उनमें आपकी उपस्थिति श्रद्धा उत्पन्न करती है। जो पहले से प्रसन्न हैं, उनकी प्रसन्नता में वृद्धि होती है, भिक्खु संघ का हर सदस्य आजीवन दायक-दायिकाओं पर आश्रित हैं। ये ही प्रत्यक्ष-अप्रत्यक्ष रूप से भिक्खुओं के चार प्रत्यय— आवास, भोजन, चीवर एवं औषधि आदि की व्यवस्था करते हैं। भिक्खु संघ के प्रत्येक सदस्य का पहला कर्तव्य यह हो जाता है कि दायक-दायिकाओं को धर्म-विनयानुसार मार्गदर्शन करें। अतएव प्रत्येक सदस्य को अपने व्यक्तिगत कार्यों को नजरअन्दाज़ कर अधिवेशन में उपस्थिति देनी चाहिए। हमारे अनेक बन्धु सुलझे एवं संवेदनशील हैं, इसलिए भिक्खु संघ के हर एक सदस्य को इस अधिवेशन में शामिल होने के लिए उत्साहित एवं प्रेरित करें।

कृ० पृ० उ०

Invitation to the 28th Annual Assembly of the All India Bhikkhu Sangha in Dhulia, 25–26 April 1998.
See translation on pp. 178–80.

(2)

औरंगाबाद और नागपुर में जो अधिवेशन हुए उनकी सफलता से आप सभी अवगत हैं। इन दोनों महानगरों के बौद्धजन, धर्म और समाज के प्रति जागृत हैं। अ० भा० भि० संघ का इस वर्ष का वार्षिक अधिवेशन धुलिया के लोगों के लिए एक नवीन जानकारी के रूप में है। इसलिए यह 28वाँ अधिवेशन महत्त्वपूर्ण होगा। यहाँ के दायक-दायिकाओं के अनुरोध पर यह सम्मेलन सम्पन्न किया जा रहा है।

आप सभी संघ के सदस्य अधिक से अधिक संख्या में उपस्थित होकर धुलिया के बौद्ध जनसमुदाय को धर्म-देशना द्वारा मार्ग दर्शन करें।

बैठक की कार्यावली

1. गत वर्ष की बैठकों की कार्यवाही का संघ द्वारा अनुमोदन।
2. वार्षिक आय-व्यय के विवरण का कोषाध्यक्ष द्वारा प्रस्तुतिकरण और उस पर विचार तथा अनुमोदन।
3. 1998-1999 सत्र के अनुमानित आय-व्यय एवं धन-संग्रह के स्रोतों पर चर्चा एवं सदस्यों द्वारा सुझाव तथा उन पर कार्यान्वयन पर गम्भीर चर्चा।
4. अ०भा०भि०संघ के निर्माणाधीन भवन-कार्य पर चर्चा एवं उसकी उपयोगिता की समालोचना।
5. मगध विश्वविद्यालय (बोध गया) के पास की अ०भा०भि०संघ की जमीन पर प्रथम चरण के कार्य को आरम्भ करना और उस कार्य के लिए धन एकत्रित करने पर विचार एवं सुझाव।
6. अ० भा० भि० सं० के प्रधान कार्यालय-सचिव के विषय में विचार विमर्श एवं उनके लिए निर्देश।
7. बोध गया स्थित महाविहार मुक्ति हेतु चर्चा एवं सुझाव।
8. अ० भा० भि० संघ के ऊपर दिल्ली की अदालत में जो मुक़दमें चल रहें हैं उनके निराकरण पर चर्चा एवं सुझाव।
9. सभापति की अनुमति से अ० भा० भि० संघ से संबंधित अन्यान्य-विषयों पर सदस्यों द्वारा विचार एवं सुझाव।

॥ भवतु सब्ब मंगलं ॥

सद्धर्म में—

R. Rasmi

महासचिव

अखिल भारतीय भिक्षु संघ

नोटः—मुम्बई की ओर जानेवाली सभी रेलगाड़ियाँ भुसावल जंक्शन पर रुकती है। अतः आप लोग धुलिया जाने के लिए वहाँ पर उतरें, और भुसावल से धुलिया जाने का प्रबन्ध किया गया है।

Invitation to the 28th Annual Assembly of the All India Bhikkhu Sangha in Dhulia, 25–26 April 1998.

All India Bhikkhu Sangha Emblem (Same address in Hindi)
Camp Office:
Wat Thai
Sarnath, Varanasi
Phone: 385001, 385744

Happiness is the Sangha's unity; happiness is the striving of the united.
Walk, o Bhikkhus, the path to salvation of many people and to the blessings of many people, out of compassion for the world.

Registered under Act XXI of 1960
Vide No. 37-1971-72 dated 10 October 1972

28th Annual Assembly of the All India Bhikkhu Sangha
25-26 April 2541/1998
Place: Dhulia (Maharashtra)

Circular Letter and Invitation

Friends in the Dharma,

It is our infinite pleasure to inform you that the 28th annual assembly of the All India Bhikkhu Sangha has been summoned on 25 and 26 April 2541/1998 in Dhulia (Maharashtra) following the invitation and request of the believing *upasakas* and *upasikas*.

You have demonstrated the unity of the *sangha* through your presence at all previous annual assemblies. During this assembly you will be presented with a report about the current projects of the *sangha*, together you will make suggestions to solve current problems, and pass on these suggestions. Due to the great number of difficulties, these are dealt with sequentially under individual heads of the agenda.

Friends! With this year the A.I.B. Sangha enters into its 28th year. You are all familiar with the tasks which had to be undertaken during these twenty-eight years. It meant, especially, the erection of a building in Bodh Gaya. This could be realized only through the efforts of our organization. Your dedication at so many places and in so many areas to the dissemination of the *dharma* and your constructive activities in service

Translation of Plates in Hindi on page 176-7

of our society, deserve the highest recognition. The A.I.B. Sangha is proud that the members of the Bhikkhu Sangha are actively and powerfully working for the well-being of so many people.

No religion in this world is free from destructive elements. Such persons act out of purely selfish reasons and harm the organization. Our Bhikkhu Sangha too is no exception in this respect. However, the number of such members is hardly of any consequence. Still, they are our friends in the *dharma*. It is our duty to collectively make an effort to appeal to their conscience. After they change their outlook, they too can constructively contribute to the activities of the *sangha*.

The annual assembly offers the opportunity to take a good look at the *sangha*. The sight of the assembled *sangha* makes everyone happy. Your presence renews the faith of the few who are dissatisfied with the harmful activities of individual members. Those who were already satisfied with the *sangha* become even more content. Each member of the Bhikkhu Sangha depends for all his or her life on lay Buddhists. They provide visibly or invisibly the four supports of a *bhikkhu*: accommodation, food, clothing, and medicine. It is the most important duty of every member of the Bhikkhu Sangha to give guidance in *dharma* and *vinaya* to the lay Buddhists. Therefore, each member should openly disclose at the annual assembly his or her personal activities. Since many of our friends are clear-thinking and feeling human beings, we wish to encourage and call upon each member of the Bhikkhu Sangha to participate in this assembly.

You know that the assemblies in Aurangabad and Nagpur were successful. In both cities attention among the Buddhists to the *dharma* and the society has been awakened. This annual assembly of the A.I.B. Sangha means a new experience for the people of Dhulia. Therefore, this 28th assembly will have a special significance. The support of the local sponsors guarantees the success of the assembly.

Therefore, you as members of the *sangha* should appear in as great numbers as possible and should grant, through instruction in the *dharma*, guidance to the Buddhists of Dhulia.

Agenda of the Session

1. Approval of the proceedings of the sessions of the previous year by the Sangha.
2. Presentation of the report and accounts by the Treasurer, discussion, and their acceptance.
3. Discussion of the expected income and expenditure for the budgetary

year 1998-9. Discussion of the sources of income, suggestions of the members, and a serious dialogue concerning these.

4. Report on the current measures of the building of the A.I.B. Sangha and a critical dialogue concerning these.
5. Suggestions about beginning with the first segment of the planned construction of the All India Bhikkhu Sangha on the piece of land near the Maghad University (Bodh Gaya). Reflections and suggestions on how the necessary financial means could be obtained.
6. Detailed discussion of the secretary in the head office and instructions for him.
7. Discussion and suggestions regarding the question of the total recovery of the Mahavihara in Bodh Gaya.
8. Report on the pending court cases against the A.I.B. Sangha in Delhi and suggestions for their termination.
9. Questions concerning the A.I.B. Sangha.

May all beings experience well-being.

In the spirit of the true Dharma
Sasanarasmi
General Secretary
All India Bhikkhu Sangha

Note: All trains coming from Mumbai (Bombay) stop in Bhusawal. So please get down in Bhusawal. Cars are provided for you to continue your journey from Bhusawal to Dhulia.

Translated from Hindi into German by Rainer Kimmig and from German into English by Hans-Georg Tuerstig.

Proceedings of the 27th Annual Assembly and the Board Meetings of the All India Bhikkhu Sangha 1997–1998

Presented for acceptance at the 28th Annual Assembly in Dhulia (Maharashtra), 25–26 April 1998

The 27th annual assembly of the A.I.B. Sangha took place on 1 and 2 March 2540/1997, after 16 years once again at the sacred Diksha site in Nagpur (Maharashtra) in a joyful, relaxed, and cheerful atmosphere. Buddhist Upasakas and Upasikas have contributed to the success of this assembly through their physical, mental, and financial support. A comparatively large number of Bhikkhus and Novices have participated in the assembly.

The assembly began on 1 March 1997 at 6:00 a.m. at the stupa of the Diksha site with the hoisting of the Panchashila flag. Following this, the Bhikkhu Sangha, the Upasakas, and the Upasikas left the Diksha site together in a procession. The procession went through the city to the Reserve Bank of India on Siddhartha Place. There the statue of Bharat Ratna Dr Babasaheb Bhimrao Ambedkar was honoured with a flower garland on behalf of the A.I.B. Sangha. Then the procession returned through the city to the Diksha site. The Bhikkhu Sangha showed its reverence for the relics of Babasaheb in the stupa on the Diksha site and honoured them with flowers. Afterwards, the Bhikkhu Sangha was fed. Thus, the 27th annual assembly of the A.I.B. Sangha began in a cheerful atmosphere.

Proceedings of the Board Meeting

The board meeting during the 27th annual assembly of the A.I.B. Sangha began on 1 March 1997 at 2:00 p.m. in the Shri Kumare Hall of the College on the Diksha Bhumi under the presidency of the eldest of the order (*Sanghanusaka*) of the A.I.B. Sangha, Ven. Dharmapala Mahathero. The Sangha opened its meeting with the worship of the Three Jewels, then the Sangha commemorated the late Ven. Dharmakirti. Ven. Shasan Rasmi Mahathero, General Secretary of the A.I.B. Sangha, briefly spoke about the life of Dharmakirti. After this, the Chairman, Ven. Dharmapala Mahathero, welcomed those present and asked the General Secretary to begin with the agenda. After that the General Secretary opened the meeting according to the agenda.

1. First, the Treasurer of the A.I.B. Sangha, Bhikkhu Gurudhammo, with

the consent of the conference leader and the General Secretary, presented to the Sangha the proceedings of the 26th annual meeting 1996 and of the other extraordinary sessions 1996-7 and asked for their sanction. The Sangha discussed the proceedings and accepted it.

2. The Treasurer presented to the board the detailed report and accounts of the past budgetary year. After a serious discussion and the correction of mistakes, the members sanctioned them. The Treasurer thanked the members of the board.
3. The General Secretary, Ven. Shasan Rasmi Mahathero, informed the Sangha about the construction of the Sangha Bhavan of the A.I.B. Sangha in Bodh Gaya and presented the plan for the enclosure of the land at Maghad University. Afterwards, he asked the Sangha for its support in raising the estimated expenses of approximately Rs 3,00,000.
4. The pending court cases against the A.I.B. Sangha were discussed. Regarding this subject, there was agreement in the session. It was decided to lead the proceedings to a solution in accordance with the legal position. In addition, Ven. Rahul Bodhi was assigned the task of contributing as much as possible to the settlement of the proceedings by being personally present.
5. Since in the current year the term of office of the governing body of the A.I.B. Sangha expires, new board members have to be elected. At the same time, the President and Vice President have to be elected. The proposal was discussed and passed by the board members, and the election was arranged.
6. The agenda for the general assembly and the election on 2 March 1997 was settled.
7. With the agreement of the Chairman, other subjects were discussed, among them the declaration given by Ven. Vishuddhananda Bodhi from Aurangabad in a Marathi newspaper. Vishuddhananda at first had asked the Sangha for forgiveness and then clarified that with this declaration he had the well-being of the Sangha in mind.
8. Because of the numerous complaints about Bhikkhu Vinayananda, who lives in the building of the Sangha in Bodh Gaya and is occupied entirely with his own self-interest and so has neglected his daily duties, the Sangha was forced to pass the resolution to remove him from his position.

With this the 27th board meeting came to an end. Finally, the General Secretary thanked the present members of the board and the Sangha, and declared the session closed.

General Assembly

The general assembly during the annual general meeting of the A.I.B. Sangha took place on 2 March 1997 at 2:00 p.m. in a magnificent tent erected on the Diksha site. Ven. Dharmapala Mahathero as President of the Sangha opened the assembly by honouring the Three Jewels. Afterwards, the President first welcomed the assembly, and then the General Secretary began with the agenda.

Successively, the following plans and suggestions were passed and approved by the general assembly:

1. First, the proceedings of last year's session was read to the Sangha. The Bhikkhu Sangha approved the proceedings.
2. The Treasurer presented the report and accounts to the Sangha.
3. The General Secretary informed the Sangha about the construction of the building of the All India Bhikkhu Sangha in Bodh Gaya and about the intended enclosure of the land near Maghad University. He urged the Sangha to make the necessary effort to raise the required monies. The Sangha agreed through its silence. The General Secretary of the A.I.B. Sangha, Ven. Shasan Rasmi, presented to the Sangha point 6 of the agenda, according to which the eldest of the order (*Sangha Nayaka*) and the members of the board had to be elected. The Sangha passed this report with its approval, and the General Secretary asked the President of the Sangha to urge the Sangha to begin with the election.

After a short address by the President of the Sangha, the General Secretary began with the election procedure. First, he dismissed the old board and then asked the Sangha to proceed with the election. The 36 board members were elected.

Officials and Board Members of the All India Bhikkhu Sangha

1. Eldest of the order *Sangha Nayaka*	Hon. Dr Medhankar Mahathero Nagpur
2. Substitute *Anu Sangha Nayaka*	Hon. Sadananda Mahathero Nagpur
3. President of the Sangha *Sanghanusaka*	Hon. Dharmapala Mahathero Calcutta
4. Vice President of the Sangha *Anu Sanghanusaka*	Hon. Vishuddhananda Mahathero Delhi

5. General Secretary	Hon. Shasan Rasmi Mahathero Sarnath
6. Treasurer	Hon. Gurudhammo Thero Sarnath
7. Secretary for Welfare	Hon. Rahulabodhi Mahathero Mumbai
8. Secretary for Culture	Hon. Buddhamitra Mahathero Kushinagara
9. Secretary for Organization	Hon. Karunananda Mahathero Delhi
10. Secretary for Education	Hon. Angulimala Mahathero Mumbai
11. Secretary for Public Relations	Hon. Sumedh Bodhi Thero Amaravati
12. Secretary for Publications	Hon. Narendra Mahathero Arunachal
13. Secretary for Administration	Hon. Sagatabodhi Thero Nagpur
14. Board Member	Hon. Dhammadarshi Mahathero Icchapur
15. Board Member	Hon. Dhammaratan Mahathero Mumbai
16. Board Member	Hon. Anuruddha Mahathero Nagpur
17. Board Member	Hon. Satyashila Mahathero Nagpur
18. Board Member	Rajguru Mahathero Calcutta
19. Board Member	Hon. Mahapanth Thero Nagpur
20. Board Member	Hon. Upagupta Thero Parbhani
21. Board Member	Hon. Nirgunananda Thero Mumbai
22. Board Member	Hon. Vishuddhananda Bodhi Thero Aurangabad
23. Board Member	Hon. Vimalananda Arunachal
24. Board Member	Hon. Amarajyoti Thero Nagpur

25. Board Member	Hon. Shantarakshita Thero Nagpur
26. Board Member	Hon. Shraddhapal Thero Nagpur
27. Board Member	Hon. Buddhaghosha Nagpur
28. Board Member	Hon. Dhammajyoti Delhi
29. Board Member	Hon. Dhammadipa Mahathero Nagpur
30. Board Member	Hon. Satyananda Madhya Pradesh
31. Board Member	Hon. Sanghananda Thero Andhra Pradesh
32. Board Member	Hon. Ananda West Bengal
33. Board Member	Hon. Aggadhammo Arunachal
34. Board Member	Hon. Udayananda Delhi
35. Board Member	Hon. Dhammapriya Haryana
36. Board Member	Hon. Shilananda Delhi

After the election, the General Secretary, Ven. Shasan Rasmi Mahathero, declared the election procedure closed and expressed his gratitude for the peaceful course of the election. With this, the 27th annual general assembly was closed.

Informal Session of the Newly Elected Board

An informal session of the newly elected board of the A.I.B. Sangha was summoned for 3 March 1997 at 2:00 p.m. In charge of the session was the newly elected eldest of the order, Ven. Medhankar Mahathero. The session was opened with the honouring of the Three Jewels.

It was the goal of the session to introduce the newly elected board members to each other and to discuss a few special topics. The central question was what role the A.I.B. Sangha plays in the efforts to free the Mahavihara in Bodh Gaya and what actions it could take in this respect.

The General Secretary, Ven. Shasan Rasmi, declared that it was the A.I.B. Sangha which first addressed the problem of the Mahavihara in Bodh Gaya. In this respect, a delegation of the Bhikkhu Sangha had visited the then Chief Minister of Bihar, Shri Laloo Prasad, and submitted the request to hand over completely the Mahavihara in Bodh Gaya to the Buddhists. The Bhikkhu Sangha, within the framework of the advisable courtesy, continues to be active in this matter. After further discussion, the decision was taken that a delegation of the entire board of the A.I.B. Sangha should visit the President (of India), the Prime Minister and the Minister for Social Welfare on 10 May 1997, hand over a memorandum concerning the Mahavihara of Bodh Gaya, and submit the demand to release the Mahavihara of Bodh Gaya to the Buddhists. In this matter, the assembly must first agree upon a date with the President and the Prime Minister. Correspondingly, letters should be written. This task was given to the secretary for organization and the board member Ven. Karunananda. Both declared their agreement. Afterwards, two further topics were discussed, and the session ended in a friendly atmosphere.

With this, the 27th annual assembly too was completed.

At the 27th annual assembly the following suggestions were passed:

Proposals passed during the 27th General Assembly of the All India Bhikkhu Sangha

1. The release of the Mahabodhi Buddha Vihara in Bodh Gaya must be pursued. The said Buddha Vihara has to be entirely given into the control of the All India Bhikkhu Sangha.
2. The officials of the All India Bhikkhu Sangha shall receive railway passes.
3. Corresponding to Sanskrit schools, special schools for the Pali, also an old Indian language, should be established.
4. The Government of India has to grant the appropriate sponsorship and protection for old historic Buddhist sites as well as historic Buddhist caves and ruins. The Government of India may summon a national meeting with participation of the *bhikkhus*.
5. The Ven. Ananda, who has lived in India for 25 years, should be awarded Indian citizenship.
6. The actions against the Chakma Buddhists are to be stopped. India has to pay them due respect and award them Indian citizenship.
7. The state may recognize the traditional Buddhist form of marriage. A corresponding proposal was passed during this assembly.

Extraordinary Session of the Board of the A.I.B. Sangha
Date: 31 July 1997. Place: Bhogal Buddha Vihara, Delhi

An extraordinary session of the board of the All India Bhikkhu Sangha was summoned on 31 July 1997 in Delhi. The session was summoned in the Bhogal Buddha Vihara in Delhi. The President, Ven. Dharmapala Mahathero, was unable to attend. For this reason, the eldest of the order, Ven. Medhankar Mahathero, assumed the chairmanship of the session. The session was opened with the honouring of the Three Jewels. Afterwards, the General Secretary welcomed first the board members and then moved on to the agenda:

1. Bhikkhu Gurudhammo read to the Sangha the proceedings of the last board meeting. The Sangha passed the report after a brief discussion.
2. The General Secretary, Ven. Shasan Rasmi Mahathero, emphasized the necessity for an enclosure for the plot near Maghad University and explained to the board members that they have to take over the responsibility in this matter. The Sangha has to raise money for this cause.
3. The General Secretary informed the Sangha about the training of *bhikkhus* and complained that there had been talk about the training of the *bhikkhus* ever since the founding of the Bhikkhu Sangha, but that each time it was declared that no place was available. However, the Thai Buddha Vihara in Sarnath now offered such an opportunity and was ready to offer the necessary support for the *bhikkhus* of the Mrigadayavana Mahavihara Samiti who were willing to undergo training. The *bhikkhus* have not yet made use of this opportunity.
4. Numerous complaints have come in against Bhikkhu Vinayananda who oversees the construction of the building of the A.I.B. Sangha in Bodh Gaya. For this reason, the board in its session came to the decision to remove Vinayananda. Therefore, it is necessary to appoint a *bhikkhu* in his place for one year. Accordingly, the General Secretary suggested that the Sangha should transfer the supervision of the building of the A.I.B. Sangha in Bodh Gaya to a suitable *bhikkhu*. The board discussed the question and finally came to the decision to entrust Bhikkhu Sagatabodhi, the secretary of administration, with this task. Bhikkhu Sagatabodhi immediately declared his agreement with this decision. The Sangha, moreover, expressed the expectation that Bhikkhu Sagatabodhi would take over the entire organization as well as the

raising of the means for the Bhikkhu Sangha. This, however, was not possible.

- At the same time it was decided that the Treasurer would take over Vinayananda's function in Bodh Gaya. Ven. Buddhamitra, Ven. Mahapanth, and Ven. Sagatabodhi would support him in this.

5. With the consent of the chairman, further topics were discussed:

   (a) The most important point was the question of the Mahavihara in Bodh Gaya. As decided during the previous session, a delegation of the A.I.B. Sangha should visit the President (of India), the Prime Minister and the Minister for Social Welfare on 10 May 1997, and hand over a memorandum. However, the Secretary for Organization was not able to put this plan, for which he had been given the responsibility, into practice.

   (b) Afterwards where the next annual assembly should take place was discussed. Ven. Upagupta suggested to the Sangha that the 28th annual assembly be summoned to Dhulia (Maharashtra). Bhikkhu Gurudhammo supported this suggestion. The suggestion was discussed by the Sangha and was accepted by voting.

Finally, general topics were discussed and the opinion of the *bhikkhus* was heard. After that, the General Secretary thanked the present board members for their support during the session. In the name of the Sangha he then thanked the leadership of the Bhogal Buddha Vihara, the Upasakas, and Upasikas for providing meals, accommodation, etc., wished them all the best, and declared the session closed.

With this the session ended.

Confirmed:
Dharmapala Mahathero
Chairman,
A.I.B. Sangha
25 April 1998

Sasanarasmi
General Secretary
All India Bhikkhu Sangha

Translated from Hindi into German by Rainer Kimmig and from German into English by Hans-Georg Tuerstig.

ALL INDIA BHIKKHU SANGHA
Temporary Office :
WAT THAI, SARNATH,
VARANASI
Tel. 385001
385744

अखिल भारतीय भिक्षु संघ
अस्थायी कार्यालय :
थाई बुद्ध विहार (वट् थाई)
सारनाथ, वाराणसी
टेलीफोन : ३८५००१
३८५७४४

॥ सुखा संघस्स सामग्गी समग्गानं तपो सुखो ॥
चरथ भिक्खवे चारिकं बहुजन हिताय बहुजन सुखाय लोकानुकम्पाय

Registered Under Act XXI of 1860
Vide No. 37-1971-72 dated 10th Oct. '72

Ref. No. AIBS/ ....

Dated 16.1. 2542/1999

Dr. Detlef. Kantowsky. Kaiserpfalz 76. D 78351 Bodman

Dear Mahā Upāsaka Dr. D. Kantowsky,

Wish you and the family very happy and prosperous New year.

We received your letter of 16.10.1998. Thank you very much for the book 'Phra Phrang', Photo post-cards and the protocol of AIBS Nagpur-Conference.

We could not send you the protocol of the Dhulia Conference for it is not yet confirmed by the Governing Body of AIBs. It will be confirmed by the Sangha in Sarnath Conference.

29 th Annual Conference of AIBs is going to be held at Sarnath from 16 th March to 17 March 1999.

You are the sponsor of this Conference, therefore, your presence at Sarnath as the Observer is pertinent and essential.

We earnestly request you to be at Sarnath in February '99, for you are free from February onwards.

With blessings and best regards.

Yours in the Sublime Dhamma
S. Rasmi
Secretary General
All India Bhikkhu Sangha

Letter of invitation by Sasanarasmi Mahathero, General Secretary of the All India Bhikkhu Sangha, in which the auhtor is requested to participate in the Sangha's 29th Annual Conference to be held at Sarnath from 16th to 17th March 1999. The concluding remark ". . . for you are free from February onwards" refers to my retirement from university duties at the end of the winter-term 1998/99 which we had often discussed during my stay in "Wat Thai", Sarnath in February/March 1998.

CHAPTER SEVEN

'Dhammagiri': The Dhamma-Mountain

IGATPURI IS located 136 km by train north-east of Mumbai and is described in an old travel guide (*Murray's Handbook* 1962: 20) in this way:

> Igatpuri, properly Wigatpura, 'the town of difficulties', so-called on account of the precipitous road, is a sanatorium, 1900 ft. above the sea, and summer resort of gentry from Bombay. Half a mile from the station a picturesque lake supplies Igatpuri and Kasara with excellent water. The line to Manmad was opened in 1861, the rails having been carted up the Thal Ghat before the work there was finished to. To the south can be seen the peak of Kalsubai (5427 ft.), the highest mountain in the Presidency, and Sivaji's hill-forts of Alang, Bitangad, Aundha and Arr.

The busy National Highway No. 3 from Mumbai to Delhi passes slightly to the south of Igatpuri, so that the old centre of town is still comparatively quiet. To the passengers sitting on the left side of the train or car a surprising view presents itself shortly before their arrival in the town. In front of a striking mountain range (see Kapadia, 1993: 67ff.) lies a wooded hill, and out of the dense green foliage shines the roof of a golden pagoda. After their arrival at the station, foreigners do not have to announce their destination. All rickshaw drivers have made the one-mile trip to Dhammagiri quite often.

In 1997, 21 ten-day Vipassana courses and 9 courses for old disciples were held there; altogether 7,350 new and 2,892 old disciples attended. 'This year', it is stated in an internal communication (*Vipassana Newsletter*, Vol. 25, No. 3, July/Septemper 1998: 3), 'the number of registrations was overwhelming: Between 1,500 and 2,000 applications for the regular ten-day courses arrived at the centre, which can accommodate only 500 disciples.'

What had begun with the purchase of an 8-hectare plot on the hill has expanded significantly in twenty years. Today, a total of 20 hectares of land belong to the grounds of the Vipassana International Academy and is enclosed to prevent overgrazing by the local cattle. The spiritual centre is a pagoda with individual rooms for a total of 300 meditators. This academy was founded by Satya Narain Goenka (born in 1924 in Burma), who practised Vipassana for the first time in 1955 under the guidance of U Ba Khin. Through this he experienced his new birth (see pp. 201f). After he renounced his very successful business in Burma, and since his return to India in 1969, Goenkaji, as he is admiringly called by his disciples, devoted himself entirely to the task of bringing the *dhamma* back to the country of its origin and to lead ten-day Vipassana courses for the self-liberating realization of the basic conditions and forms of universal truth.

The Vipassana movement thus created has spread all over the world. In the annual report for 1997, which was submitted in 1998 at the annual international conference in Dhammagiri, it is said in this respect (*Vipassana Newsletter*, Vol. 25, No. 3, 1998):

Ehi passiko

The year 1997 was marked by a rapid and extensive growth of the *dhamma*, not only in India, but in the entire world. In spite of 43 established centres and 400 teachers and assistant teachers, the demand for Vipassana courses exceeds the present possibilities for holding them. Many factors are responsible for the growth of Vipassana, among them the service rendered worldwide and in various ways by several thousands of disciples. But the main factor is the quality of the *dhamma* itself: *Ehi passiko*—come and see.

The Great Vipassana Pagoda

On 26 October, in a public ceremony, the foundation stone for the great Vipassana pagoda in Mumbai (Bombay) was laid. During this historically important occasion, the Mahabodhi Society of India handed over relics of the Buddha for the shrine in the pagoda. An information gallery inside the pagoda will inform visitors about the life of the Buddha and describe the positive effects of practising Vipassana. The compound will also include a large Dhamma Hall, which can accommodate 10,000 meditators. The completion of the building of the pagoda is planned for the end of 1999, a suitable appreciation of Vipassana at the opening of the twenty-first century. At the same time, this project marks the centenary of the birth of Sayagyi U Ba Khin.

During the ceremony for the consecration of the pagoda, Myanmar (Burma) and Taiwan were represented by large groups of visitors, including monks and nuns who, after the ceremony, participated together in a ten-day course in Dhammagiri in the presence of Goenkaji.

At the same occasion, the CD-ROM of the *Pāli-Tipitaka* was officially introduced. This CD-ROM was produced by the Vipassana Research Institute and is the first in the world, to contain the entire *Tipitaka* and the corresponding commentaries in Devanagari as well as Roman and Burmese scripts. It is based on the authorized text of the Sixth Buddhist Council, which was held in this century (1956) in Burma. The CD-ROM preserves the authentic words of the Buddha in modern electronic form. It simplifies the search for this extensive literature and is a valuable resource for research. The CD-ROM is given free of charge to institutions, scholars, and other interested people.

The method of self-observation, the conscious awareness especially of physical sensations, which has been described in the shorter and longer sermons on the basics of awareness (*Satipatthana Sutta*), is sufficiently known and has been explained as "The Heart of Buddhist Meditation" (Nyanaponika, 1972) for Western practitioners as well. Publications of the Vipassana Research Institute inform about the special experiences that have occurred in Dhammagiri as well as in other Indian centres—and recently even in Indian prisons! (cf. *Vipassana Newsletter*, 1991, 1994, 1995, and 1997).

An earlier experience of a course with U Ba Khin in 1960 from a Christian perspective was reported by Winston L. King (1990: 225-35). Also very vivid and precise is the report of a 'hippie' who participated in the first course offered by Goenka in a camp near Pratapgarh (Maharashtra) in 1973 (Rahula, 1985: 251–70). Three years later, he was ordained in Sri Lanka as a monk with the name Yogavacara Rahula. Meanwhile, he is well known in Germany as well and gives courses regularly in the "House of Silence" in Roseburg, near Hamburg, Germany (see *Nachrichten aus Roseburg*, 1998).

A description of Goenka's methods is available in a German translation authorized by him (Hart, 1996), and the dissertation by Gerhard Scholz (1992) discusses Vipassana as the heart of the Buddha's teachings within an activity-oriented yet theoretical context and with special reference to its importance for drug therapy. Gerhard Scholz himself lived for two years at the Vipassana Research Institute in Dhammagiri.

Finally, two internal publications inform the reader in great detail about the content of a ten-day course (Goenka, 1995) as well as the understanding of *dharma* (Goenka, 1997) conveyed during this course. The code of discipline which all participants at the beginning of a course

Vipassana Meditation Centres

Vipassana International Academy, *Dhamma Giri*
Igatpuri, 422 403 Dist. Nasik, Maharashtra
☎(02553) 84076, 84086, Fax:[91] (02553) 84176

Vipassana Centre, Dhamma Thalī
PO Box 208, Jaipur 302 001, Rajasthan
☎(0141) (Off.) 49520, (T.R.) 49311

Vipassana International Meditation Centre, *Dhamma Khetta*
12.6 km. Nagarjun Sagar Rd,
Kusum Nagar Vanasthali Puram,
Hyderabad 500 070, Andhra Pradesh
☎(040) 4020290, 4021746

Kutch Vipassana Centre, *Dhamma Sindhu*
Village-Bada, Dist. Mandvi, Kutch 370 475, Gujarat
☎(028347) 3303, 3304

Vipassana Centre, *Dhamma Gaṅgā*
Bara Mandir Ghat, Harishchandra Dutta Road,
Panihati (Sodepur), Dt. 24 Parganas, W.B. 743 176
☎(033) 553 2855, City Off.: (033) 251 767, 258 063

Dhamma Sikhara, Dharamsala, H.P
Dhamma Sota, Haryana (near New Delhi)
Dhamma Tihār, Tihār Jail, Delhi
Dhamma Salila, Dehradun, UP
Dhamma Cakka, Sarnath, UP
Dhamma Vimutti, Kushinagar, UP
Dhamma Suvatthi, Savatthi, UP
Dhamma Licchavī, Muzzaffarpur, Bihar
Dhamma Bodhi, Bodhgaya, Bihar
Dhamma Upavan Baracakia, Bihar
Dhamma Kānana, Balaghat, MP
Dhamma Ketu, Bhilai-Durg, MP
Dhamma Pāla, Bhopal, MP
Dhamma Pīṭha, Ahmedabad, Gujurat
Dhamma Koṭa, Rajkot, Gujarat
Dhamma Nāga, Nagpur, Mah.
Dhamma Sarovara, Dhule, Mah.
Dhammālaya, Hatkangale, Kolhapur, Mah.
Dhamma Setu, Madras, Tamil Nadu
Dhamma Sumana, Bangalore, Karnataka

Countries with Vipassana Centres:
Australia, New Zealand, France, UK, Germany, USA, Nepal, Sri Lanka, Myanmar, Combodia, Thailand, Japan.
For courses in these centres and for non-centre Vipassana courses in other countries contact:
VIA, *Dhammagiri*, Igatpuri (see address above) or
Vipassana Meditation Centre, *Dhamma Dharā*
P.O. Box 24, Shelburne Falls, MA 01370
☎ [1] (413) 625 2160; Fax [1] (413) 625 2170
E-mail: vmcdhara@aol.com

Vipassana Centres in India.

vow to keep (see pages 207–12, and the addresses of all centres in India (see page 193), are the additional sources of information offered here. The German version of the quarterly *Vipassana Newsletter*, which is published by the Vipassana Vereinigung in Germany, includes information about the courses, especially in Western countries.

There is enough information material available in English and German, and in the Hindi and Marathi languages as well, to enable one to find out about Goenka and his movement. How is it judged by Indian Buddhists?

New Buddhists, when one approaches them to discuss Goenka: 'That's again nothing else but an attempt of the Hindus to absorb Buddhism!' Or: 'Goenka gives a good conscience to the Bania-elite (i.e. the businessmen) of Bombay. His entire movement and all centres are financed with black money.' Or: 'We as good Buddhists do not go there. There are only upper-class Hindus who despise us *Nao-Buddhas*.'

One exception in this overall negative assessment from outside is D.C. Ahir. In a recent book, he portrays S.N. Goenka's Vipassana movement as very important for the re-introduction of Buddhism into India (Ahir, 1998: 133–43; see also Ahir, 1999). But then, where does the open mistrust, the hostile rejection of most New Buddhists come from? Why do not they go there and see for themselves? In my opinion, there are two main reasons:

1. S.N. Goenka and the Vipassana movement are recognized by the Hindu establishment. This became very obvious during the solemn ceremony to mark the laying of the foundation stone of the new Shwegadon Pagoda near Mumbai on 26 October 1997. The President of India congratulated the movement for the noble project and pointed out that Buddhist *karuna* (compassion) is of central importance for our time. The Maha Bodhi Society welcomed Goenka as an old friend (*kalyan mitra*) and donated some of their relics of the Buddha for the new pagoda in order to enhance the influence of this large-scale project aimed at 10,000 meditators. Among the many messages of greeting, however, the All India Bhikkhu Sangha as well as the TBMSG were missing.

If one is familiar with the history of the life and suffering of Buddhists in India today, it becomes understandable that such high recognition, especially by the Maha Bodhi Society, may seem suspicious to them. They argue that precisely because of this, Goenka could not afford to call himself a Buddhist since his Hindu followers would understand this as solidarity with the New Buddhist movement of the Ambedkarites, which they despise.

2. New Buddhists see the fact that Goenka does not call himself a Buddhist as annoying and at the same time as a sign of the ever-present Hindu inclusivism (Hacker, 1983). In an introductory verse to his treatise on *Dharma and Sectarianism*, he wrote in this context:

   Dharma is not Hindu nor Buddhist
   not Sikh, Muslim, nor Jain;
   Dharma is purity of heart,
   peace, happiness, serenity.
   (Goenka, 1997)

But if one compares the second accusation with the 'Pali Passages quoted in the Discourses' (Goenka 1995: 66–87), one notices that all participants during a ten-day course are systematically led to the core of the Buddha's teachings, in order to do on the tenth day what Buddhists do everywhere for the mutual confirmation of their common basic orientation—the joint recitation of the Threefold Refuge, the Five Shilas, and the Eightfold Path.

The core of a system of practices which was orally transmitted by the teacher Gautama more than two thousand five hundred years ago is today appreciated once more in Dhammagiri and elsewhere. In doing so, one does not bother much about the scholastic disputes which began with the writing down of the teachings, and even more so, without marking oneself off with the confession that one is a Buddhist against the mass of dissenting Hindus. Everywhere and at any time, a community of like-minded people can come together, can form a refuge for each other, and can convey an experience of the liberating effect of the practices for overcoming discriminatory ways of thinking and acting. An entrance sign proclaiming '*Buddhism*' is not necessary for such a practice hall, and nobody has to put on a Buddhist club badge at the entrance.

It may be that such a basic understanding of the teachings makes it indeed easier for Hindu pandits to integrate the new challenges of the *dhamma*, the way it is taught by Goenka, into the unquestionable oneness and general validity of all, which is the Hindu philosophy of life: The Buddha as a reformer of Hinduism and Goenka as a modern mediator of well-known Indian techniques for individual self-realization within a secular India, where untouchability has been legally prohibited with

Independence and where Buddhist symbols have been adopted or rather newly interpreted in the national flag and the emblem of the state. (See plate on page 215). In his preface to the official government commemorative publication *2500 Years of Buddhism*, to which Lama Anagarika Govinda and Sangharakshita also contributed essays, the then President of India, Sir Sarvepalli Radhakrishnan (1956, IX and XV/XVI), described this Brahmanical view in this way:

> The Buddha did not feel that he was announcing a new religion. He was born, grew up, and died a Hindu. he was restating with a new emphasis the ancient ideals of the Indo-Aryan civilization.
>
> The Buddha utilized the Hindu inheritance to correct some of its expressions. He came to fulfil, not to destroy. For us, in this country, the Buddha is an outstanding representative of our religious tradition. He left his footprints on the soil of India and his mark on the soul of the country with its habits and convictions. While the teaching of the Buddha assumed distinctive forms in the other countries of the world in conformity with their own traditions, here, in the home of the Buddha, it has entered into and become an integral part of our culture. The Brahmans and the Sramanas were treated alike by the Buddha and the two traditions gradually blended. In a sense, the Buddha is a maker of modern Hinduism.

Whatever attributions and social constructs may guide the actions of people in India today, the fact remains that in the courses on the Dhamma Mountain and in other places of practice of the Vipassana movement in India, we meet almost exclusively Hindus and occasionally Jains and Indian Christians. Self-declared Buddhists mostly arrive from Western countries in order to directly experience in Igatpuri the special power of the Dhamma Mountain. For the Indian New Buddhists, however, the place is seen through an attitude of anti-Hindu resentment, which they are not (yet) able to let go of.

30.000 Vipassana-Meditatoren bei erster Steinlegung von Shwedagon-Reproduktion

New Delhi, 26. Oktober 97 - Am 26. Oktober wurde in Mumbai im indischen Staat Maharashtra der erste Stein für den Bau eines fast hundert Meter hohen goldenen Stupa's gelegt. Den Anstoß für den Bau hat der bedeutende Vipassanā-Lehrer Sayagyi S.N. Goenka (Foto rechts), ein früherer erfolgreicher Geschäftsmann und Lehrling des burmesischen Meditationslehrers Sayagyi U Ba Khin. Mumbai wird als günstiger Platz für diesen Stupa betrachtet, da die Stadt die größte Anzahl Vipassanā-Studenten in der Welt hat. Alle zwei Wochen beginnt ein Zehntagekursus in Dhammagiri in nahegelegenen Igatpuri. Bei der Einweihung waren mehr als 30.000 Vipassanā-Übende anwesend. Die Initiative für den Bau des Stupa kommt aus Taiwan. Die Baukosten werden auf knapp 10 Millionen DM geschätzt, die durch Vipassanā-Studenten in der ganzen Welt finanziert werden sollen. Die Stupa wird nach dem Modell der 116 Meter hohen Shwedagon Pagoda in Yangon (Rangoon), Myanmar (Burma) gebaut, dem Land, in dem die Vipassanā-Technik weiter bewahrt wurde, nachdem sie 500 Jahre nach Buddha aus Indien verschwunden war. „Die Essenz des Stupa soll die Begegnung mit der echten Übung von Vipassanā darstellen," so sagte S.N. Goenka.

Sayagyi ('Lehrer' in Burmesisch) S.N. Goenka erklärte bei dieser Gelegenheit: „Während der vergangenen zweitausend Jahre ist nicht nur allein die Wahrheit über das Leben und die Lehre des Buddha aus Indien verschwunden, sondern es sind auch falsche Informationen verbreitet worden, die aus ihm eine mythologische Figur gemacht haben und wodurch seine historische Wirklichkeit vergessen wurde. Darüberhinaus wurden seine rationellen, wissenschaftlichen Lehren total verkehrt begriffen und zu unrecht als eine der vielen sektiererischen Dogmen und religiösen Lehrweisen betrachtet. Eine erleuchtete Person ist nie an der Stiftung einer Religion oder dem Verbreiten eines sektiererischen Dogmas interessiert. Er unterweist allein den Dhamma oder das universelle Gesetz der Natur, das für die ganze Menschheit anwendbar ist. Der praktische Pfad aus dem Elend in ein glücklicheres Leben. Vipassanā ist die Essenz des Dhamma -eine analytische Studie von geistigen und körperlichen Erscheinungen, die den Geist von der Basis her säubert und sein negatives Gewohnheitsmuster durchbricht." Mit dem Vipassanā-Stupa will man die Wiederentdeckung des Buddha als universellen 'Super-Wissenschaftler', der die fundamentalen Gesetze der Natur durch direkte Erfahrung realisierte, in Erinnerung rufen. Nicht nur den Buddha als Stifter einer Religion.

Der Stupa soll im Innenraum hohl sein und eine zirkelförmige Galerie, in der das Leben des Buddha abgebildet ist sowie eine riesige Halle, in der 10.000 Menschen bei den Reliquien des Buddha meditieren können, bergen.

Die wichtigsten offiziellen Gäste bei der Steinlegung waren der erste Minister Joshi und Gouverneur Alexander von dem indischen Teilstaat. Die Mahā Bodhi Gesellschaft von Indien wurde durch den ehrw. Wipulasāra Mahāthera vertreten. Der goldene Stupa soll Ende 1999 vollendet sein. Dies ist das Jahr des hundertsten Geburtstages von Sayagyi U Ba Khin. Der erste Minister Joshi von Maharashtra kündigte an, daß alle Regierungsangestellten 10 Tage bezahlten Urlaub bekommen können, um Vipassanā-Meditation zu üben.

The Laying of the Foundation Stone, New Stupa, Mumbai.
See translation on p. 198.

A translation of the German report on page 197 of the initial event of a new stupa in Mumbai:

30,000 Vipassana Meditators attend the Laying of the Foundation Stone of Shwedagon Model Stupa

New Delhi, 26 October 1997. On 26 October in Mumbai in the Indian state of Maharashtra, the first stone was laid for the construction of an almost three-hundred-foot-high golden stupa. This construction was initiated by the eminent Vipassana teacher Sayagyi S.N. Goenka (photo on page 200), a former successful businessman and a student of the Burmese meditation teacher Sayagyi U Ba Khin. Mumbai is considered an auspicious place for this stupa, since the city has the largest number of Vipassana students in the world. Every two weeks a ten-day course begins in Dhammagiri in nearby Igatpuri. More than 30,000 people who practice Vipassana were present during the consecration. The initiative for the construction of the stupa comes from Taiwan. The construction costs are estimated at nearly 5 million US dollars and are supposed to come from Vipassana students from around the world. The stupa will be modelled on the 116-meter (380 feet) high Shwedagon Pagoda in Yangon (Rangoon), Myanmar (Burma), the country in which the Vipassana technique was preserved after it had disappeared from India 500 years after the Buddha. 'The essence of the stupa shall depict the meeting with the true practice of Vipassana', said S.N. Goenka.

Sayagyi (*teacher* in Burmese) S.N. Goenka declared at this occasion:

> Not only has the truth about the life and teaching of the Buddha disappeared from India during the past two thousand years, but false information has been disseminated which has turned the Buddha into a mythological figure, and his historical reality has been forgotten. Moreover, his rational scientific teachings were totally misunderstood and [were] wrongly considered one of many sectarian dogmas and religious teachings. An enlightened person is never interested in founding a religion or in disseminating a sectarian dogma. He teaches nothing but the *dhamma* or the universal law of nature which is applicable to the entire humanity: the practical path out of misery into a happier life. Vipassana is the essence of the *dhamma*, an analytical study of physical and mental appearance, which purifies the mind from its base on and breaks through its negative habitual patterns.

With the Vipassana-stupa one wants to remind everyone of the rediscovery of the Buddha as a universal *super-scientist* who realized the fundamental laws of nature through a direct experience, and not just of the Buddha as the founder of a religion.

The stupa is hollow inside and contains a circular gallery in which the Buddha's life is depicted, as well as a huge hall in which 10,000 people can meditate near the relics of the Buddha.

The most important guests during the laying of the foundation stone were Chief Minister of Maharashtra, Manohar Joshi and P.C. Alexander, the Governor of this Indian state. The Maha Bodhi Society of India was represented by the Ven. Wipulasara Mahathera. The golden stupa should be completed by 1999. This is the year of the centenary of the birth of Sayagyi U Ba Khin. The Chief Minister Joshi of Maharashtra announced that all government employees could receive ten days paid holidays to practice Vipassana-meditation.

Buddhayana Zeitung, Vol. 9, No. 3,
January 1998/2541: 1 and 6.

Satya Narain Goenka, 1991.

Forty Years of a New Life

S. N. GOENKA

'FORTY YEARS OF a New Life' first appeared in the *Vipassana Patrika* in the autumn of 1995, marking the fortieth anniversary of the beginning of the practice of Vipassana. This article has been made available to Dr Kantowsky by the Vipassana Academy in Igatpuri.

The first ten days of September 1955 were the most precious of my life. Sitting at the feet of the supremely compassionate householder-saint, Sayagyi U Ba Khin, I learned the pristine art of observing the truth within. It was a great fortune, an exalted *parami* (wholesome deed) of some past life that had borne a priceless fruit. I could never have dreamed that these sacred moments would happen. It was a new birth.

My first birth had taken place thirty-two years earlier. Now I was truly twice-born. This second birth was indeed a worthy birth. Like a bird born of its mother, encased in a shell, my first birth was shrouded in the darkness of deep ignorance. A bird's second birth is its true birth—when it breaks the eggshell and emerges into the light. Just as the little bird blinks its eyes when it emerges from its shell into the sunlight, so was I astounded when the dark layer of ignorance was penetrated for the first time and I glimpsed the rays of true understanding. Indeed, the darkness of ignorance is darker than the absence of light within an eggshell or the womb.

Hitherto, I had not even remotely perceived the truth within. Yet how well I experienced it in those ten days. This perishable, material body, which had always seemed so solid and heavy—now its every atom trembled and came alive. Yet a still greater achievement was that I found a simple and scientific method of eradicating mental defilements. By realizing the true relationship between the body and the mind, the shackles of those deep-rooted mental defilements now began to disintegrate. I had read or heard about the highly valued stages of meditation practice, and now I was experiencing them. My heart overflowed with gratitude toward my Teacher, Sayagyi U Ba Khin.

After returning home, I practised Vipassana every morning and evening without a break, despite the acute demands of my busy schedule. This brought about fundamental changes, and my profound gratitude toward my revered teacher deepened immensely.

Vipassana became a part of my life. The mind that had burned incessantly in the fires of passion, anger, and ego now experienced a rare spiritual peace and calm. Where it had been plagued by the constant tension of myriad domestic, business, and social responsibilities, my mind was now enriched by happiness and health. Vipassana did not draw me away from my worldly responsibilities; rather it gave me renewed energy to fulfil them dispassionately. Consequently, my capacity for work increased significantly.

For years I had been immersed in serious scriptural studies and steeped in sentimental devotional practices, tremulously praying to the deities my family worshipped. Despite these practices, deep-seated defilements remained. But now they began to weaken due to this simple and natural process of meditation. My heart overflowed with thankfulness.

Since my childhood I had been conditioned by beliefs about our family deity. Although it was taught that the Lord Buddha was the ninth and most evolved incarnation of the god Vishnu, his teachings were portrayed as being oriented toward magic; they were considered unfit for true believers. These beliefs were stumbling blocks, which caused me to hesitate to join my first course of Vipassana.

But I had also heard that the Buddha was deeply compassionate. As a child I had read the story in which his cousin Devadatta had wounded a swan with an arrow and how young Gotama compassionately saved it. I had also observed that the people of Myanmar (Burma) were simple, straightforward and guileless. A question arose in my mind: if the Buddha's teachings were wrong, then how could his followers be such decent people?

Confounding my mind still further were blind beliefs that I had clung to since childhood. Some came from one of my uncles who held a high position in my father's firm. He was much older than I and a Sanskrit scholar. He had read the scriptures extensively and his frequent weapon in an argument was: 'The scriptures say so.' Immersed in rites and rituals, he prayed and worshipped for four or five hours every day. His daily chants were impressive; from a young age they inspired me to recite important scriptural passages for which I am grateful to him. I enjoyed these daily morning recitations; the words reverberated in my mind long afterward. My entire family was deeply devoted to the gods Vishnu, Krishna, and Shiva. My chants further strengthened this inherited devotion.

My uncle was extremely strict. Though he did not oppose the Lord Buddha, he strongly opposed his teachings. I, on the other hand, often visited the famous Mahamuni (Buddhist) temple in Mandalay with my grandfather, and felt very peaceful there. My uncle often said to me, 'The old man has become senile, but you are still young and should refrain from taking the wrong path.' But I continued to visit the temple even after my grandfather's death. The peace and cleanliness of the Buddha's temples attracted me. I knew nothing about meditation then, but whenever I visited the Mahamuni temple I felt very calm.

I finally joined a Vipassana course after speaking with Sayagyi U Ba Khin. His explanations, given with deep compassion and *metta* (loving kindness), allowed me to understand how blemish-free this meditation practice is. In the very first course I realized how false and misleading was the centuries-old propaganda against the Buddha's teachings.

I now saw clearly: What can be wrong in practising a meditation which is based on universal truth and can bring this wild, unruly mind to one-pointed concentration? What, indeed, can be wrong in establishing the mind in wisdom and knowledge based on one's own experience—a mind that hitherto had depended on somebody else's wisdom? Can anything be wrong in learning the art of leading a new life, the result of a mind cleansed and purified from defilements, and filled with *metta*, *karuna* (compassion), *mudita* (sympathetic joy) and *upekkha* (equanimity)? I had read and heard about the importance of these subtler qualities since childhood. Now I felt: If someone teaches the experiential aspects of the eternal truth—which had only been described in empty rhetoric—then how can these teachings be considered false, illusory, or magical? I found the Vipassana practice faultless.

I then decided to read the Buddha's words, thinking that perhaps I would find something false or misleading lurking there. But as I read the scriptures I saw with increasing clarity that *dhamma* was sublime and pure, beneficial to one and all.

In those days, I used to come to India to visit established *ashrams* (centres for spiritual practice) and meet various religious leaders. I wanted to determine if I had, perhaps, started walking on a wrong path, if I had become entangled in a delusion. I also sought to learn: If Vipassana was a proper path, how could I progress beyond what I had already learned? Alas, after these explorations, I felt certain that India had become spiritually poorer since losing the sublime knowledge of the Buddha's teaching.

India's neighbour Myanmar is truly blessed in having preserved these priceless jewels in their pristine purity: not only Vipassana meditation, but the original Buddhist scriptures which were lost due to our Indian ancestors' lack of wisdom. I now clearly understood the way in which misinformation had been propagated all over India, whereby the Buddha was praised but his teachings were denounced. I was saddened and dismayed when I realized how the educated classes of India had been duped and so lost our country's ancient, timeless, priceless treasure. It was time for the country to awaken.

Besides my daily practice of meditation, I visited my revered Sayagyi at his centre in Yangon every Sunday morning at 7:00 for group meditation and I continued to go deeper in Vipassana *panna* (experiential wisdom) by taking at least one ten-day course a year. At times I also undertook longer, more intensive retreats. Gradually I came to realize the true purpose of human existence. The reality of the senses at the mental and physical levels, their universal characteristics of *anicca* (impermanence), *dukkha* (suffering), and *anatta* (egolessness) became increasingly clear experientially. I could see the truth as obviously as a piece of fruit held in my hand.

The state of total dissolution that I had experienced so naturally and effortlessly in my first course had created the illusion that this was indeed the permanent, eternal, absolute state; whereas in reality, this dissolution was nothing but physical and mental sensations, clearly within the realm of *anicca* (rising and passing away).

Subsequently, when I experienced even subtler realities and their concomitant states of deep peace and sublime bliss and joy, I realized the importance of experiencing these states with increased alertness. This is essential to prevent the seeker from getting stuck in this elevated but illusionary experience, which is still in the field of mind and matter. The meditator must clearly perceive whether this blissful state is one of heightened awareness of the senses, or the experience which transcends the senses. In this experience beyond the senses, the senses do not work;

if this has not happened, then one is still in the field of mind and matter. With deepened awareness I experienced rising and falling in this profoundly subtle realm also. Without the awareness of *anicca*, this state would have trapped me with the illusionary thought of 'me', 'my', 'mine'," and 'permanent, eternal, absolute soul'. That is why it is vital to remain totally aware of the reality of this experience.

Through practising constant awareness and experiencing the various stages on the path to total liberation, all doubts were gradually dissolving. At every step, the sublime purity and spiritually beneficent aspects of *dhamma* manifested themselves. Naturally, my heart overflowed with feelings of gratitude, gratitude toward Gotama the Buddha who, despite tremendous hardships, rediscovered the technique of Vipassana, which had been lost for eons—the only technique which leads to mental purification and total liberation. Not only did he seek out the path and liberate himself, but with boundless compassion he shared it with one and all.

Deep gratitude flows toward the unbroken tradition of teacher-student, diligently maintained in India and thereafter in Myanmar, which preserved the basic tenets of this knowledge in total purity. Gratitude flows toward my *dhamma* father, Sayagyi, who taught me Vipassana with such compassion, and who firmly established me in the theoretical and practical aspects of pure *dhamma*.

When I survey the last forty years of my new life on the path of Vipassana, my heart brims with deep satisfaction and joy. In the worldly sphere, during these forty years, there have been so many ascents and descents, so many springs and autumns, so many turns of the tide. But the daily practice of Vipassana never failed to help me to develop equanimity in all situations.

My life is fulfilled. From the abundant compassion of my respected teacher, I have received incomparable sustenance, and I continue to receive it in such abundance. The rejuvenating medicine of *dhamma* gives me confidence to move firmly on. It continues to benefit me so much and uplifts so many others also. Pondering this, a spark of gratitude toward my respected teacher rekindles in my heart.

The river of *dhamma* that started flowing 25 centuries ago through the efforts of the supremely compassionate Buddha—may it spring forth once again in the current era due to the efforts of my deeply revered Sayagyi. May it liberate all those who are enchained, who are tired and thirsty, who are in pain and sorrow. May it benefit all, may it uplift all—this wish of goodwill flows from my heart.

Having experienced and appreciated the Buddha's teaching, deep like the ocean, broad like the vast earth, and high like the Himalayas, I feel very comfortable in accepting, practising, and passing it on in its pristine purity. There can be no question of practising or teaching anything but this wonderful *dhamma*. *Dhamma* is *paripunna*—it is complete, there is nothing to add. And it is *parishuddha*—so pure that there is nothing to be removed.

Code of Discipline
for
Vipassana Meditation

Vipassana International Academy
Dhammagiri, Igatpuri- 422 403,
Dist. Nasik, Maharashtra, India.
Tel. (02553) 84076, 84086 & 84302.
Fax : [91] (2553) 84176

introduction to the technique

Vipassana is one of India's most ancient meditation techniques. Long lost to humanity, it was rediscovered by Gotama the Buddha more than 2,500 years ago. Vipassana means to see things as they really are, it is a process of self-observation. One starts by observing the natural breath to concentrate the mind. With this sharpened awareness one proceeds to observe the changing nature of body and mind and experiences the universal truths of impermanence, suffering and egolessness. This truth-realisation by direct experience is the process of purification. The entire Path (Dhamma) is a universal remedy for universal problems and has nothing to do with any organised religion or sectarianism. For this reason, it can be practised freely by all without conflict with race, caste or religion, in any place, at any time and will prove equally beneficial to one and all.

Vipassana meditation aims at the highest spiritual goals of total liberation and full enlightenment. Its purpose is never simply to cure physical diseases, but as a by-product of mental purification, many psychosomatic diseases get eradicated. Actually, it is an art of living which eliminates the three causes of all unhappiness: craving, aversion and ignorance. With continued practice, the meditation releases the tensions developed in everyday life and opens the knots tied by the old habit of reacting in an unbalanced way to pleasant and unpleasant situations and develops positive creative energy for the betterment of the individual and society.

The process of self-purification by introspection is certainly never easy: one has to work really hard at it. By his own efforts the student arrives at his own realisations; no one else can work for him. Therefore, the meditation will suit only those willing to work seriously and observe the discipline, which is actually for their own benefit and protection. The rules and regulations are an integral part of the meditation practice.

code of discipline

Ten days is certainly a very short period in which to penetrate to the deepest levels of the unconscious mind and learn how to eradicate the deep-lying complexes. Continuity of practice in seclusion is the secret of success of this technique. The rules and regulations have been formulated keeping this practical aspect in view. The rules are not for the benefit of the Teacher or the Management, nor are they negative expressions of tradition, orthodoxy or blind faith in some organised religion. Rather, they are based on the practical experience of thousands of meditators over the years and are scientific and rational. Keeping the rules creates a very conducive atmosphere for meditation; breaking them pollutes it.

A student will have to stay on for the complete ten days. Besides this, the other rules should also be read and carefully considered. Only those who feel that they can honestly and scrupulously follow the discipline should apply for admission.

Code of Discipline.

Those not prepared to make full-hearted efforts will only waste their time and worse still, cause a disturbance to those others who wish to work seriously. An intending student is warned that it would be both harmful and unpleasant to have to leave without finishing the course if he finds the discipline too difficult. Likewise, it would be most unfortunate, if in spite of repeated warnings he does not follow the rules and has to be asked to leave.

the precepts:

All students will have to observe rigorously the following precepts:

Abstention from killing.
Abstention from stealing.
Abstention from all sexual activities.
Abstention from telling lies.
Abstention from all intoxicants.

Old students will observe three more precepts :

Abstention from taking food after 12 noon.
Abstention from sensual amusements and bodily decorations.
Abstention from using high and luxurious beds.

Old students will observe the sixth precept by taking only lemon water at the 5 pm break, whereas the new students will take milk or tea and fruits. The Teacher may excuse an old student from observing this precept for health reasons.

acceptance of the teacher and technique:

For the period of the course the student must surrender himself completely to the Teacher and the technique of Vipassana which includes all the rules, regulations, code of discipline and the course timetable. Only with this attitude of surrender can one work diligently and thoroughly. The surrender should be with discrimination and understanding, not with any blind faith. Such confidence in the Teacher and technique is essential for the student's proper guidance and protection.

rites, rituals and other techniques:

For the period of the course it is absolutely essential that all rites and rituals, such as burning incense and lamps, counting beads, reciting mantras, singing and dancing, total fasting, praying etc. be totally suspended. All other meditation practices should also be suspended without condemning them. This is enjoined for the reason that the student may be able to give a fair trial to the Vipassana technique in its pristine purity and he may ensure his own protection. Students are strongly warned against mixing any type of practice with Vipassana. Despite repeated warnings by the Teacher, there have been cases in the past where students have deliberately mixed Vipassana with some other ritual or practice and seriously harmed themselves. Students joining a course will be expected to work exactly as they are instructed by the Teacher without missing any step or adding anything extra. Any doubts or confusions which may arise can always be clarified by meeting the Teacher.

Code of Discipline.

yoga and physical exercise:

Although physical Yoga and other exercises are compatible with Vipassana, they should also be suspended because, at present, proper secluded facilities are not available at the Academy. Students may exercise by walking in the areas set aside for this purpose.

meeting the teacher:

Problems or confusion about the meditation should be taken only to the Teacher for clarification. The time between 12 noon and 1 p.m. is set aside for these private interviews at the Teacher's residence. Questions may also be asked between 9 p.m. and 9.30 p.m. in the meditation hall, as well as during short rest breaks.

These question times are solely for the purpose of clarifying actual practical problems relating to the Technique. They should not be taken as an opportunity to indulge in philosophical discussions or intellectual arguments.

noble silence:

Students must observe Noble Silence from the start of the course until 10.00 a.m. on Day 10. Noble Silence is silence of body, speech and mind. Any form of communication, whether by physical gestures, written notes, sign language, etc., is prohibited. However, the student may speak to the Teacher whenever necessary.

He may also contact the Management with any problems concerning accommodation, food, etc. All these contacts should be kept to the minimum.

couples:

Complete segregation of the sexes must be observed within the Academy.

talismans, rosaries, sacred threads etc:

All such items should not be brought to the Academy. If they are brought inadvertently, they should be deposited with the Management for the duration of the course.

valuables:

Students are also requested not to bring any jewellery or valuables with them as proper arrangements for their safe-keeping do not exist. If however these items have been brought, they may deposit them with the Management at their own risk.

shopping:

As there are no proper facilities for shopping, students should bring all their requirements such as soap, toothpaste, mosquito repellent, torch, etc. The Academy will provide mattresses and meditation cushions. Students should bring their own bedsheets.

intoxicants and drugs:

The laws of this country prohibit the possession of hashish, marijuana, etc. Bringing these into the Academy is strictly forbidden. Those taking medicines or drugs on doctor's prescription should notify the Teacher.

Code of Discipline.

smoking:

Smoking or chewing tobacco is not allowed inside the Academy.

clothing:

There should be modesty and decorum in dress within the Academy, suited to the serious nature of the work. Backs, chests, legs etc. should be kept covered, even during hot weather. Women must wear bras or use a shawl. Transparent and revealing dresses are not allowed and sun-bathing is forbidden.

cleanliness:

Students are required to live and work in common rooms, so it is essential that they bathe daily and keep their clothes clean.

A laundry service is provided at a reasonable cost.

outside contacts:

Students will have to remain inside the Academy for the entire course. They may leave only with the specific consent of the Teacher. All telephone calls, letters and contacts with visitors will have to be suspended. In any emergency a visitor may contact the Management. Students are also requested not to communicate with the Academy staff (except the Management).

food:

It is not possible to cater to the special food requirements of all the students, coming as they do from so many different countries and cultures. The students are kindly requested to make do with the simple Indian vegetarian menu provided. If a student has been prescribed a special diet because of ill-health, he should inform the Management at the time of registration.

reading and writing:

No writing or reading materials, religious works and even books on Vipassana, should be brought into the Academy. Students should not distract themselves by taking notes. The restriction on reading and writing is to emphasise the strictly practical nature of this meditation.

tape recorders and cameras:

These can be used only with the specific permission of the Teacher.

passports and visas:

All foreigners must bring the appropriate passports and visas with them, valid for the period of the course. They are requested to submit these to the Management for the period of the course.

cost of boarding and lodging:

There is absolutely no charge for the Dhamma Teaching. The cost of all boarding and lodging is met by donations of past students and these donations also cover all other expenses such as administration, salaries, postage, taxes, light, water, overheads etc. The

Code of Discipline.

Academy has no other source of income. The construction of the Academy was also made possible by the donations of students and the proposed new construction work will have to be financed in the same way. But according to the tradition of pure Dhamma, donations small or large are accepted only from such students who have actually benefited themselves by taking a Dhamma course and who have developed a strong wish that the Wheel of Dhamma may keep turning so that more and more people can be benefited by it with adequate facilities.

For this reason, no donation is accepted from a new student on his joining the course. However, at the end of the course he is welcome to express his feeling of satisfaction and goodwill by offering donations in keeping with his volition.

It may be that a student cannot understand the practical reasons for one or several of the above rules. Rather than allowing himself to develop negativity and doubt, he should immediately seek clarification from the Teacher or management.

Finally, students should note that their progress in Vipassana depends solely on their own Paramitas (previously accumulated merits) and five factors: full-hearted efforts, faith, sincerity, health and wisdom.

the timetable

The following timetable has been designed to maintain the continuity of practice. Students are advised to follow it as closely as possible for best results.

4.00 am		Morning wakeup bell
4.30	- 6.30	Meditation in hall or residence
6.30	- 8.00	Breakfast break
8.00	**- 9.00**	**Group Meditation in hall**
9.00	- 11.00	Meditate in hall or residence, as per instructions of the Teacher.
11.00	- 12.00	Lunch
12.00	- 1.00	Rest
1.00	- 2.30	Meditation in hall or residence
2.30	**- 3.30**	**Group Meditation in hall**
3.30	- 5.00	Meditate in hall or residence, as per instructions of the Teacher
5.00	- 6.00	Tea break
6.00	**- 7.00**	**Group Meditation in hall**
7.00	- 8.30	Teacher's discourse in hall
8.30	**- 9.00**	**Group Meditation in hall**
9.00	- 9.30	Question time in hall
9.30 pm		Retire to own room. Lights out.

Note: During group sittings no one should leave the hall.

May the above rules and regulations, code of discipline and timetable help you to obtain maximum benefit from your meditation course!

May All Beings Be Happy !

Rules of conduct for those practising Vipassana.

राष्ट्रपति
भारत गणतंत्र
PRESIDENT
REPUBLIC OF INDIA

MESSAGE

Lord Buddha's timeless message of 'Karuna', equality and a life of harmony, balance and moderation is of profound contemporary relevance to human society.

I am glad to learn that the foundation stone laying ceremony for a magnificent Vipassana Stupa is being organized in Mumbai in October. I extend my greetings to all associated with this noble project and wish them success in their endeavours.

Narayanan K.R.

(K.R. NARAYANAN)

New Delhi
October 20, 1997.

Message of greeting from the President of India.

NAMO BUDDHAYA

Maha Bodhi Society of India

(Founded by Anagarika Dharmapala in 1891)
[Registered under W.B.S.R. Act 1961 - Regn. No. S/2666/61 of 1916-16]

Post Box No. 12365 • Grams : "BUDDHIST" Calcutta • Phone : 2415214
Fax : 91-33-241-5214 / 91-33-241-2100 ATN : MIF-34

Headquarters :
4A, BANKIM CHATTERJEE STREET, CALCUTTA-700 073, INDIA.

Ref. No...........   Date 97 . 7 . 25

To,

Kalyana Mitra Sri S.N. Goenka,
Global Vipassana Foundation,
Green House, 2nd Floor,
Green Street, Fort,
Bombay-400 023.

Dear Kalyan Mitra Sri S.N. Goenkaji,

I am extremely pleased to receive your cordial invitation to me to join the auspicious foundation laying ceremony of the grand Vipassana Dhamma Stupa at Buddha Dweep in Mumbai, the largest consmopolitan commercial city of India on 26th October 1997. With a height of over 300 feet, it will be one of the highest monument of its type in the world. This monument with its gallery of exhibits showing the life and teachings of the Buddha will certainly help in educating the people of India and of the whole world, the true significance of Buddha's teachings which was readily adapted in the past by people around the world as it gave wonderful results.

Those who are Vipassana meditatiors will be able to get the benefit of sitting around the relics of the Enlightened One and meditate.

I shall be happy to donate a portion of the genuine Buddha's relics from the Mahabodhi Society for enshrining in the new Pagoda. Enshrining the Buddha's relics in such Pagoda will be a real honour to the relics, and will be as per Buddha's last instructions. The relics so enshrined will be a source of immense enthusiasm among the faithful, and also help the Vipassana meditators to take advantage of its strong vibrations by meditating in its close proximity in the Pagoda.

I send you my best wishes for the successful completion of this noble project. May this monument bring peace and harmony to all.

Yours in the Dhamma,

Ven'ble Dr. D. Rewatha Thera)
General Secretary,
Maha Bodhi Society of India
Headquarters, Calcutta.

Message of greeting from the General Secretary of the Maha Bodhi Society.

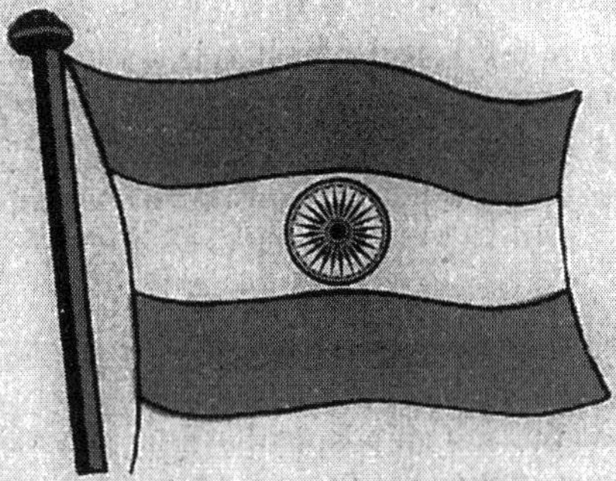

National Flag and National Emblem of India.
See p. 216 for comments.

National Flag

The National Flag is a horizontal tricolour of deep saffron on the top, white in the middle, and dark green at the bottom, all in equal proportions. The ratio of the width to the length of the Flag is two to three. In the centre of the white band there is a wheel in navy blue to represent the *Chakra*. Its design is that of the wheel which appears on the abacus of the Sarnath Lion Capital. Its diameter approximates to the width of the white band and it has 24 spokes.

The National Flag was adopted by the Constituent Assembly of India on 22 July 1947.

National Emblem

The National Emblem of India is an adaptation from the Sarnath Lion Capital of Asoka as it is preserved in the Sarnath Museum. In the original, there are four lions, standing back to back, mounted on an abacus with a frieze carrying sculptures in high relief of an elephant, a galloping horse, a bull, and a lion each separated by intervening wheels (*Chakras*) over a bell-shaped lotus. Carved out of a single block of polished sandstone, the Capital was crowned by the Wheel of the Law (*Dharma Chakra*).

In the National Emblem adopted by the Government of India on 26 January 1950, only three lions are visible, the fourth being hidden from view. The wheel appears in relief in the centre of the abacus, with a bull on the right and a horse on the left and the outlines of the other wheels on the extreme right and left. The bell-shaped lotus has been omitted. The words 'Satyameva jayate', from the *Mundaka Upanishad* meaning 'Truth alone triumphs', are inscribed below the Emblem in the Devanagari script.

Comments

ELEANOR ZELLIOT

A Report on the Literature on the New Buddhists

TERMINOLOGY. Dr Kantowsky's original publication used the term Neo-Buddhist. Since this term is unacceptable to many of the Buddhists of the recent conversion movement, he graciously agreed to change the designation to 'New Buddhist'. The meaning of new and neo is technically the same, but *neo* seems to carry the connotation of inferiority (it is not used for Christian or Muslim converts) and *new* is simply a reference to the fact that the conversion took place after the conversion of Dr B.R. Ambedkar in 1956. Another possible term is Ambedkarite Buddhist, but this is unsatisfactory as being too limiting. Some scholars have invented a new term, Navayana Buddhism, the new vehicle, analogous to Mahayana Buddhism, the great vehicle, and Hinayana, the lesser vehicle (a designation unacceptable to Theravadins).

Another problem with terminology is the designation of Dr Ambedkar as a Bodhisattva. Dr Kantowsky originally wrote that hundreds of thousands of Mahars took *diksha* (conversion) in 1956 following the example of Dr Ambedkar, whom they honoured as Bodhisattva. I changed this to 'some' honoured him in this way because the appellation seems to have been made popular by Bhandant Anand Kausalyayan, a traditionally trained *bhikkhu* originally from the Punjab, *after* Ambedkar's death and is used chiefly by the less educated to mean 'the one who brought us to Buddhism'. However, one educated Buddhist claimed in 2002 that the Dalai Lama at a public meeting just before Ambedkar's death addressed him as Bodhisattva. I think it is not an appellation that would have pleased Ambedkar, who spoke against *manus bhakti* or *vyakti puja*, devotion to a human being, and based his Buddhism on Theravada texts which do not honour *bodhisattvas*.

The Available Literature. Although some studies, such as that of Neera Burra (1996) (see main bibliography), are very good, all available studies so far published ignore urban activity, which must be investigated city by city, locality by locality, to understand the religious and social work promoted by individual Buddhists. That is where the life is! We may turn to the following examples, all in Maharashtra State: the Modi Khana *vihara* in Pune is the site of weekly Buddhist chanting by a mixed caste group, and in a community room to the rear, a dedicated Buddhist woman teaches the children of the slum every evening. A lowly employee of Milind College in Aurangabad built a *vihara* himself, and designed a metal grill for the closure decorated with an abstract Buddha which is a remarkable work of art. A railway employee in Wardha raised money through the years, rupee by rupee, to build a *vihara* which features a library and a kindergarten as well as a place for Buddhist religious gatherings. The owners of a bookstore in central Pune on the edge of the red light district try to educate their neighbours in the ways of health care as well as provide books on Buddhism and social action for all who come.

We could cite many more examples: a doctor left his practice to found sixty-seven 'Bodhi convent' schools which teach children about the Buddha and Dr Ambedkar as well as reading and writing. His work inspired a civil servant to found a school in a small city in a backward area of Maharashtra which welcomes Muslims as well as Buddhists and gives preference to the children of rickshaw drivers and labourers. A Buddhist in Pune made an arrangement with his wife before their wedding that they would live on her school teacher's income and his earnings from his profession as a house painter would be spent on Buddha images. There is now a museum of those Buddhist images from all over Asia in a special room in the Dr Babasaheb Ambedkar Sanskriti Bhavan in Pune. A Buddhist in a small town puts out a weekly newspaper entitled *Kalman* (Measure of the Times) which features the Buddhist wheel as logo and sketches of 'the sons of revolution', the Buddha, Mahatma Phule, and Dr Ambedkar. He also runs a school in the slums in which he lives. (There are dozens of such locally produced Buddhist news sheets.) A Buddhist woman in Mumbai edits and publishes a magazine for women called *Maitrani* (informal term for a woman friend), which includes much material on Buddhism; she has attended international women's Buddhist conferences.

Now, this activity does not show up in any study so far, and I do not know how to quantify it or evaluate its importance or relate it to spiritual qualities, but I could give many more examples of individual commitment to Buddhist study and action which should be recognized as a phenomenon of the Buddhist conversion movement. I should add that an educated group of 'digital Dalits' have a Buddhist circle e-mail network which extends the life found in the city to participants all over India and abroad. Their concern is to understand Buddhism and to extend their religion to social action.

The 1999 Ph.D. thesis of Johannes Beltz in Lausanne in French does include comments on Buddhist life based on extensive urban travel. It will be published in English as 'Mahar, Buddhist and Dalit: Religious conversion and socio-political emancipation of castes in India'. He agrees with me that the only way to study the full range of Buddhist influence is to learn Marathi, to look at action in the city and although he finds much questioning of Hinduism among Buddhists, he finds more carry-over of worship of Hindu Gods than I did in my extensive tour of India thirty-five years ago.

Community Occasions. There is much on the Kumbh Mela, Hindu pilgrimage, the importance of Varanasi, etc., but there is so far no writing on the massive festive and community occasions of the Buddhist movement. The vast crowds that flock to Mumbai every year on the Death Day (6 December) of Ambedkar experience feelings of belonging to a community at the Chaitya Bhumi in Dadar, and also have an opportunity to buy books and cassettes (which are not usually sold in ordinary stores), to learn from the hospitality of Mumbai Buddhist groups, and to see the Buddhist art at the Prince of Wales Museum (Zelliot, 2002). Ambedkar's birthday on 14 April is celebrated in most localities with meetings, speeches, theatre, and music. But especially impressive are the anniversaries of the conversions in Chandrapur and Nagpur which bring literally hundreds of thousands together for *vandana* (recital of Pali texts), religious discourses, music and, at times, drama. Chandrapur celebrations are limited to religious activity; the Nagpur celebrations include political figures as guests and a wide array of subsidiary activity such as booths for human rights campaign signatures, Tibetan freedom, music cassettes related to Ambedkar and Buddhism, a number of book displays (there are at least four Buddhist publishing and/or distribution centres), several banks offering information on savings and loans, etc. Both celebrations include the presence of a number of *bhikkhus* and offer opportunities for conversion ceremonies.

THE BHIKKHU SANGHA AND ORDINATION

I am not aware of any study or even comment on the *bhikkhus* moving about among the New Buddhists. Those whom I have met: a Bengali *bhikkhu* at the *vihara* in the Government Quarters in Bandra; a Sri Lankan *bhikkhu* at the Todiwalla Road *vihara* in Pune; a highly educated *bhikkhu* teaching at Siddharth College; a *bhikkhu* who divides his time between England and Nagpur; several trained by Bhandant Kausalyayan at the opening of a *vihara* in Wardha; a number of *bhikkhus* with Surai Sasai at Chandrapur and Nagpur at the time of the Diksha commemorations—these individual cases do not confirm what would be called in Marathi *jungli* behaviour, the crude ways noted by Dr Kantowsky. But it is true that no towering intellectual has arisen among them. The *bhikkhu* with the largest following is the Japan-born Surai Sasai of Nagpur, who has won the respect of many Ambedkar Buddhists through his building of *viharas* as well as his teaching and his leadership of the Bodh Gaya campaign. He was chief guest at the opening of a Dalit (oppressed, ex-Untouchable) art exhibition featuring the work of Savi Savarkar at the time of the Dhamma Diksha Parivartan (conversion commemoration) in Nagpur in 2000 and although I could not understand a word of his guttural Hindi, the audience laughed or applauded appreciatively a number of times. I should also note that Dr Kantowsky has not investigated the training school for *bhikkhus* at the Diksha grounds in Nagpur founded by Bhandant Kausalyayan—nor has anyone else.

Dr Kantowsky's excellent observation that the *bhikkhu's* robe does not stand out, since India is filled with yellow-orange-purple robed ascetics, leads to another point. Many educated (and some uneducated) Indians have no use for *swamis*, *gurus*, *babas* and the plethora of holy men in general. Some of this distrust may transfer to the robed *bhikkhus* of the Ambedkar following, and may even mean that the best and the brightest do not consider joining the religious order. It must also be said that many who do well academically are expected to help their family financially and are thus not encouraged to become penniless *bhikkhus*.

An interesting addition to Dr Kantowsky's report of the ordination of *bhikkhus* and *bhikkhunis* at Bodh Gaya is the fact that 28 women from Maharashtra went to Bodh Gaya in 1999 for ordination (see Zelliot, 2000: 264–5, 269). Reports of the event indicate that the women who took ordination spoke only Marathi and were very poor but very eager. I have met only one of these women, a *bhikkhuni* who led a lengthy *vandana* and chanting at a meeting of Buddhist women in Mumbai, but who said nothing on her own. A small group of English-speaking New Buddhist women attended the Sakyadhita (daughters of the Buddha) conference at Lumbini in 2000. They found that their entrance into the international world of Buddhist women, encouraged by the Sakyadhita founder, Karma Lekshe Tsomo, an American ordained in Korea, was very meaningful. Only one, however, intends to leave married life and become a *bhikkhuni*, and that too not until her family responsibilities are over.

TBMSG

The TBMSG is less centralized in Pune now. Lokamitra has stepped back and does not have his office at the central building in Dapodi. He has been successful in raising money in Taiwan for new buildings, both for education and teaching and for retreats. He is also an honoured guest and speaker at the conversion celebrations and other occasions, where he speaks only on the *dhamma*. I think the circle of the TBMSG may be broader than Dr Kantowsky indicates. I have seen that the hostels for girls in Pune and Nagpur, which are run by very impressive women administrators, do bring in a wide range of students, as do the retreat centres. When I was at Bhaja recently, I ran into seven young men who had come down to the village from the TBMSG retreat centre across the valley from the first century Buddhist caves to buy vegetables. They came from Nagpur, Wardha, Amaravati and two nearby small towns and none was highly educated.

It should be added that Lokamitra himself is concerned about the limits of the TBMSG. He has founded a new organization named Jambudvipa, the ancient Buddhist name for India, which hopes to extend the horizons of the present movement.

Vipassana

The Buddhist e-mail circle mentioned above has been filled with comments on Vipassana, some recognizing the criticism that it may be Hinduized meditation, but in general the young Buddhists contributing to the debate find Goenka and the Vipassana technique very acceptable to the Buddhist movement. One such entry is by a New Buddhist who is a medical doctor with psychiatric training who wrote:

> In the last two weeks I have sent two people in distress to Goenkaji's vipassana, which is non sectarian. . . . After the course I teach them whatever little I know with the most skillful means I know. First I let the person benefit from the

mechanistic improvement and then I introduce him to the essence of Buddhism.
In fact that seems to be Goenkaji's plan too; otherwise he wouldn't be singing songs about *dhamma* in his mission nor translating all Buddhist works. There is a subtle evangelism [for Buddhism] in Goenka's activities. He is dependent on *savarnas* [high castes] for funds, mind you. I think some Scheduled Castes and others take at times a position that Goenka is practicing Brahmin Buddhism. I disagree.

I have no idea of the numbers on either side of the Vipassana debates. I do know there is a circle of Buddhist students at Jawaharlal Nehru University who have attended meditation courses and hold meditation sessions. I know there is much discussion on Ambedkar's views on meditation, especially since he left no written record of his thoughts on the subject, although an acquaintance of his in Myanmar (Burma) says that Ambedkar spoke favourably of meditation when he met him at the Buddhist conference there in 1955. I also know that Goenka himself is very sympathetic to Ambedkar Buddhism. He conducted a Vipassana session in the very place that Ambedkar took *diksha*, the stupa in the Diksha Bhumi grounds of Nagpur. Some of the Brahman teachers in his classes may not be as understanding. One said to me, 'I don't know why these Ambedkar people come. They know nothing of Buddhism.' I thought she might have concluded from this that they came to learn, but evidently that possibility did not occur to her.

Dr Kantowsky does not include all the reasons that Brahmanized Buddhism is unacceptable to Ambedkar's followers. Goenka himself gives a hint of this when he says he was taught as a youth that the Buddha's ideas concerned magic. In the Hindu religion, the Buddha is not only the ninth incarnation of Vishnu but also 'according to most theologians the god became Buddha in order to delude the wicked and to lead them to deny the Vedas and thus ensure their damnation' (Basham, 1954: 306). It is impossible for a New Buddhist to believe this. And it is impossible for most to honour a leader in the Maha Bodhi Society who is also a member of the Vishva Hindu Parishad, the organization held to be one of those responsible for violence against Muslims, most recently in Gujarat.

Another sticking point is the Hindu idea of *karma*, birth determined by previous deeds, which justifies the lowly place of the Untouchable and encourages him only to accept his fate and fulfill his *dharma*, his duties. Instead, Pauline Kolenda has shown that Untouchables have rarely accepted this theory, but have created myths that tell stories of great mistakes that result in unjustified untouchability, and the Buddhists of the Ambedkar movement certainly do not believe their suffering is caused by their actions in a previous life. I wonder how the New Buddhists interpret the idea of merit, particularly influential in South-East Asia, which can be transferred to dead ancestors. I have heard no comment on the incident cited in Dr Kantowsky's chapter on Bodh Gaya of 'the special puja for the departed nun in order to share their [the Buddhists at ordination ceremonies] merit with the deceased'. I expect most New Buddhists would classify this as superstition; this as well as the rejection of *karma* determining their status as Untouchables is an area in which Ambedkar's ideas differ from those of traditional Buddhism. The best analysis of the hermeneutics of Ambedkar's Buddhist thought is by Christoher Queen, 1996.

Those who criticize the emphasis laid by Ambedkar on the need to abandon Hindu gods and practices might look at the history of the Protestant revolution in Europe. Catholic practices were, to say the least, discouraged. Many, including Ambedkar, think of Buddhism as a *protestant* religion, not an offshoot of or a part of Hinduism. And it should be recognized that in no country now Buddhist did the dominant religion before Buddhism stigmatize a group of people who then could not combine the old religion with the new Buddhism.

REFERENCES

I have included a number of my own articles not in the main Bibliography, since, as Dr Kantowsky notes, some are difficult to find. The studies by Beltz and Omvedt are important for the New Buddhist movement but are not yet published.

Basham, A.L., *The Wonder That was India*. New York: Grove Press, 1954.

Beltz, Johannes, 'Mahar, Buddhist and Dalit: Religious conversion and socio-political emancipation of castes in India', English translation of 1999 Ph.D thesis in French, not yet published.

Beltz, Johannes and Surender Jondhale, eds. The papers from the 1998 conference on Ambedkar's Buddhism in Pune are in the process of publication.

Kolenda, Pauline, 'Religious Anxiety and Hindu Fate', *Journal of Asian Studies*, Vol. XXIII, 1960: 71–81.

Omvedt, Gail, A study on Buddhism and Brahminism, title as yet undetermined, to be published by Sage, New Delhi.

Queen, Christopher S., 'Dr. Ambedkar and the Hermeneutics of Buddhist Liberation', *Engaged Buddhism: Buddhist Liberation Movements in Asia*, Christopher S. Queen and Sallie B. King, eds., Albany: State University of New York Press, 1996.

Zelliot, Eleanor, 'The Indian Rediscovery of Buddhism, 1855-1956', *Studies in Pali and Buddhism*, A.K. Narain, ed. (Jagdish Kashap Memorial Volume), New Delhi: D.K. Publishers and Distributors, 1978.

———, The Buddhist Literature of Modern Maharashtra, *Minorities on Themselves*, Hugh van Skyhawk, ed. as Vol. 11 of the *South Asia Digest of Regional Writing*, South Asia Institute, University of Heidelberg, 1985: 134–49.

———, 'Buddhist Women of the Contemporary Maharashtrian Conversion Movement', in *Buddhism, Sexuality and Gender*, Jose Cabezon, ed., Albany: State University of New York Press, 1992: 91–107.

———, 'Religious Leadership among Maharashtrian Buddhist Women', in *Women's Buddhism; Buddhism's Women*, Ellison Banks Findly, ed., Summerville, MA: Wisdom Publications, 2000: 259–74. The volume also contains an excellent article by Owen Lynch on 'Sujata's Army: Dalit Buddhist Women and Self-Emancipation', about the organization of Buddhist women in Agra: 247–57.

———, *From Untouchable to Dalit: Essays on the Ambedkar Movement*. Third Edition with new introduction and up-to-date bibliography, New Delhi: Manohar, 2001 (1992, 1996).

———, 'Bombay/Mumbai and the Ambedkar Movement: Past and Present', in *Thinking Social Science in India: Essays in Honour of Alice Thorner*, ed. by Sujata Patel, Jasodhara Bagchi and Krishna Raj, New Delhi: Sage Publications, 2002.

Postscript

DETLEF KANTOWSKY

I AM VERY GLAD that Eleanor Zelliot took the initiative to have an English translation of my study on *Buddhists in India Today* published in India so that whatever I had to say on the subject in 1998 is now available for English readers. How much I owe to India and its people I have described elsewhere (Kantowsky, 1993), and that I am not an unconcerned observer of its socio-cultural developments has been brought out by my studies on Sarvodaya (1980) and on the mis-interpretation of Max Weber's studies on Hinduism through the American translations of his texts (1982, 1984). Therefore, the following remarks on my colleague's comments should be taken as what they are meant to be: an honest protocol of a re-thinking process that has been set in motion after her comments reached me here at Lake Constance, Germany, in February 2002.

1. Regarding 'terminology', I am of the opinion that 'Ambedkar Buddhists' would be the most appropriate label if any special connotation has to be given to people (mostly) from Maharashtra who have taken Ambedkar's Buddhist's Oaths (see text on p. 26). I have some knowledge of Buddhist practice in other Asian countries like Nepal, Sri Lanka, Thailand, Japan, and Taiwan, and I do not know of any other Buddhist denomination with such an anti-pathetic appeal as is contained in the first eight of the twenty-two oaths that the followers of Ambedkar's movement have to take. Whereas the Buddha himself took people for what they were and never did argue against their ancestral gods, Ambedkar Buddhists have to admit that the religion of their Hindu heritage is 'detrimental to the emancipation of human beings' (Oath No. 19). Though I do very well understand that a Mahar Indian intellectual who emancipated himself from the fate of untouchability through post-graduate studies in Western universities had to see things that way, I nevertheless maintain that this is

a socio-political stance and as such an un-Buddhist attitude as far as the early teachings are concerned. No wonder that *bhikkhus* from the Maha Bodhi Society had and still have difficulties with Ambedkar's re-interpretations of traditional *dhamma* so as to fit it into the programme of a social reform movement for the uplift of his caste brethren. A logical consequence of the success of the movement was, however, that Ambedkar Buddhists were re-integrated into Hindu society and its protective discrimination through The Constitution (Scheduled Castes Orders) Amendment Act, 1990 (see fn. 5 on p. 52).

2. The available literature shows that there is dissent on terminology (all references are to the literature noted in the bibliography): M. Baumann (1991), a very sympathetic observer of the Ambedkar movement, used the term 'neo', as did S. Linsley (1988). D.K. Samanta (1991) spoke of 'the Nava Bouddha of Maharashtra', whereas R.W. Taylor (1972) wrote about 'Ambedkarite Buddhists' in his contribution to a volume on 'the Neo-Buddhist Movement' edited by the Christian Literature Society in Madras. Finally R.H. Kamble (1995) wrote of 'Nav Bouddhas', and I have used 'Neo-Buddhists' in the sub-title (only) of my survey of the literature available on 'Buddhists in India'. Though we should not add too much importance to labels, there is nevertheless a 'diplomacy by terminology' which is often not un-biased, to put it mildly. But why is the available literature mostly written by outsiders, many of them not even from India like Zelliot and Kantowsky ? Do we miss the mainstream of the intellectual thinking of the New Buddhists since we do not have sufficient access to regional journals and various accounts in the 'native languages'? Why do we not know of evaluations of such community occasions as mentioned by Zelliot, written by New Buddhists of the urban middle-class milieu ? Have they forgotten their past or do they not want to 'come out'?

3. It is too early yet to assess whether the identity card scheme of the All India Bhikkhu Sangha will suffice to guarantee a proper training of new Indian *bhikkhus* to come. Ultimately, their support will anyhow depend not upon identity cards but on individual charisma and the right livelihood they manifest in close neighbourhood contacts with their supporters.

Whether the Taiwan-sponsored mass ordination of new *bhikkhunis* in Bodh Gaya in February 1998 will have sown the right seeds to re-establish an accepted nuns' order of the Theravada tradition in India, I have reason to doubt, since I have been a very close witness not only to the proceedings but also the non-acceptance of the *bhikkhunis* at the

AIBS headquarters in Bodh Gaya, where they were given shelter in the assembly hall. We should, moreover, keep in mind that the demand for spiritual equality of women was introduced from the West ever since the first conference of Buddhist women and nuns was held under the patronage of the Dalai Lama in Bodh Gaya from 11 to 17 February 1987 to discuss 'suitable means' of re-establishing equality in religious practice in countries where the Buddhist clergy have great reservations about the matter. Hence, it was no coincidence that the second conference (1991) took place in Bangkok, and the third (1993) in Sri Lanka.

How will the classical schools of Buddhism react? Will they accept that a 'new world' has new needs, or will they resort to the 'old strategies of avoidance' of their respective traditions? Could the question of 'feminism' even provoke a schism in Buddhism between the old Eastern and the new Western Orders?

4. As I have tried to document, the TBMSG has certainly achieved remarkable results in the field of Buddhist-oriented education and for the patterning of a new form of lay Buddhist activists. Whether the high standards of performance set so far can be maintained, should outside resources become scarce, is still an open question. But even so, the Mahasangha, and especially its founder, has had a lasting impact on Dr. Ambedkar and his followers since it was from a young English monk called Sangharakshita that he came to know how easy it would be to embrace Buddhism (Sangharakshita, 1986: 19–20).

5. On Goenka's Vipassana movement I have not much to add to Zelliot's observations except an expression of sincere gratitude for what I have learned from a ten-day course which I attended in Igatpuri in March 1999. Having analysed the videos of such a ten-day course afterwards, and of the seven-day course on the *Satipatthana Sutta* as well, I wonder, however, how Goenka can maintain that his teachings are neither Buddhist, nor Hindu, nor Muslim, nor Christian, since suffering is universal. As far as I have understood, he not only teaches a basic Buddhist technique of mindful self-observation of impermanence (*anicca*) and non-self (*anatta*) within one's own body and its sensations, but he does in fact relate the functioning of this so-called neutral technique with almost every sentence to a very unique Buddhist theory of knowledge and perception, and it is only within this non-theistic frame of reference that it becomes meaningful to overcome *dukha*.

But it may be that this is only a concern for a German Buddhist's mind.

REFERENCES

Kantowsky, D., *Sarvodaya. The Other Development*. New Delhi: Vikas Publishing House, 1980. Hindi translation: *Ek aur Sarvodaya*. Delhi: Gandhi Peace Foundation, 1986.

———, 'Max Weber on India and Indian Interpretations of Weber', in *Contributions to Indian Sociology*, New Series, Vol. 16, No. 2, 1982: 141–74.

———, 'Max Weber's Contributions to Indian Sociology', in *Contributions to Indian Sociology*, New Series, Vol. 18, No. 2, 1984: 9–43.

———, 'Learning in and from South Asia', in *Contributions to Indian Sociology*, New Series, Vol. 27, No. 1, 1993: 105–18.

Bibliography

Ahir, D.C.

Maharashtra. The Land of Buddhism, New Delhi: Dalit Sahitya Prakashan, 1988.

The Pioneers of Buddhist Revival in India, Delhi: Sri Satguru Publications, 1989.

Buddhism in Modern India, Delhi: Sri Satguru Publications, 1991.

Himalayan Buddhism, Past and Present. Mahapandit Rahul Sankrityyan Centenary Volume, Delhi: Sri Satguru Publications, 1993.

Buddha Gaya through the Ages, Delhi: Sri Satguru Publications, 1994.

(ed.) *A Panorama of Indian Buddhism. Selections from the Maha Bodhi Journal (1892-1992)*, Delhi: Sri Satguru Publications, 1995a.

Gandhi and Ambedkar. A Comparative Study, New Delhi: Blumoon Books, 1995b.

(ed.) *Selected Speeches of Dr. B.R. Ambedkar (1927-1956)*, New Delhi: Blumoon Books, 1997

Buddhism. India, Fifty Years of Independence: 1947-1997. Status, Growth and Development. Delhi: B.R. Publishing Corporation, 1998.

(ed.) *Vipassana: A Universal Buddhist Technique of Meditation*, Delhi: Sri Satguru Publications, 1999.

Akanda, L.

Buddhism in Bangladesh. A Brief Background and History', *Bodhi - Enlightenment*, Dhaka: Fine Art Press, pp. 11–15.

Ambedkar, B.R.,

The Buddha and His Dhamma, Aurangabad: Siddharth College Publications, 1957, 1974, 1984, 1991. Also published as Volume 11 in *Dr. Babasaheb Ambedkar Writings and Speeches*, Bombay: Education Department, Government of Maharashtra, 1992.

Anagarika Dharmapala (see Guruge 1965)

Anisuzzaman

'Carypada and Bengali Literature', *Bodhi - Enlightenment*, Dhaka: Fine Art Press, 1990, pp. 22–6.

Asian Buddhists Conference for Peace

Bodhi - Enlightenment, Dhaka: Fine Art Press, 1990.

Barua, D.K.

Buddha Gaya Temple. Its History, Bodh Gaya: Buddha Gaya Temple Management Committee, 1975, new edition 1981.

Barua, K.

'A Glimpse into Buddhist Heritage in Bangladesh', *Bodhi - Enlightenment*, Dhaka: Fine Art Press, 1990, pp. 22–6.

Barua, S.B.

Buddhism in Bangladesh, Chitagong: Prajna Printers, 1990.

Baumann, M.

'Neo-Buddhistische Konzeptionen in Indien und England. Zum 100. Geburtstag Bhimrao Ramji Ambedkars', *Zeitschrift fur Religions- ünd Geistesgeschichte*, Vol. 43, No. 2, 1991, pp. 97–116.

Bechert, H.

'Contemporary Buddhism in Bengal and Tripura', *Educational Miscellany, a Quarterly Journal of the Directorate of Education*, Tripura, 1967–8, Vol. IV, Nos. 3–4, pp. 1–25.

'Buddhism in East Pakistan', *Vision Magazine*, Karachi, 1968, pp. 11–16.

'The Chakmas: A Buddhist Community in Bangla Desh', *Jagajiyoti, a Buddha Jayanti Annual*, Calcutta: Bauddha Dharmankur Sabha (Bengal Buddhist Association), 1973a, pp. 13–15.

'Buddhism and Buddhist Culture in Bangla Desh', *The Buddhist*, Vol. 44, No. 3, 1973b, pp. 5–9.

'Zur Geschichte des Theravada-Buddhismus in Ostbengalen', *Beitrage zur Indienforschung*, Berlin: Museum fur Indische Kunst, 1977, pp. 45–66.

'The Chakmas, an Ancient Buddhist Population in the Indian Subcontinent', *Abhinandana-Bharata. Professor Krishna Kanta Handiqui Felicitation Volume*, Gauhati: Assam Research Society, 1982, pp. 130–2.

Buddhismus, Staat und Gesellschaft in den Landern des Theravada-Buddhismus, Part 1, Grundlagen, Ceylon (Sri Lanka), 1988. Mit einem Register versehener, unveranderter Nachdruck der Ausgabe von 1966, Gottingen: Veroffentlichungen des Seminsras fur Indologie und Buddhismuskunde der Universitat Gottingen.

Beltz, J.

'Spiritualiser Le Dhamma? L'Implantation Contestee du Trailogya Bauddha Mahasangha en Inde', *Asiatische Studien, Zeitschrift der schweizerischen Asiengellschaft*, Vol. 51, Part 4, 1997, pp. 1055–71.

(See also References in Zelliot, *Comments*, in this volume.)

Buddha Dharmankur Sabha

Hundred Years of the Buddha Dharmankur Sabha 1892-1992, Calcutta: Rev. Dharmapala Mahathera, General Secretary, Bauddha Dharmankur Sabha.

Brauen, M, and D. Kantowsky

Junge Tibeter in der Schweiz. Studien zum Prozess kultureller Identifikation, Diessenhofen: Verlag Ruegger, 1982.

Burra, N.

'Caste, Conversion and Identity: A Case Study of Village Mahars', *Caste. Its Twentieth Century Avatar*, M.N. Srinivas, ed., New Delhi: Viking by Penguin Books, 1996, pp. 152–73.

Buss, J.

'Die Wiederbelebung des Buddhismus sudasiatischer Pragung in Indien seit dem Tode von B.R. Ambedkar', Universitat Gottingen: Philosophische Fakultat, MA Arbeit, 1998, 91 pp.

Central Institute of Higher Tibetan Studies

Catalogue 1997, Sarnath, 36 pp.

A Profile, 1993, Sarnath, 8 pp.

Chowdhury, H.B.

'Kripasaran Mahathera', *Kripasaran Mahathera 125th Birth Anniversary Volume*. Calcutta: Bauddha Dharmankur Sabha (Bengal Buddhist Association), 1990, pp. 1–10.

Conrad, D.

'The Personal Law Question and Hindu Nationalism', *Representing Hinduism. The Construction of Religious Traditions and National Identity*, V. Dalmia and H.V. Stietencron, eds., New Delhi: Sage Publications, 1995.

Coward, H.G.

'The Revival of Buddhism in Modern India', *Religion in Modern India*, Robert D. Baird, ed., New Delhi: Manohar, 1995, pp. 274–97.

Crook, J. and H. Osmaston, eds.

Himalayan Buddhist Villages. Environment, Resources, Society and Religious Life in Zangskar, Ladakh, Bristol: University of Bristol, Office of the Secretary, 1994.

Daijo Graph

Special Number: The Unveiling of the Great Buddha Statue, Bodh Gaya, Daijo Graph, No. 5, issued on 1 July 1990, Nagoya City: Daijokyo Sohonzan Temple, 4–7-Sotodoi-cho, Atsuta-ku, Nagoya City, Japan.

Dalit International Newsletter

1996—Thrice yearly, P.O. Box 932, Waterford, Connecticut, 06385, USA.

Das, Anjana R.

'Der Theravada-Buddhismus als Minderheitenreligion in Bangladesh', *Studien zur Indologie und Buddhismuskunde. Festgabe des Seminars fur Indologie und Buddhismuskunde fur Professor Dr. Heinz Bechert*, Reinhold Grunedahl, ed., Bonn: Indica et Tibetica Verlag, 22, 1993, pp. 65–76.

Dhammika, S.

Middle Land, Middle Way. A Pilgrim's Guide to the Buddha's India, Kandy: Buddhist Publication Society, 1992.

Doyle, Tara

Bodh Gaya. Journeys to the Diamond Throne and the Feet of Gayasur. Cambridge, Mass: Harvard University Ph.D. thesis, 1997.

Evangelischer Pressedienst

'Indien, Dalits im Aufbruch', *Entwicklungspolitic*, Part 14, 1994.

'Nicht länger mehr "unberührbar." Indische "Dalits" fordern Gerechtigkeit', *Dokumentation*, No. 1, 1995.

Fischer, E.

'Zwei Begegnungen', *50 Jahre Buddhistisches Haus gegrundet von Dr. Paul Dahlke, 1924-74*, Berlin-Frohnau: Im Auftrag der German Dharmadatu Society Colombo herausgegeben von Sri Gnanawimala Maha Thero, 1974, pp. 78–9.

Fiske, A.M.

'The Understanding of "Religion" and "Buddhism" among India's New Buddhists', *Ambedkar and the Neo Buddhist Movement*, T.S. Wilkinson and M.M. Thomas, eds., Madras: Christian Literature Society, 1972a, pp. 103–28.

'Scheduled Caste Buddhist Organizations', *The Untouchables in Contemporary India*, J. Michael Mahar, ed., Tucson: University of Arizona Press, 1972b, pp. 113–42.

Fitzgerald, T.

'Buddhism and Social Change in Maharashtra', *Aichi Gakuin University Bulletin* 3, Aichi, Japan, 1989, pp. 50–73.

'Buddhism in Maharashtra: a Tri-partite Analysis—A Research Report', *Dr. Ambedkar, Buddhism and Social Change*, A.K. Narain and D.C. Ahir, eds., 1994, Delhi: B.R. Publishing Corporation, pp. 17–34.

'Ambedkar Buddhism in Maharashtra', *Contributions to Indian Sociology*, New Series, Vol. 31, No. 2, 1997, pp. 225–51.

Fo Kuang Shan

Our Report. What has Fo Kuang Shan Achieved? Taiwan: Ta Shu, Kaohsiung, 84010, ca. 1996.

Goenka, S.N.

The Discourse Summaries. Talks from a Ten-Day Course in Vipassana Meditation, condensed by William Hart, Igatpuri: Vipassana Research Institute, 1995 (1st edn. 1987).

The Gracious Flow of Dharma, Igatpuri: Vipassana Research Institute, 1997 (1st ptg. 1994).

Gokhale, J.B.

'The Socio-political Effects of Ideological Change: the Buddhist Conversion of Maharashtrian Untouchables', *Journal of Asian Studies*, Vol. XLV No. 2, 1986, pp. 269–92.

From Concessions to Confrontation: the Politics of an Indian Untouchable Community, Bombay: Popular Prakashan, 1993.

Guru, G.

'Hinduisation of Ambedkar in Maharashtra', *Economic and Political Weekly*, Vol. XXVI, No. 7, 16 February 1991, pp. 339–41.

'Appropriating Ambedkar', *Economic and Political Weekly*, XXVI, No. 27, 6–13 July 1991, pp. 1697–9.

Guruge, A.

Return to Righteousness. A Collection of Speeches, Essays and Letters of the Anagarika

Dharmapala, Ceylon: Anagarika Birth Centenary Committee, Ministry of Education and Cultural Affairs, 17 September 1965.

Hacker, P.

'Inklusivismus', in G. Oberhammer (Hgb.), *Inklusivismus. Eine indische Denkform*. Wien: Institut für Indologie der Universität Wien, Sammlung de Nobili, 1983, pp. 11-28.

Haque, E.

'Buddhist Sculpture in Bangladesh', *Bodhi - Enlightenment*, Dhaka: Fine Art Press, 1990, pp. 16–18.

Hart, W.

Die Kunst des Lebens, Vipassana-Meditation nach S.N. Goenka, Frankfurt a.M.: Fischer Taschenbuch Verlag, 1996.

Hecker, H.

(ed.), *Der erste deutsche Bhikkhu. Das bewegte Leben des Ehrwurdigen Nyanatiloka (1878 - 1997) und seine Schuler*, Universitat Konstanz: Forschungsprojekt 'Buddhistischer Modernismus' (Forschungs-Bericht No. 10), 1995.

Lebensbilder deutscher Buddhisten. Ein biobliographisches Handbuch, Band I: *Die Grunder*, Universitat Konstanz: Forschungsprojekt 'Buddhistischer Modernismus' (Forschungs-Bericht No. 13), 1996.

Hiramani, A.B.

Social Change in Rural India. A Study of Two Villages in Maharashtra, Delhi: B.R. Publishing Corporation, 1977.

Hossain, S.

'Ancient Buddhist Monastic Establishments in Bangladesh', *Bodhi - Enlightenment*, Dhaka: Fine Art Press, 1990, pp. 19–21.

Jatava, B.R.

The Critics of Dr. Ambedkar, Jaipur: Surabhi Publications, 1997.

Jogdand, P.G.

'Dalits in Maharashtra. Challenges Ahead', *Economic and Political Weekly*, Vol. XXXII, No. 51, 20 December 1997, pp. 3249–50.

Jurgens, B.S.

B.R. Ambedkar - Religionsphilosophie eines Unberuh baren, Frankfurt: Peter Lang, 1994.

Kadam, K.N. (ed.)

Dr. B.R. Ambedkar. The Emancipator of the Oppressed. A Centenary Commemoration Volume, Bombay: Popular Prakashan, 1993.

Kamble, R.H.

'Social Meanings of Conversion: To Buddhism among Nav-Bouddhas', *Indian Missiological Review*, March 1995, pp. 25–30.

'Being a Buddhist: A Case Study in Bombay', *Journal of the Asiatic Society*, Vol. 38, No. 1, 1996, pp. 81–90.

Kantowsky, D.

Sarvodaya. The Other Development, New Delhi: Vikas Publishing House, 1980.

Hindi translation: *Ek Aur Sarvodaya*, Delhi: Gandhi Peace Foundation, 1984.

An Indian Village through Letters and Pictures, Delhi: Oxford University Press, 1995.

'Satipatthana - Der Einzige Weg', *Lotusblatter, Zeischrieft fur Buddhismus*, Vol. 11, April 1997 and January 1998, pp. 4–11.

Kapadia, H.

Trek the Sahyadris, Bombay: R.S. Limaye, Indu Villa, 51 Shivaji Park, Bombay 400 028, 1993.

Kausalyayan, Bhadant A.

Dr. Ambedkar, the Liberator, tr. by Bhikkhu Chandra Bodhi. Bangkok: International Network of Engaged Buddhists, 1991.

Kenadi, L.

Revival of Buddhism in Modern India: The Role of B.R. Ambedkar and the Dalai Lama XIV, New Delhi: Ashish Publishing House, 1995.

Khare, R.S.

The Untouchable as Himself: Ideology, Identity, and Pragmatism among the Lucknow Chamars, Cambridge: Cambridge University Press, 1984.

King, W.L.

Buddhism in Contemporary Burma, Foreword by Edward Conze, Berkeley: Asian Humanities Press, 1990 (1st ptg. 1964).

Landerbericht Indien

Landerbericht Indien, Wiesbanden: Statistisches Bundesamt, 1995.

Leoshko, J., ed.

Bodh Gaya—The Site of Enlightenment, Bombay: Marg Publications, 1988.

Ling, T.

Buddhist Revival in India. Aspects of the Sociology of Buddhism, London: McMillan Press, 1980.

'Buddhists, Urban and Rural, in Bengal', *Jagajiyoti, Kripasaran Mahathera 125 Birth Anniversary Volume 1990*, Calcutta: Bauddha Dharmankur Sabha, pp. 18-29.

Linsley, S.

'Ideology and Practice in a Neo-Buddhist Organization in Western India', University of Durham (England), Department of Anthropology, BA thesis, 1989.

Lokamitra, Dh.

'Ambedkar and Buddhism', *Economic and Political Weekly*, Vol. XXVI, No. 20, 18 May 1991, pp. 1303–4.

'Sangha and Social Change', *Dr. Ambedkar, Buddhism and Social Change*, A.K. Narain and D.C. Ahir, eds., Delhi: B.R. Publishing Corporation, 1994, pp. 49–65.

'Buddhism in Maharashtra with special reference to Trailokya Bauddha Mahasangha (Ideology and Programmes)', Pune University: National

Seminar on the Post Ambedkar Dalit Movement in India, 27–29 March 1997 (Manuscript).

Lynch, O.

The Politics of Untouchability. Social Mobility and Social Change in a City of India, New York: Columbia University Press, 1969.

'Dalit Buddhism: The Liberate Bodh Gaya Movement', *Dalit International Newsletter*, Vol. 3, No. 1, February 1998, pp. 1–11.

Macy, J.R. and E. Zelliot

'Tradition and Innovation in Contemporary Indian Buddhism', *Studies in the History of Buddhism*, Papers presented at the International Conference on the History of Buddhism at the University of Wisconsin, Madison, 19–21 August 1976, A.K. Narain, ed., Delhi: B.R. Publishing Corporation, 1980, pp. 133–53.

Maha Bodhi Journal

The Maha Bodhi Centenary Volume, Calcutta, 1992.

(Also see Ahir, 1995a.)

Mathiassen, Ch.

'Tibet—The Creation of a Myth', *Newsletter, Nordisk Institute of Asian Studies*, Copenhagen, No. 2, 1996, pp. 14–18.

Middle Way Travels

Map courtesy of Mr. Shahabuddin, Bodh Gaya.

Milinda

Questions of King Milinda, T.W. Rhys Davids, ed. and tr., Sacred Books of the East series, Vols. 35-6, Oxford: Clarenden Press, 1890–4. Reprinted by Motilal Banarsidass, Delhi, 1965, 2 vols.

Nachrichten aus Roseburg

Roseburg: Haus der Stille, No. 84, December 1998.

Monlam Office

Map distributed by the Kagyud Monlam Office, Bodh Gaya, 1997.

Narain, A.K. and D.C. Ahir, eds.

Dr. Ambedkar, Buddhism and Social Change, New Delhi: B.R. Publishing Corporation, 1994.

Nyanaponika

The Heart of Buddhist Meditation (Satipatthana). London: Rider, 1962.

Omvedt, G.

Dalits and the Democratic Revolution. Dr. Ambedkar and the Dalit Movement in Colonial India, New Delhi: Sage Publications, 1994.

Padmasuri (Hilary Blakiston)

But Little Dust. Life among the Ex-Untouchable Buddhists of India. Birmingham: Windhorse Publications, 1997 (1st pub. 1990).

Palakshappa, T.C.

Tibetans in India. A Case Study of Mundgod Tibetans, New Delhi: Sterling, 1978.

Pilchick, T. (Dharmachari Nagabodhi)

Jai Bhim! Dispatches from a Peaceful Revolution, Glasgow: Windhorse Publications, 1988.

Prajavangsha

'The Buddhist Community of Bangladesh. A Brief Survey', *Bodhi - Enlightenment*, Dhaka: Fine Art Press, 1990, pp. 41–7.

Queen, C.

'Ambedkar, Modernity and the Hermeneutics of Buddhist Liberation', A.K. Narain and D.C. Ahir, eds., *Dr. Ambedkar, Buddhism and Social Change*, 1994, pp. 99–122.

Radhakrishna, S.

'Foreword', in *2500 Years of Buddhism*, P.V. Bapat, ed., New Delhi: Ministry of Information and Broadcasting, 1956, pp. v–xvi.

Rahula, Y.

One Night's Shelter. The Autobiography of an American Buddhist Monk, Colombo: The Public Trustee, 1985.

Ramteke, D.L.

Revival of Buddhism in Modern India, New Delhi: Deep and Deep Publications, 1983.

Redmond, G.P.

'Is There a Specifically Buddhist Approach to Social Ethics?' A.K. Narain and D.C. Ahir, eds., *Dr. Ambedkar, Buddhism and Social Change*, 1994, pp. 123–35.

Saklanie. G.

The Uprooted Tibetans in India, New Delhi: Cosmo Publications, 1984.

Samanta, D.K.

The Dominant Weak. A Case Study of the Nava Bouddha of Maharashtra, Calcutta: Anthropological Survey of India, Memoir No. 86, 1991.

Sangharakshita

Ambedkar and Buddhism, Glasgow: Windhorse Publications, 1986

Scholz, G.

'Vipassana Meditation und Drogensucht,. Eine Studie uber den Ausstieg aus der Herrschaft der Attraktion Droge', Universitat Zurich: Philosophische Fakultat I, Dissertation, 1992.

Shastree, U.

Religious Converts in India. Socio-Political Study of Neo-Buddhists, New Delhi: Mittal Publications, 1996.

Somananda, A.

Theravada Buddhism in Bangladesh. On the Occasion of the Cremation of the Remains of His Holiness the Late Supreme Patriarch Abhayatissa Sangharaja Mahanayakathera, the Seventh Supreme Sangharaja of Bangladesh, Bangkok: The Religious Affairs Press, 1975.

Sponberg, A.

'TBMSG: A Dhamma Revolution in Contemporary Asia', *Engaged Buddhism.*

Buddhist Liberation Movements in Asia, C. Queen and S. King, eds., New York: State University of New York Press, 1996, pp. 73–120.

Subhuti, Dh. (Alex Kennedy)

Buddhism for Today: A Portrait of a New Buddhist Movement, Salisbury, Wiltshire: Element Books, in Association with the Friends of the Western Buddhist Order, 1983.

Tartakov, G.M.

'Art and Identity: The Rise of a New Buddhist Imagery', in A.K. Narain and D.C. Ahir, *Dr. Ambedkar, Buddhism and Social Change*, 1994, pp. 175–94.

'New Paths to Sanchi', in Vidya Dahejia, ed., *Unseen Presence: The Buddha and Sanchi*, Mumbai: Marg Publications, 1996.

Taylor, R.W.

'The Ambedkarite Buddhists', *Ambedkar and the Neo-Buddhist Movement*, in T.S. Wilkinson and M.M. Thomas, eds., Madras: Christian Literature Society, 1972, pp. 103–28.

Trevithik, A.M.

'A Jerusalem of the Buddhists in British India, 1874-1949', Cambridge, Mass: Harvard University Ph.D. thesis, 1988.

Tsomo, K.L., ed.

Tochter des Buddha. Leben und Alltag spiritueller Frauen im Buddhismus heute, Munchen: Diederichs Verlag, 1991.

Sakyadhita: Daughters of the Buddha, Ithaca, New York: Snow Lion Publications, 1988. Also published by Sri Satguru Publications, Delhi, 1998.

Vipassana Newsletter

Informationen zur Vipassana Meditation in der Tradition von Sayagyi U Bha Kin, wie gelehrt von S.N. Goenka. Oldenberg: Vipassana-Vereinigung, Junkerstrasse 30, D-26123.

Vipassana Pagoda

Souvenir, 26 October 1997, Mumbai: Global Vipassana Foundation.

Vipassana Research Institute

A Collection Commemorating the Teaching of Sayagi U Bha Kin, Igatpuri: Vipassana Research Institute, 1994 (1st ptg. 1991).

Vipassana. Its Relevance to the Modern World. An International Seminar held at the Indian Institute of Technology, Delhi, 15-17 April, 1994, Igatpuri: Vipassana Research Institute, 1994.

Dharma—Its True Nature. An International Seminar held at Dhammagiri, 6–7 May 1995, Igatpuri: Vipassana Research Institute, 1995.

Wege zu einer gerechten Gesellschaft, 1996

'Beitrage engagierter Buddhisten zu einer internationalen Debatte', Hamburg: Evangelisches Missionswerk, 'Weltmission heute', Vol. 23.

Wilkinson, T.S.

'Buddhism and Social Change among the Mahars', *Ambedkar and the Neo-Buddhist Movement*, in T.S. Wilkinson and M.M. Thomas, eds., Madras: Christian Literature Society, 1972, pp. 71–100.

Zelliot, E.

'Religion and Legitimation in the Mahar Movement', *Religion and the Legitimation of Power in South Asia*, in Bardwell L. Smith, ed., Leiden: E.J. Brill, 1978, pp. 88–105.

From Untouchable to Dalit: Essays on the Ambedkar Movement, New Delhi: Manohar, 3rd revd. edn. 2001 (1992, 1996).